indexed

Beside the

Still Waters

volume three

Daily Devotional

BESIDE THE STILL WATERS VOLUME 3

ISBN-10: 1-932676-52-X
ISBN 13: 978-1932676-52-5

Also Available as Ebook at www.vision-publishers.com
ePUB-10: 1-932676-53-8
ePUB-13: 978-1932676-53-2

ePDF-10: 1-932676-54-6
ePDF-13: 978-1932676-54-9

Printed in the United States of America

Layout and Cover Design: Lanette Steiner

All scriptures taken from the King James Version

For special discounts on bulk purchases, please contact:
Vision Publishers Orders by phone: 877.488.0901

For Information or Comments, please contact:
Vision Publishers
P.O. Box 190 • Harrisonburg, VA 22803
Phone: 877.488.0901
Fax: 540.437.1969
E-mail: orders@vision-publishers.com
www.vision-publishers.com
(See order form in back)

Holmes Printing Solutions
8757 County Road 77 • Fredericksburg, OH 44627 • 888.473.6870

TABLE OF CONTENTS

INTRODUCTION

Jesus said, Come unto me, all ye that labor and are heavy laden, and I will give you rest (Matthew 11:28).

Life does have many burdens and trials. It can be very perplexing and disturbing.

Jesus calls for all who are experiencing such to go to Him and find rest for the soul.

Thou wilt keep him in perfect peace, whose mind is stayed on thee: because he trusteth in thee (Isaiah 26:3).

As evil and corrupt men grow worse and worse, as nations move farther and farther away from God there is a need for something that is dependable in whom man can put his trust. These devotionals are intended to lead one's thoughts to God and His Word. God's Word is more certain than gold that perishes. God's Word is a reservoir of help in our need. It is that because it springs from One Who is the Rock that is unmovable.

Volume 3, of the Beside the Still Waters devotional series is drawn from the seventh, eighth, and ninth years of the bi-monthly devotionals, by the same name, that are mass produced and sent out to tens of thousands of subscribers. We are grateful for the privilege to reproduce these devotionals, written by many men from different walks of life.

Like the two previous volumes, this devotional is indexed by Contributor, Scripture, and Subject.

We pray that many will take the time to allow these devotionals to minister to their hearts and lives.

A portion of each sale will go to the Still Waters Ministries of Clarkson, Kentucky.

– The Publishers

January 1

Bible Reading: Philippians 3:10-21, Titus 2:11-15

One Year Bible Reading Plan: Matthew 1, Genesis 1, 2

Where there is no vision, the people perish:
but he that keepeth the law, happy is he.

- PROVERBS 29:18

INVENTORY AND NOBLE GOALS

As we did our year-end inventory and evaluated our tax preparation sheet and annual financial statement, we noticed that in many areas we could have done better. But the year is gone. The money is spent. The only thing left to do is to learn from those mistakes and set better goals for the next year.

Isn't that exactly how it is in our spiritual life? When we meditate and remember the past year, take a look at each incident we were involved in, and evaluate the bottom line, we can see where we failed and fell short in many accounts. But the year is gone and we can't change it. God forgives our sins.

But let's learn from our failures of the past year, and with the Lord's help, set better goals for the future. We do need goals in our businesses, but spiritual goals are much more important. Parents, let's set our goals to do our best with the help of our Lord, so all our children and their children's children come to the knowledge of the truth and reach that heavenly crown.

Let's set goals that each member of the church can grow in the knowledge of the truth. It should be our goal that not one be doomed to eternal hell, but that all may live eternally in that glorious eternal heaven. Yes, it is God's will. "Who will have all men to be saved, and to come unto the knowledge of the truth" (1 Timothy 2:4).

Andrew M. Troyer, Conneautville, PA

No man can be a workman for God until he
is the workmanship of God.

January 2

Bible Reading: Nehemiah 4

One Year Bible Reading Plan: Matthew 2, Genesis 3–5

Now I beseech you, brethren . . .
that ye all speak the same thing.
- 1 CORINTHIANS 1:10

ONE MIND WITH GOD

A congregation once decided to add to their church building. They sat together to discuss on which side of the building to build. One option would take out a large oak tree which had stood there for many years. The oak had provided nice shade for many church picnics. It seemed this was a good option, but one of the older men of the congregation, who had been a member for many years, thought they should build in another direction and save the oak. The tree had been his favorite.

The vote carried to remove the tree to build the addition, with the older man being the only one to vote against it. They planned a work bee to cut down the tree. And much to the surprise of the members, the first one to arrive was the old man who had voted against the plan.

How many of us are willing to sacrifice our ideas for the sake of the brotherhood, for the sake of unity and peace, for the sake of perfect love and consideration, for the sake of Jesus Christ?

Human nature wants its own way. Human nature loves self-indulgence, but God can change that. He says He'll take out the stony heart and give us a new one that will be workable and pliable. As God takes our heart and forms it for Himself, our heart beats with His. We become more like Him and then more like each other. Only then will we be able to be of one mind.

Harold R. Troyer, Kiev, Ukraine

It's not so much that we think alike, but that we think together.

January 3

He that is faithful in that which is least is faithful also in much.

- LUKE 16:10

FULFILLING OUR RESPONSIBILITY

As we approached the village, we passed Brother Juan (not his real name) walking away from the village. We had been asked to go to the church that Sunday morning to share the Word. Brother Juan was the minister, but he had become discouraged and had stopped preaching. I didn't expect to see him leaving the village at the time for the service to begin. The people were slow in coming to the service. When it was time to start singing, no one led out. It was hard for me to lead a song in another language, but somehow I managed to start one. When it was time for devotions, no one was ready. It reminded me of a dead church. They were like sheep without a shepherd. After the service, no one talked, and it seemed like greeting each other was a real burden.

Six months later, I was again asked to share with this church. During those six months, Brother Juan had confessed his sin of discouragement and disregard of his responsibility to the church. After a time of proving himself, he again took up his leadership position as minister of the church. As we came near the church house that morning, we could see the members joyfully walking to church from all directions. The building was almost full. Brother Juan opened the service. Someone else led the spirited singing. Another brother had a meaningful devotional. After the service, the brothers and sisters talked and shared and willingly greeted each other.

A number of brethren thanked me for sharing the Word with them. I was amazed at the difference I saw. The church was alive. They had a leader, a shepherd, and the flock was following.

What has God called us to? Are we fulfilling our responsibility, or are we causing others to stumble and falter? In the church, home, school, or job, may we be faithful to what God has called us.

David Good, Punta Gorda, Belize

Faithful is He that calleth you, who also will do it.

January 4

Bible Reading: John 11:25-46

One Year Bible Reading Plan: Matthew 4, Genesis 9–11

I am the way, the truth, and the life:
no man cometh unto the Father, but by me.

- JOHN 14:6

JESUS, OUR FAITHFUL GUIDE

The path we are on will take us somewhere. Every person that has lived on earth will end up either in heaven or in hell. We want to consider carefully the rich man in Luke 16:19-31. After he found himself in hell, there was no release, no exit, and no entrance for someone to come to his rescue. He was utterly helpless. He had lived for self, indulging too much in the things this world had to offer, not considering others. He chose his destiny. Jesus was not his choice.

If we are traveling to a place we have never been before, it would be unwise not to consider the road map carefully to know which route will lead us where we want to go. "Search the scriptures; for in them ye think ye have eternal life: and they are they which testify of me" (John 5:39).

Have you ever read a book when your heart wasn't in it? Sometimes pupils end up with a failing grade because their heart wasn't in the book. They had other interests and goals that were more important to them.

If our hearts are not set on Jesus and on His words, we are like a ship at sea with no captain, tossed to and fro without a goal. Even if one survives the storms of life, there is one storm that no one will survive without Jesus. The only way we will survive the day of judgment is with Jesus, our faithful Guide, to take us through. Study the Book, heed the signs along life's pathway, allow Jesus to be your Guide, and you will make it in safely.

Tobe Y. Hostetler, Danville, OH

We must either die or live. Choose Jesus, and you will live.

January 5

Bible Reading: Ephesians 4:11-32

One Year Bible Reading Plan: Matthew 5:1-26, Genesis 12–14

Wherefore putting away lying, speak every man truth
with his neighbour; for we are members one of another.
- EPHESIANS 4:25

YOUR SINS WILL FIND YOU OUT

It was Friday, and four boys planned to go fishing after school. They had their fishing gear loaded and ready. On the way to school, the temptation was too great. They decided to fish awhile and still get to school on time. But the fish were biting well, and they arrived at school an hour late.

"What will we tell the principal?" the boys asked, as they walked toward the schoolhouse.

"I will tell him we had a flat tire," the driver volunteered. They arrived at the principal's office and explained that they had a flat tire.

The principal was very understanding. "Anyone can have a flat tire," he said, as he handed each boy a slip of paper. "I have just one question, though, before you go to your classes. Jot down which tire was flat."

Lying is not only sinful, it is very inconvenient. I am amazed at how many church-going people carry grudges, bitterness, and hatred in their hearts. When we profess to be followers of Jesus, but refuse to heed His commands, we are lying. When I say I love the Lord, but fail to love those around me, I am living a lie.

I knew a man who would often say, "Give me a few minutes, and I will tell you something that sounds reasonable." If we always speak the truth, we will never need to come up with an explanation that sounds reasonable.

Melvin L. Yoder, Gambier, OH

We will tell the truth, or suffer the consequences.

January 6

Bible Reading: Psalm 37

One Year Bible Reading Plan: Matthew 5:27-48, Genesis 15–17

Rest in the Lord, and wait patiently for him: fret not thyself because of him who prospereth in his way.

- PSALM 37:7

CONTENTMENT GOD'S WAY

How does peer pressure affect me? Can I rejoice when someone else prospers, when his business or farming operation is profitable, or when he finds a suitable life companion? Or am I not satisfied until I do just as well or better?

When our children were younger, they often said things like, "David's dad got another truck last week. Don't you think our old truck should be replaced?"

"Rebecca has another new dress. I wish I could make one, too."

"Our tractor doesn't have air conditioning or even a cab."

"But it still works well, and it's paid for," I would remind them.

As parents, it seems we hear of every new purchase, every trip taken to visit relatives in other congregations far from home, every wedding, and every reunion. But does that mean we have to do the same things just because we can? In 1 Timothy 6:6 we read, "Godliness with contentment is great gain."

I grew up in a home where not much, if anything, was bought new, and the latest gadgets were never even considered. One of Dad's favorite sayings was, "Use it up, wear it out, make it do, or do without."

I believe the church today could learn from this small bit of wisdom. We can be just as happy without the newer vehicles and nicer furniture and still rejoice with those who are able to have these things. Credit cards, charge accounts, higher wages, and a booming economy are detrimental to the spiritual growth of God's people. Could we still be faithful and happy without the prosperity we enjoy now? Someday we might experience trials as our forefathers did. What of peer pressure then?

John Freeman, Albany, KY

Poor indeed is the man who cannot enjoy the simple things of life.

January 7

Bible Reading: 1 Timothy 6:6-21

One Year Bible Reading Plan: Matthew 6, Genesis 18, 19

For whatsoever is born of God overcometh the world:
and this is the victory that overcometh the world, even our faith.
- 1 John 5:4

LIFE'S END—A VICTORY OR A DRAW?

A seventy-eight-year-old prominent actor and president of an influential political lobbying group was recently told by his doctor he had symptoms of Alzheimer's disease. His public response was that he would not give up, but would continue to be the fighter others had known him to be. Then he added, "It's just that someday I'll need to call it a draw."

The definition of draw is to "leave a contest undecided; to come out even in a contest." When a game ends in a tie, you could call it a draw. Now consider the concept of the end of life that this man expressed when he said, "I'll need to call it a draw."

Calling it a draw is being unwilling to face the consequences of life's choices and its fights. Having our own way will never end in a draw, but only defeat. With whom would we tie, God or Satan? To call it a tie with God is near blasphemy, and ending in a draw with Satan is unacceptable.

The Christian also fights in life. He fights the Devil, his own flesh, and the forces of this world. The battle is arduous and long, and at times we become weary. But we dare never call it a draw. Nor do we want to, for that is less than winning. Victory is our goal, and we expect a crown of life at the end. Should our life end sooner than we expected, or should we contract Alzheimer's, we can be "more than conquerors through him that loved us."

Paul understood the concept when he said, "I have fought a good fight, I have finished my course, I have kept the faith." Victory is not a draw with God, but rather a success under His blessing and direction.

Delmar R. Eby, London, KY

*Not to the strong is the battle; not to the swift is the race;
but to the true and the faithful, victory is promised at last.*

January 8

Bible Reading: 1 Corinthians 10:1-13

One Year Bible Reading Plan: Matthew 7, Genesis 20–22

Surely the serpent will bite without enchantment; and a babbler is no better.
- ECCLESIASTES 10:11

OVERCOMING THAT OLD SERPENT

A big snake was climbing toward a nest of young birds. The starlings squawked with such distress that robins joined them in trying to overcome this dreaded foe. About twenty birds were frantically diving and pecking the snake's head, but it kept climbing despite the obstacles and successfully reached the nest.

Many people are simply terrified at the sight of a snake. A brother once commented, "In their fear of snakes, women are scriptural." He was referring to Genesis 3:15: "I will put enmity between [the serpent] and the woman."

I have to think of the biblical description of "that old serpent, called the Devil, and Satan" (Revelation 12:9). He is out to destroy our precious children and grandchildren. He may attack them in deceptive ways by causing them to doubt the authenticity of the Scriptures or by seducing them into worldliness and materialism. Many people who are very frightened at the sight of a snake (which are usually small, harmless snakes) don't seem to be afraid of the chief of serpents which is the Devil. They even laugh at the thought of him and make light of him as if he were but a joke and a myth. How sad that multitudes of souls will finally be in the lake of fire with that old serpent, the Devil— the one they sported with in life.

Let us overcome the serpent by the blood of Jesus Christ, the Lamb of God, which "taketh away the sin of the world."

Willis Halteman, Carlisle, PA

Snakes are known to go crooked, but true Christians are known to go straight.

January 9

Bible Reading: 1 Peter 5

One Year Bible Reading Plan: Matthew 8, Genesis 23, 24

Be sober, be vigilant; because your adversary the devil,
as a roaring lion, walketh about, seeking whom he may devour.

- 1 PETER 5:8

BEWARE. DANGER AHEAD!

Several weeks ago our son bought a bull to run with his beef cows. It was soon evident the bull was becoming sick. The vet determined his illness as shipping fever and treated him for it. We were told to follow up with a shot for several days.

When the bull was very sick, it was easy to chase him between two steel gates and give him a shot, but as he grew better it was a different story. One morning we arranged the gates and tried to chase him in, but he stood his ground and even took a step toward me. After a quick prayer for protection and for courage to proceed, I determined I would show the bull I was not afraid. When I continued prodding him, he suddenly charged me, knocking me flat on the concrete. For a split second I lay helplessly, expecting some unmerciful mauling. The bull backed off, and it took me only a few seconds to reach a place of safety.

Do I sometimes make unwise decisions that give the enemy an opportunity to destroy my soul? Will I be able to humble myself and take advice from someone older or wiser when I'm obviously headed for real danger? Or will I prod till the enemy charges me with a ferocious, deadly blow?

Only by the grace of God did I have the opportunity to walk away unharmed after foolishly prodding something that could have destroyed my life. I pray that God will always protect me and humble me so I will immediately choose? safety when there is spiritual danger ahead.

Daniel Mast, Orrville, OH

Any man can commit a mistake, but a fool will continue in it.

January 10

It is good for a man that he bear the yoke in his youth.
- LAMENTATIONS 3:27

THE YOKE

We read of quite a few different kinds of yokes in the Bible: The yoke of learning (Matthew 11:29), the yoke of bondage (Galatians 5:1), and the yoke of transgression (Lamentations 1:14), to name a few.

What is a yoke? It is a piece of wood placed over the necks of two oxen. It binds two animals together to pull whatever they are hitched to. Although yokes of this type are a thing of the past for most of us, they are still used in some places.

Whenever there was a young ox to train, an older, well-trained ox was yoked to the young one, and they were turned out to pasture. Wherever the older ox went, the young one had to follow. This is called the yoke of learning.

Isn't this the yoke Jesus is speaking of in Matthew 11:29? When we take Jesus' yoke upon us, we tie ourselves together with Him and learn from Him. We will follow wherever He goes and learn of His ways. His yoke is easy and His burden light.

In Galatians 5:1 we are admonished to break away from the yoke of bondage. In 2 Corinthians 6:14 we are told to not be unequally yoked with unbelievers, so we do not learn their wicked ways. Let us be careful with whom we are yoked. If we yoke ourselves to an unbeliever, we will learn more of his ways. This is a dangerous yoke.

Daniel Miller, Dunnegan, MO

There is no greater joy than to be yoked to Jesus.

January 11

They profess that they know God; but in works they deny him,
being abominable and disobedient, and unto every good work reprobate.
- TITUS 1:16

JONAH'S INCONSISTENT PROFESSION

We know Jonah as a prophet of God who was assigned a mission of great importance. God's love was reaching out to the vilest of sinners, to invite them into fellowship with Him. He chose Jonah to be a vessel to carry His invitation.

But under the influence of Jonah's humanity and his Jewish pride and nationalism, he disobeyed the heavenly calling. He fled—not just from his task, but from the presence of the Lord. Then he found himself in an inescapable situation. A terrible storm threatened to destroy the ship, and the sailors questioned this sleepy passenger.

He came up with two contradictory claims about himself. He told them he feared God, but he was fleeing from the presence of God. Did Jonah realize the incongruity of his confession? His fear was not strong enough to move him to obedience.

But then the question arises: How often do my words contradict my actions? We say to the world around us that we are plain people. But when our worldly neighbors observe our homes or businesses, do they reveal plainness? We say the Christian doesn't live for money, but how much effort do we expend trying to get the last dollar in our dealings with others? We say we believe in evangelism. But how often do we say something to the neighbor or salesman about salvation?

Let us not say "I fear God" from one side of our mouth, and "I want to please myself" from the other. An inconsistent profession brings reproach on God and takes God's name in vain. Let us say "I fear God" and show it by obedience to His direction.

Delmar R. Eby, London, KY

If I fear God, then I will hear God and draw near God.

January 12

Bible Reading: Hebrews 12:1-17

One Year Bible Reading Plan: Matthew 10:1-23, Genesis 29, 30

Now no chastening for the present seemeth to be joyous, but grievous: nevertheless afterward it yieldeth the peaceable fruit of righteousness unto them which are exercised thereby.

- HEBREWS 12:11

STEPPING STONES OR STUMBLING BLOCKS

The legend is told of a stoop-shouldered old man called Grandfather Time. He travels around delivering a package to every newborn baby. Everyone's package contains the same thing—the troubles of life. Everybody hates these packages, but they cannot figure out how to get rid of them.

The story continues and most people open their packages and spread them helter-skelter over the highway of life. They wander around, aimlessly stumbling over first one and then another. Happily, a few people have figured out what to do with their troubles. They also spread them over the road of life. Then they proceed to step on top of each trouble as they run up against it. They make stepping stones of their troubles instead of stumbling blocks.

This legend is fanciful, of course, but it illustrates the difference between the Christian's view and the non-Christian's view of the troubles of life. The non-Christian faces troubles hopelessly and aimlessly. The Christian knows that troubles can become stepping stones and even blessings with the aid of God and the Holy Spirit.

"And we know that all things work together for good to them that love God" (Romans 8:28). God promises that good can come from even the worst troubles of life.

Often a Christian can see good coming out of his problems. Perhaps they help him rely upon God more or give him experience to help others who face similar problems. Even if we do not understand the whys, God may allow us to face problems to test us, to see if our commitment to Him is genuine. This is called the chastening of the Lord. "For whom the Lord loveth he chasteneth" (Hebrews 12:6).

Roger Berry, Seymour, MO

Use your problems as stepping stones to keep you close to God.

January 13

Bible Reading: Genesis 3:1-13

One Year Bible Reading Plan: Matthew 10:24-42, Genesis 31, 32

The serpent beguiled me.

- GENESIS 3:13

SATAN MAY LOOK BEAUTIFUL—AT FIRST

As a young unbeliever, I was vacationing with a Christian friend. One sunny morning I snorkeled alone in the clear, warm water just off the shore. My snorkeling adventure was filled with sudden bursts of colorful schools of fish.

I began to swim back to shore, but I caught a glimpse of a beautiful sea creature gliding along the sandy bottom. I followed this creature from above. The sunrays penetrated the clear water and reflected many colors off the creature's back. I was mesmerized by its beauty. Suddenly, without warning, the creature turned and swam toward me. I froze in fear. But the creature inexplicably stopped within arm's reach and quickly swam away from me. I decided it was time to swim to shore!

When I came ashore, my friend seemed agitated and repeatedly asked, "Are you okay?" My friend had been praying for me a few moments earlier out of concern for my safety.

Shortly after I returned home, I was shocked to stumble across a picture of the sea creature. The deadliest snake in the world! It was a sea snake, in the middle of its mating season (when they are the most aggressive and relentless), and it had nearly attacked me. If it had bitten me, I would have experienced respiratory failure within a few seconds and drowned. I would have died an unbeliever, without hope and separated from God forever.

Then I realized the truth of God's salvation. I was following after Satan who, like the sea snake, seemed beautiful, exciting, and peaceful. But my life was full of loneliness, emptiness, and fear. Satan and the sea snake are both deceitful and deadly. My Christian friend had cried out to the Lord for my soul. I repented and gave my life to the Lord, and the angry serpent was turned away from me forever.

Bruce Files, Lyndon, KS

Seek the Lord, not the old subtle serpent.

January 14

Bible Reading: Ephesians 6:10-20

One Year Bible Reading Plan: Matthew 11, Genesis 33–35

Watch ye, stand fast in the faith, quit you like men, be strong.
- 1 CORINTHIANS 16:13

STANDING FOR GOD

Because of the sin of Adam and Eve, we are all born with a sinful nature. Satan works on us from within (our sinful nature) and from without (temptation). He wants us to fall. God wants us to stand. Ephesians 6:11 says we are to put on the armor of God so we can stand against the schemes of the Devil. God provides all we need to stand for Him. The challenge is for us to make use of the armor and stand for God.

There are many examples in the Bible of those who stood for God. Daniel and Joseph stood in difficult times. Christ stood during His time of temptation in the wilderness.

Scripture tells us to be brave like men and stand fast in the faith. We can only stand as we yield ourselves to the power of God and put on the whole armor that He provides. If we face the world without this armor, we are sure to fall.

Will I stand for God now? Revelation 20:12 tells us that we will all stand before God at the Judgment. If I stand for Him now, I will be ready to stand then. Jesus also stands and knocks at the door (Revelation 3:20). He stood and knocked at our heart's door. Can we stand for Him?

Scripture tells us that Christ now is at the right hand of the Father. When Stephen was stoned, he saw Jesus standing at the right hand of God. When God calls us home, I believe Jesus will stand to welcome us home. Will we stand for Him now?

David Good, Punta Gorda, Belize

If I want to walk with God, I must stand up.

January 15

Bible Reading: Isaiah 55

One Year Bible Reading Plan: Matthew 12:1-21, Genesis 36, 37

Incline your ear, and come unto me: hear, and your soul shall live; and I will make an everlasting covenant with you, even the sure mercies of David.
- ISAIAH 55:3

STOP, LOOK, LISTEN

A few decades ago, the above three words were commonly found at railroad crossings. Nearly a hundred years ago, the largest railroad company in our country saw the danger and death that so often resulted from the collision of its steel locomotives with vehicles at railroad crossings. The company offered a prize of $2,500 to the person who would suggest the three best words to be used as warning words at railroad crossings. The person wise enough and fortunate enough to win the prize offered these three words: Stop, Look, Listen. Each word played a special part in the safety of the lives of the people. It did not work for the people just to stop but not look and listen. But their safety was granted as they obeyed the whole sign.

Many times we come to railroad crossings in our spiritual life. When God speaks to us, do we stop and listen to what He wants to share with us? Do we look into God's Word for guidance from day to day? Too often our prayer line is clogged so that we cannot hear what God is trying to tell us. The cares of this world, the deceitfulness of riches, or the unknown future can drag us down spiritually.

It is God's desire to communicate with man and to lead him in the ways of righteousness and true holiness.

Samuel Beachy, Belvidere, TN

Stop when God stops. Move when God moves.

19

January 16

Bible Reading: Matthew 10:7-42

One Year Bible Reading Plan: Matthew 12:22-50, Genesis 38–40

For they being ignorant of God's righteousness, and going about to establish their own righteousness, have not submitted themselves unto the righteousness of God.

- ROMANS 10:3

CONFESS CHRIST TODAY

Tell someone about Jesus today. Maybe we say, "I don't know how," or "I am slow of speech," like Moses said when God called him to deliver the Israelites. Maybe we just feel bashful talking about Jesus and what He has done for us. What if they laugh or mock or get angry? What will I do then? If I don't want to do something, there is almost no end to reasons and excuses for not doing it. According to Matthew 10:32, 33, if we are ashamed of Jesus, He will also be ashamed of us.

Many people are hurting deeply and crying for help on the inside. They may look fine on the outside, but on the inside they are a crying, seeking child. Some will even mock or ridicule you, but on the inside they wish someone would just reach out and tell them that Christ can satisfy their longing and fill their void. They are potential Christians.

It is not always someone out in the world who is hurting. Perhaps it is my very own brother in the church or at home who needs a word of encouragement or a helping hand.

Our key verse says that they are ignorant of God's righteousness so they try to establish their own righteousness. To be ignorant is simply not to know through lack of information or intelligence. We need to be willing to tell them that Christ loves them and can fill them with His love.

May Christ fill us with His Spirit and power so we can burn brightly for Him.

Sanford Nissley, Catlett, VA

If we won't speak for Christ today, He won't speak for us on Judgment Day.

January 17

Bible Reading: Matthew 3

One Year Bible Reading Plan: Matthew 13:1-32, Genesis 41

Cast away from you all your transgressions, whereby ye have transgressed;
and make you a new heart and a new spirit: for why will ye die,
O house of Israel?

- EZEKIEL 18:31

REPENTANCE IS THE WAY TO GOD

John the Baptist preached repentance. Jesus preached repentance.
Men still preach repentance today.

So what is the message? What is the idea? Why preach repentance?
Is there something wrong among us? Maybe we think that those
preaching are just trying to make us feel guilty.

Whatever the case, repentance is absolutely necessary to gain
God's forgiveness. We cannot come into the presence of God without
first repenting of sin. Ungodliness separates and bars us from God
and His approval and blessings. Repentance and faith in Christ's
atoning blood restores man into full fellowship with His Creator.

Repentance is detesting sin and self enough to ask God to cleanse
us from it. When we're sick enough of sin to pray that God would give
us a new heart, then we are on the way to gaining God's forgiveness.

Repentance is not a one-time-cure-all either. Man is likely to fall at
times in his walk with God even after he seeks a changed heart. We
must continue to deal with the sin problem and continue to repent.

Repentance isn't always easy, but it's always worth it. When we
stand before God, we will be glad we were simple enough to believe
that repentance makes a difference.

To repent is to admit and confess our sins. "For all have sinned, and
come short of the glory of God" (Romans 3:23). No one is exempt from
the act of repentance and confession.

May we repent of sin and be ready when we meet God face to face.

Harold R. Troyer, Belleville, PA

---

*We have two options: Repent today and believe on Jesus or be
damned tomorrow!*

January 18

Bible Reading: Luke 13:1-16

One Year Bible Reading Plan: Matthew 13:33-58, Genesis 42, 43

And he answering said unto him, Lord, let it alone this year also,
till I shall dig about it, and dung it.
- LUKE 13:8

SOLVING ROOT PROBLEMS

A friend of mine told of a tree that, every spring when it was time to bud and grow leaves, it appeared to be split right down the center. One half was nice and full, but the other half looked shaggy. He said they fertilized it to try to get the other half to grow out, too, but it didn't work. Finally, after some thinking and studying, they decided something must be wrong with the roots. They got someone in to dig down to the roots on the side where the tree didn't look as nice. Sure enough, a big rock was hindering the roots from spreading out and getting the nourishment they needed. They removed the rock and filled the hole with good dirt. The next spring the tree was no longer lopsided. It looked nice all around.

If the man had decided just to cut off some branches from the good side to balance the tree, the whole tree would have looked shaggy. He did try to feed it, but that didn't help either. He looked deeper and found the problem was underneath where no one could see it. After he removed the problem, the tree could grow out nicely.

Root problems can also hinder growth and beauty in the family or in the church. How often do we start at the top, picking at this or that, thinking it will solve the problem, only to find things in worse shape than they had been? Often if we see a problem such as rebellion, the root of the problem is underneath where man cannot see it. Although we may see signs on the outside, the real problem is on the inside.

Joe Miller, Hartville, OH

Keep your roots in the Word of God

January 19

Bible Reading: Luke 10:30-42

One Year Bible Reading Plan: Matthew 14:1-21, Genesis 44, 45

And the barbarous people shewed us no little kindness: for they kindled a fire, and received us every one, because of the present rain, and because of the cold.
- ACTS 28:2

LORD, GIVE US EYES

Several years ago, my sister placed a note in my lunch box.

Lord, give me eyes that I may see
Lest I as people will,
Should pass by someone's Calvary
And think it just a hill.

Do you care enough to go bind the wounds and heal the broken-hearted? Do others know you will care and understand? God cared enough for us to send His only son to earth to die. Jesus cared enough to allow men to ridicule Him, nail Him to a tree, and accuse Him falsely. He could have called ten thousand angels, but He died alone for you and me. He showed great mercy and compassion for humanity!

If we could grasp the compassion and caring heart of Jesus, maybe we could better understand each other. Those who repent in sackcloth and ashes, receive Jesus as their Savior, and see themselves as unworthy, really care. Otherwise, we're too proud to care.

There are many hurting people in our world today. People have problems in the home, health problems, problems at work, and problems in the church. Does anyone care? I thought of a few ways we could care. Listen to the stories and problems of those who hurt and tell them you'll pray for them. Develop a relationship with those who want help. Make a phone call. Send a note of encouragement. Send a bouquet of flowers. Ask God to guide you to someone today who needs a helping hand. Keep your eyes on Jesus, and you will care.

Harold R. Troyer, Belleville, PA

People do not care how much you know until they know how much you care.

January 20

Bible Reading: Matthew 25:14-30

One Year Bible Reading Plan: Matthew 14:22-36, Genesis 46–48

And unto one he gave five talents, to another two, and to another one; to every man according to his several ability.

- MATTHEW 25:15

TALENTS FOR GOD'S GLORY

The day was cold and snowy. I could not help but think about my boss who was enjoying the warm weather in the Dominican Republic. He was filling in for a mission family for several months while they were on furlough. Suddenly I was struck with the thought, *He has gone to a faraway country and has entrusted his business into my care. What kind of report will I have to give when he returns?*

Jesus spoke about this very issue. How are we using the talents our heavenly Father has entrusted to us? "Oh, but I do not have the ability as some others," we may say. Or like Moses, "I cannot speak well." Or like Saul, we may hide behind our stuff.

When the lord returned, he did not ask for more than simply that the servants made increase of what was entrusted to them. His requirement was to make gain. No two people will perform equally, as is shown in our Scripture today. Our Lord does not ask of us any more than to make spiritual gain according to our ability. Then when He returns, we can report gain, even if it is only interest.

Oh, that men would cry out to God like Paul, "What wilt thou have me to do?" Or like Isaiah, "Here am I; send me!" Then we can rejoice because it is God who works in us to do His good pleasure.

Nelson Gingerich, Richfield, PA

Utilized talents make gain.

January 21

Bible Reading: Luke 12:35-48

One Year Bible Reading Plan: Matthew 15:1-20, Genesis 49, 50

And whatsoever ye do, do it heartily, as to the Lord, and not unto men.
- COLOSSIANS 3:23

RELUCTANT SERVICE

One of our elderly church sisters was moving, and I felt responsible to help her. Because her health was poor, she did little housecleaning, and her furniture certainly showed it. My son and I did the job as quickly as possible. After we were finished, I felt as though a shower and change of clothing were necessary. Well, I did my duty helping this elderly lady. Looking back, however, it was no credit to my account because I did it reluctantly.

We should have asked the church sisters to help clean her house and arrange the furniture. I should have taken my time, speaking words of encouragement to comfort her during this stressful time. What an excellent opportunity I had missed! There was no blessing for me from this experience.

We may be giving reluctant service to our parents, our employer, or worst of all, to our Lord. How do we deal with such an attitude? Our key verse exhorts us to serve as if we were doing it for the Lord. If we are going to do what is necessary, why miss the blessing? Loving service will have a pleasing effect not only on those we help and to our Lord, but also on ourselves.

God told the prophet Jonah to go to Nineveh to preach. Jonah tried to run away, but God intervened, and Jonah went to Nineveh. A great revival resulted. Jonah was displeased with the revival when he should have been rejoicing. He did his duty, but what a blessing he missed because of his attitude!

May our reluctance be changed to voluntary, loving service. Only the Lord knows how many will be blessed.

Norman Wine, Lebanon, PA

God has a purpose for each life,
A work for all to do,
And in His kingdom there's a plan
No one can fill but you. - Ada Wine

January 22

Who is this King of glory? The LORD strong and mighty,
the LORD mighty in battle.

- PSALM 24:8

THE VANITY OF MAN

If you have ever witnessed the majestic glory of a western thunderstorm, you know why I call it majestic. Continuous lightning and rolling thunder give witness to the tremendous power of God. God is the creator of this incredible motion picture.

Thousands of years ago, God came down upon Mount Sinai. When the Israelites saw the lightning and the smoking mountain, and heard the noise of the trumpet, they moved away and stood far off.

The psalmist David said, "O God, thou art my God; early will I seek thee: my soul thirsteth for thee . . . to see thy power and thy glory, so as I have seen thee in the sanctuary" (Psalm 63:1-2).

When Isaiah saw the Lord sitting on a throne, he said, "Woe is me! for I am undone . . . for mine eyes have seen the King, the LORD of hosts" (Isaiah 6:5). Moses wanted to see the glory of God, but God said, "Thou canst not see my face: for there shall no man see me, and live" (Exodus 33:20).

God's glory can only be seen in part by mortal eyes. Only after death will we see God face to face. We observe His glory and majestic power only in part in our lives. His goodness is beyond measure.

God told Job, "Deck thyself now with majesty and excellency; and array thyself with glory and beauty" (Job 40:10). Job replied, "I abhor myself" (Job 42:6). May we in humble reverence bow our knees and hearts before God.

Harold R. Troyer, Belleville, PA

And God said unto Moses, I AM THAT I AM.

January 23

Redeeming the time, because the days are evil.
- EPHESIANS 5:16

REDEEMING THE TIME

Time is a precious commodity. Each of us has only so much of it, so we need to make the best of every opportunity. Wasting time in activities that leave us feeling empty and unfulfilled is not redeeming the time.

We are prompted to redeem the time . . .

• when we consider the brevity of life (Psalm 90:12). We need to realize our days are numbered.

• by youthful piety (Ecclesiastes 12:1). We should remember our Creator in the days of our youth. There is no better time to start redeeming the time—while the evil days come not when we say, "I have no pleasure in them."

• by subordinating earthly duties to Heavenly duties (1 Corinthians 7:29). Here it speaks of being married or single. Being married should not hinder our goals in Christian attainment; it should enhance them.

• by serious living (Ephesians 5:15-16). We must not be flippant, but exercise the use of talents in ways that produce increase.

• by a consistent example before the world (Colossians 4:5). We redeem the time by behaving in a way that the world will see our deep dedication to God by our words and actions.

• by taking every opportunity to be in the assembly of the saints (Hebrews 10:25).

If we have failed in the past, now is the time to start using our time for God only.

Wilmer S. Beachy, Liberty, KY

Our days are identical suitcases, all the same size, but some people pack more into them than others.

January 24

Bible Reading: Genesis 6

One Year Bible Reading Plan: Matthew 17, Exodus 7, 8

Thus did Noah; according to all that God commanded him, so did he.

- GENESIS 6:22

PREPARING AN ARK

When God talked to Noah about building an ark, the earth was a corrupt and violent place. Wicked giants lived with all their desires and selfish lusts. A grieved God, looking down from heaven, repented of having made man whose heart was evil. Can we imagine one man in the midst of all this evil finding favor with God? Noah was a just and perfect man who did all that God had commanded him. Being a preacher of righteousness, he warned the corrupt and fearless people about their sinful ways.

After Noah got his instructions from God for building the ark, he probably did not spend much time bemoaning his foolish, self-centered neighbors. Maybe they were not willing to help, or possibly they mocked Noah's family and their strange ideas. Instead of complaining, Noah got to work. Through faith and obedience to God, Noah and his family found grace and a safe haven.

The blessings of being obedient are far-reaching and eternal. What can we learn from the life and times of Noah?

1. One man can make a great difference if he takes the narrow path.

2. It is important to obey in faith.

3. We desperately need an Ark [Jesus] for the saving of our souls.

Am I preparing an ark for my soul and the souls of my family by trusting in and obeying Christ?

Roy Keim, West Union, OH

Doing the will of God involves a personal choice—an act of the will.

January 25

For that which I do I allow not: for what I would, that do I not;
but what I hate, that do I.

- ROMANS 7:15

THE STRUGGLE WITHIN

"I am carnal, sold under sin" means that, though the "law is spiritual" because it is God's law, the old nature is not spiritual. It seeks to rebel and be independent of God. If I, being a Christian, try to struggle with sin in my own strength, I will slip into the grasp of sin's power.

Paul gives three lessons that he learned in trying to deal with his old sinful desires.

1. Knowledge is not the answer (Romans 7:9). Paul felt fine as long as he did not understand what the law demanded. When he learned the truth, he knew he was doomed.

2. Self-determination does not succeed (Romans 7:15). Paul found himself sinning in ways that were not even attractive to him.

3. Becoming a Christian does not stamp out all sin and temptation (Romans 7:22-25). Being born again takes a moment of faith, but becoming like Christ is a lifelong process. Paul likens Christian growth to a strenuous race or fight (1 Corinthians 9:24-27; 2 Timothy 4:7).

As Paul emphasized throughout the book of Romans, no one in the world is innocent. No one deserves to be saved. We all must depend on the work of Christ for our salvation. We cannot earn it by our good behavior. This inward struggle with sin was as real for Paul as it is for us. From Paul we learn what to do about it. Whenever he felt lost, he would return to the beginning of his spiritual life, remembering that Jesus Christ had already freed him.

When you feel confused and overwhelmed by sin's appeal, follow Paul's example. Thank God that He has given you freedom through Jesus Christ. Let the reality of Christ's power lift you up to real victory over sin.

Marvin C. Hochstetler, Nappanee, IN

When we fall, He lovingly reaches out to help us up.

January 26

Bible Reading: Matthew 18:1-14

One Year Bible Reading Plan: Matthew 18:21-35, Exodus 11, 12

As newborn babes, desire the sincere milk of the word,
that ye may grow thereby.

- 1 PETER 2:2

A LITTLE CHILD SHALL LEAD THEM

Perhaps one of the most touching letters in the White House collection came from a child. It was addressed to President Cleveland and written in September, 1895. This is what the letter said:

> Dear President, I am in a dreadful state of mind, and I thought I would write and tell you all. About two years ago, as near as I can remember, I used two postage stamps that had been used before on letters. It may have been more than two. I can only remember doing it twice. I did not realize what I had done until lately. My mind is constantly turned on that subject, and I think of it night and day. Now, dear President, would you please forgive me for this and I will promise you I will never do it again. Enclosed find the cost of three stamps, and please forgive me for I was but thirteen years old when this happened, and I am very sorry for what I have done.

I also read of a little girl that was in the hospital and was to have a dangerous operation. She was placed on the table and the surgeon was about to give her ether. So he told her, "Now, before we can make you well we must put you to sleep." She spoke up sweetly and said, "Oh, if you are going to put me to sleep, I must say my prayers first."

So she got on her knees and began: "Now I lay me down to sleep. I pray the Lord my soul to keep. If I should die before I wake, I pray the Lord my soul to take."

That evening, as that surgeon was ready to go to bed, he said a prayer for the first time in thirty years.

Eli A. Yoder, Stuart's Draft, VA

All who would reach the Mount of Transfiguration must go by the way of the Valley of Humiliation.

Bible Reading: Luke 3:1-18

One Year Bible Reading Plan: Matthew 19:1-15, Exodus 13–15

He must increase, but I must decrease. He that cometh from above is above all: he that is of the earth is earthly, and speaketh of the earth: he that cometh from heaven is above all.

- JOHN 3:30-31

MINE OR GOD'S?

John the Baptist was a man of the wilderness. He was likely not a very pretty picture in his rough clothing, long hair, and skin darkened by the blazing desert sun. He was not a man whom someone would travel long distances to see because of his outstanding personal qualities.

But John had a message from the God of heaven, and when God called him to begin his ministry, he obeyed. He could have said, "No one will listen to me. I'm not like other people. They will never accept me." He did not question the call but began preaching repentance and baptism.

His message cut to the hearts of those who heard him. Conviction was stirred, and people from all around came to hear this wild man with the powerful message. He became so popular that people began to look to him for answers. Even soldiers asked him, "Master, what shall we do?"

John the Baptist now faced a crisis in his own life. The people did listen to him. Many did accept his message. Here was a great opportunity to begin a movement and to be their leader. Some people were even beginning to wonder if he was the Christ. All they needed was a little encouragement from John.

What did John do? His response was, "One mightier than I cometh, the latchet of whose shoes I am not worthy to unloose (Luke 3:16). He must increase, but I must decrease" (John 3:30). Did John really decrease after that? Yes, he even gave his head for the cause of Christ.

Where does my life point others? Do I promote a kingdom for me or the kingdom of Christ, who alone is worthy to receive all glory?

Nelson Rohrer, Harriston, ON

---

*Let my hands perform His bidding, Let my feet run in His ways,
Let my eyes see Jesus only, Let my lips speak forth His praise.*

January 28

And he sat down, and called the twelve, and saith unto them,
If any man desire to be first, the same shall be last of all, and servant of all.
- MARK 9:35

ME B4 U

The big Lincoln Continental slowly cruised by on my left and pulled steadily ahead when I noticed the license plate. At first I was amused, but I was soon displeased. The more I thought about it, my displeasure was replaced with indignation.

The proud spirit screamed so loudly it could not help being heard. I lead; you follow. I am the head; you are the tail. I am in; you are out. I am up; you are down. But that is the human, worldly spirit that prevails. Be a leader, excel, get ahead, have others look up to me. I am the boss; you are my servant. The irony of it all is that he paid extra to have that put on his license plate. He probably thought he had plenty of money, so it wouldn't matter. But to me it was galling.

As a Christian, it caused me sobering thoughts. Am I willing to be plain me, working behind the scenes unnoticed and unremembered? Am I content with food and raiment? Am I willing to be a humble, cross-bearing follower of Jesus? Am I taking the rebuffs humbly and without retaliation, always a ready representative of my heavenly Leader?

I am without station in life and have no noticeable prominent position, yet I have all the riches showered upon me by Christ. If I remain faithful, I will someday see His glorious face, and it won't matter about ME B4 U.

Wilmer S. Beachy, Liberty, KY

An egotist is me-deep in conversation.

January 29

Bible Reading: Jeremiah 29:1-14

One Year Bible Reading Plan: Matthew 20:1-16, Exodus 19–21

For I know the thoughts that I think toward you, saith the LORD,
thoughts of peace, and not of evil, to give you an expected end.
- JEREMIAH 29:11

WHAT DOES GOD THINK OF YOU?

Often when we have done wrong, we wonder what others think of us. Even if we haven't done wrong, we still wonder what others think of us. But have we stopped to think what God thinks of us? Jeremiah said that the thoughts of God toward us are of peace and not of evil or calamity.

It is a great promise and comfort to know that, even when we do wrong, God still wants us to come to Him. Why, to give us a whipping or a tongue lashing? No! He wants to give us peace. It is a joy to have our sins forgiven and washed away and even buried in the deepest sea. That is just one of the things that God thinks toward us (See John 14:27 and 16:33).

God is not willing that any of us perish but wants every person to be saved. The choice is ours. God wants to bless us, but unless we go to Him, we cannot experience that wonderful promise.

He promised to hear us. "Call unto me, and I will answer thee, and show thee great and mighty things, which thou knowest not" (Jeremiah 33:3). See also 2 Chronicles 7:14 and Jeremiah 29:12-13. If we call on Him, we can be assured that He hears us.

What a great and marvelous God we have! Oh, if we would only trust Him more!

Mark G. Meighn, Belize City, Belize

No God - No Peace; Know God - Know Peace

January 30

Therefore thou art inexcusable, O man, whosoever thou art that judgest:
for wherein thou judgest another, thou condemnest thyself;
for thou that judgest doest the same things.

- ROMANS 2:1

PASSING THE BUCK

When my wife, Melissa, was a little girl, she decided to do some crayon art on the wall. Of course, her mother wasn't too happy when she discovered it. "Did you do this?" she asked sternly.

Melissa gave her most innocent look and pointed to the dog. "Ralph did it."

"Passing the buck," as it is commonly called today, is a part of the old nature. It dates as far back as the Garden of Eden. When Adam was confronted with his disobedience, he said, "The woman whom thou gavest to be with me, she gave me of the tree, and I did eat" (Genesis 3:12). Eve said, "The serpent beguiled me, and I did eat" (Genesis 3:13). Neither one was willing to accept any of the blame.

In Exodus 32:19-24, Aaron excused his making of the golden calf by blaming it on the people. When King Saul neglected to utterly destroy Amelek, he passed the blame (1 Samuel 15:20-21). And so it goes throughout history.

What a contrast from David's response to Nathan in 2 Samuel 12:13, "I have sinned against the Lord." No wonder David is referred to as a man after God's own heart.

As Christians, we need to have a heart like David. We should be honest in our evaluation of a situation and accept whatever it reveals. Even if I feel someone else is 99 percent to blame and I am only 1 percent to blame, I have a responsibility to take care of that 1 percent in humility and sincerity. I need to realize that in the other person's eyes, I may be the one who is 99 percent to blame (see Matthew 7:1-5).

With God's help let us strive to take full responsibility for our every action. Only then can we have true unity within the Church.

Joseph Jones, Ash Fork, AZ

There is no shame in accepting the blame.

January 31

Bible Reading: Daniel 3

One Year Bible Reading Plan: Matthew 21:1-22, Exodus 25, 26

But he knoweth the way that I take: when he hath tried me,
I shall come forth as gold.

- JOB 23:10

WHY SUFFERING?

Daniel's three friends faced a big decision. The king commanded them to worship the golden image or be thrown into the fiery furnace. They chose to follow God even if it would cost them their lives. They went against the king's command, stood alone, and experienced a fiery furnace trial.

In life we face painful experiences. Beautiful traits in our life are sometimes the result of pain. Suffering is unpleasant, but as we accept it, it can bring honor and glory to God.

A rose is a beautiful flower, but it also has thorns amidst its beauty. Sometimes it takes the thorns of life to bring out our true beauty. Roses shed their sweetest fragrance in the darkest hours of their life. If we are going through a dark valley in our life, let us take courage and not give up. May we produce sweet fragrance in the darkest hours.

God is trying to mold us and shape us to His honor and glory. Our master Sculptor may sometimes see some flaws in our life, which He desires to chisel out. We sometimes cringe as He chisels away at impure things in our life. But let's be patient, knowing that the trial of our faith works patience. Though suffering is painful, let us accept the unpleasant things of life.

Let us keep our eyes on Jesus, and someday we can experience the eternal bliss of heaven. In heaven, there will be no more pain, heartache, or suffering.

Samuel Beachy, Belvidere, TN

Though trials are unpleasant, they can produce precious fragrance.

February 1

But thou, when thou fastest, anoint thine head and wash thy face; that thou appear not unto men to fast, but unto thy Father which is in secret: and thy Father which seeth in secret shall reward thee openly.

- MATTHEW 6:17, 18

PROCLAIM A FAST

Today's Bible reading touches on an important point in the life of many godly people through the history of the Bible. Fasting has been a way of appealing to God for mercy, compassion, and release from the many afflictions we as humans suffer because of our fallen nature. Many examples can be drawn from the saints in the Bible who fasted. In 1 Samuel 7 we read of a great battle the Israelites won against the Philistines after they fasted and confessed their sins to God. When Haman plotted to kill all the Jews, Queen Esther proclaimed a fast for three days and nights and they were marvelously delivered from the hands of the enemy.

Another outstanding testimony is when Jesus sent out His disciples two by two and gave them power over unclean spirits (Mark 6:7). They were confronted with a case where their power was defeated. Jesus was grieved by their lack of faith, and after He cast out the unclean spirit, His disciples were informed that such only go by prayer and fasting.

By the power of the Holy Spirit, Jesus was able to resist the Devil, when He fasted forty days and forty nights in the wilderness.

In these last perilous days when iniquity abounds and the love of many waxes cold, may we join hands to pray and fast in the spirit that God chose in Isaiah 58. Not only can the participant in a fast see God at work, but he is purged from his own transgression and can enjoy a closer walk with God.

Chester Mullet, Belle Center, OH

By eating the forbidden fruit, sin was brought into the world. By fasting and prayer we may be released from sin.

February 2

Bible Reading: Psalm 139

One Year Bible Reading Plan: Matthew 22:1-22, Exodus 29, 30

Let me be weighed in an even balance, that God may know mine integrity.

- JOB 31:6

SELF-EXAMINATION

There was a man named Louie. He came to his minister one day and said he had a lot of problems. The minister told him what to do. But he came back awhile later and said, "I tried it, but it didn't work."

Finally the minister said, "Louie, I've told you all I know. Why don't you go and talk to other ministers? Maybe they can help you."

Sometime later Louie came back and said, "I've seen them all, and none of them know any more than you do."

One evening this minister had an appointment to preach at another church, so he asked Louie to go along. Late that night on the way home, they stopped at a restaurant to get a sandwich. While they were sitting there eating, all at once Louie said, "I've got it, I've got it!" He brought his fist down on the table hard enough that everybody heard it.

"Well, quiet down," the minister said. "What is it you've got?"

"I've got the answer to my problem. The reason everything goes wrong with myself is that I am wrong." He discovered that, when a person really gets spiritual power and moves away from weak, defeated self, he can have a victorious life.

Quite often the reason people have many problems in life is because they have sin in their lives.

Eli A. Yoder, Stuarts Draft, VA

Life with Christ is an endless hope; without Him it is a hopeless end.

February 3

Bible Reading: 1 Kings 3:16-28

One Year Bible Reading Plan: Matthew 22:23-46, Exodus 31–33

Humble yourselves in the sight of the Lord, and he shall lift you up.
- JAMES 4:10

BUT A CHILD

Every day many babies are born into the world. Some are born into Christian homes, others into non-Christian homes, and still others are born and have no home. God loves children. Childlikeness is one of the attributes He wants to see in His people. Jesus said, "Except ye be converted, and become as little children, ye shall not enter into the kingdom of heaven."

Children play a vital part in our world. How would it be not to have any children around? How would it be never to hold a baby, never hear their cry, and never feel their smallness?

Children somehow touch our hearts and we love them. Maybe it's because of their smallness. Maybe it's because of their simplicity and lack of arrogance. A young child would never think to be someone great. Perhaps we love them because they are willing to be taught. Or could it be because they love and adore us? There are many reasons we love babies and children.

Solomon said, "I am but a little child" (1 Kings 3:7). Jeremiah said, "Ah, Lord God . . . I am a child" (Jeremiah 1:6). Remember, unless we become as little children we can't go to be with God, because God loves children. He loves us when we remember that we are small.

Babies are helpless and need constant care and attention. God can help us only after we realize we are totally helpless. He wants to help us. He wants to teach us. He wants to lead us. He wants to hold us. But maybe we think we're too big for that. We say we'll take care of ourselves, and we lose a big blessing. God wants to take us as a little baby in His arms and say, "Let's go this way." Let us never think we're too big for that!

Harold R. Troyer, Kiev, Ukraine

The strongest faith is often found in a child's heart.

February 4

Bible Reading: 2 Peter 3:1-14

One Year Bible Reading Plan: Matthew 23:1-22, Exodus 34–36

But the day of the Lord will come as a thief in the night; in the which the heavens will pass away with a great noise.

- 2 PETER 3:10

BE READY

It was a lovely, peaceful evening in late summer in northern Pennsylvania. Folks were going about their normal duties, doing chores in the barn, washing dishes in the house, or simply relaxing.

Suddenly there was a loud boom. I left the barn and went outdoors to investigate. The sky was clear. Then there was a lesser boom followed by a series of rumbles for a minute or two. Phones started ringing as people became alarmed. Scanners reported a possible jet crash in our area. Cars started racing toward the supposed crash site. One man, who was away from home, drove ninety miles per hour when he heard that the crash was near his home.

After investigating, it was concluded there was no jet crash. But evidence was found to confirm that a meteorite had struck the atmosphere and had caused the eruption, resulting in the unusual noise that caused alarm.

This is a vivid reminder of the words of Peter telling us that the heavens shall pass away with a great noise. We are told that in the last days scoffers will come, saying, "Where is the promise of His coming?" There may be frightening events that take place, causing people to think seriously for a time, but they soon forget, thinking that everything will continue as normal. But our text reminds us not to be ignorant of the fact that the Lord is not slack concerning His promise. "Seeing then that all these things shall be dissolved, what manner of persons ought ye to be in all holy conversation and godliness."

We can look forward to Jesus' return with joyful anticipation, rather than suffer the consequences of the wrath of God on the wicked.

Willis H. Martin, Wellsboro, PA

In trouble and distress, Jesus speaks, saying, "Be of good cheer, it is I."

February 5

Bible Reading: Revelation 7:1-3, 9-17; 13:11-18

One Year Bible Reading Plan: Matthew 23:23-39, Exodus 37, 38

In whom also after that ye believed, ye were sealed with that holy Spirit of promise, Which is the earnest of our inheritance.
- EPHESIANS 1:13, 14

SEALED OR MARKED?

Identification is an important issue in the world today. The government is making more effort than ever to know who is moving and operating within its borders. For most of us, social security numbers, passports, and driver's licenses are only a routine seal of our identity. They actually help us access the goods and services we wish to acquire, and provide measures of security.

Identification becomes a burden to others. Photo IDs may give them away. Passports and visas are forged to give them a false identity. Why is this necessary? They are marked by the government as criminals, troublemakers, or even as terrorists. These marks of identification are dead give-aways as to who they really are.

The children of God possess bona fide identification. They have been redeemed from sin. They have changed their loyalty from Satan and the world, to God and the Church. In that conversion experience, God graciously seals their commitment to righteousness with the Holy Spirit of promise. That seal is the earnest or down payment guaranteeing that God can and will do for them all that He has promised as they faithfully serve Him. It is God's commitment to them that He will protect and help them if they remain in His love. It is seen by all as they allow Him to produce in their lives the fruit of the Spirit.

The wicked and unregenerate people are not so blessed by God. They serve a different master. He wishes to enslave them. But his service leaves scars, not seals. His servants become marked by the rigors and harshness of sinful living. Their lives are marked by discontent, hatred, and immorality. Often it shows on their faces and in their lack of joy in living. Finally, "the wages of sin is death."

The choice is ours. Are we marked or sealed?

Delmar R. Eby, London, KY

Seals secure and preserve; marks identify for destruction.

February 6

Bible Reading: Ecclesiastes 10:1-12; 3:1-15

One Year Bible Reading Plan: Matthew 24:1-22, Exodus 39, 40

As we have therefore opportunity, let us do good unto all men, especially unto them who are of the household of faith.

- GALATIANS 6:10

OPPORTUNITY KNOCKS

Can I be too busy? "I'd like to help you, but I'm busy," I say. Do you ever hear yourself say that? How do you know when to deny yourself of work in order to help someone with a less valuable project? We cannot do everything for everyone, but we ought to be willing to do work that requires sacrifice of ourselves. What is first in my life if I am unavailable to help my neighbor but wash my car instead? God has given us brethren in the church to help each other, though it may not always suit to help.

To understand His will, we need to look at the Word and make it precious in our lives. "Whatsoever thy hand findeth to do, do it with thy might, for there is no mark, nor device, nor knowledge, nor wisdom, in the grave, whither thou goest" (Ecclesiastes 9:10). Take into consideration that a chance to help someone may never come again. Opportunities are given by God. It is our choice whether we allow our self-life to control us or not.

"While we look not at the things which are seen, but at the things which are not seen: for the things which are seen are temporal; but the things which are not seen are eternal" (2 Corinthians 4:18). Eternal values are established when we do more than our personal interests. We should voluntarily take time to help with a cottage meeting or visit an elderly person. We won't find an opportunity to share our life with someone else unless we give up ourselves to love others as Christ loved us. It is our responsibility to share joy, hope, and comfort with those who need it. "I must work the works of him that sent me, while it is day: the night cometh, when no man can work" (John 9:4).

Nevin Landis, Kalona, IA

Work for the Savior Who loves souls.

February 7

Bible Reading: Ezekiel 33:1-20

One Year Bible Reading Plan: Matthew 24:23-51, Leviticus 1–3

Go ye therefore and teach all nations.

- MATTHEW 28:19

REACHING OUT TO HELP

The news came through at 2:00 a.m. on the morning of July 25, 2002. Bill Arnold and his family awoke to the unusual barking of his dog. He got up and looked out of his bedroom window and saw a commotion going on at the coal mine site on his farm. He told his wife he was going over to see what it was all about. Arnold found out there was a mining accident, and nine men were trapped under his farm land 240 feet below the surface. What shocking news for the surrounding area of Somerset, Pennsylvania, let alone to the families of the nine miners who were trapped. The news spread rapidly. Rescue crews rushed in. Drilling rigs arrived. First, a small hole was drilled in order to pump out water and to send down hot air and oxygen for the men to survive. Another rig began drilling a thirty-six-inch hole to bring the men to the surface as soon as possible.

People were asked to pray for the safety of the trapped men and for the grieving families. The drilling continued day and night for seventy-two hours after the accident. The cry was not, "Can we save them?" but "We will save them!" What rejoicing when the last of the nine men was lifted to safety!

This happening should awake each one of us Christians to the great task of reaching out to those who are buried in sin. For if they do not repent, they will be lost forever and ever, without any hope of escape! Let us be desperate to point a lost and dying world to Jesus Christ. We need to persevere, pray, and witness, pointing them to Jesus Christ, whose blood will wash away their sin. Come, let us shoulder our responsibility and reach out to help.

Amos B. Stoltzfus, Honey Brook, PA

Rescue the perishing, care for the dying.

February 8

Bible Reading: Acts 4:31-37, 5:1-11

One Year Bible Reading Plan: Matthew 25:1-30, Leviticus 4–6

I have no greater joy than to hear that my children walk in truth.

- 3 JOHN 4

TRUTH IS UNCHANGING

The story is told of Franz and Grandfather walking to town. A rabbit ran across the road.

"What a big rabbit!" said Grandfather.

"Why, that was nothing," said Franz. "Once I saw a rabbit as big as a cow."

"Really!" Grandfather exclaimed. "How interesting, and have you heard the tale about the bridge we're coming to? The tale is that when someone crosses over it who doesn't tell the truth, it breaks down."

"Uh, perhaps the rabbit was only as big as a goat," said Franz.

"Perhaps," said Grandfather.

"Or maybe it was only as big as a dog," Franz continued.

"Maybe," said Grandfather.

They came to the bridge. Franz stopped.

"Now I remember," he said. "It was only as big as a . . ."

"A rabbit?" asked Grandfather.

"Yes," said Franz. "A rabbit."

Too often we stretch the truth a long ways. It should probably be called a lie, but it sounds so good to say. We think just maybe we'll get by with it. Truth is truth and it will never change, just like God never changes.

Someone once said that you can stretch, change, or revise the truth and it will still be the truth. But that's a lie, because unless it's the pure truth, it's not the truth. You can't change the truth, revise it, or even stretch it, because then it will no longer be the truth.

God said, "Adam and Eve, if you eat of that tree you shall surely die." Satan told them a lie: "You will not surely die, but will become as gods, knowing good and evil." Maybe he just stretched the truth. What do you think? Wasn't part of what he said right?

Harold R. Troyer, Kiev, Ukraine

The worst lies are those that most resemble truth.

February 9

Bible Reading: 1 John 2:12-17, Jude 11-19

One Year Bible Reading Plan: Matthew 25:31-46, Leviticus 7–9

And the world passeth away, and the lust thereof: but he that doeth the will of God abideth for ever.

- 1 JOHN 2:17

LOVE NOT THE WORLD

While I was at church one evening, my Bible was open and I saw these underlined words: "Love not the world." I whispered, "Lord, please, create in me a living hatred for the world, Satan, and sin." Later the words, "Love not the world" were still running through my mind.

"Love not the world . . ." In these four little words we see what one preacher was saying about love. He said, "Love is a decision." The Lord has created us with a free will. We can choose what to do. Even though sometimes we get angry with someone and we want to get revenge, it is still a decision, and we can decide either to hate or to love.

We have two forces pulling against each other within us–the spirit and the flesh. It's just as the Indian told his pastor. He said, "Pastor, it is as if there were two dogs fighting within me. The one I encourage the most is the one who always wins."

We are in a real and living fight. I feel it in me quite often. Sometimes I feel the world's mighty wind trying to blow me off course and roll me down to destruction. If I don't keep my eyes on Him, if I'm not tied to my Anchor, my soul will shipwreck.

Do we love the world more than we love the Father? Do we love the world more than we love our brothers? Our personal appearance, our speech, and the places we go must identify us with the saints rather than with the world. Would our Father recognize us as His possession?

The lust of the flesh, the lust of the eyes, and the pride of life are not of the Father, but of the world.

Let's choose not to love the world or the things that are in the world. "If any man love the world, the love of the Father is not in him" (1 John 2:15).

Richard del Cristo, Piedra Blanca, Dominican Republic

No power can make a man do wrong without his consent.

February 10

Bible Reading: 1 Corinthians 3

One Year Bible Reading Plan: Matthew 26:1-19, Leviticus 10–12

Therefore thus saith the Lord God, Behold, I lay in Zion for a foundation a stone, a tried stone, a precious corner stone, a sure foundation: he that believeth shall not make haste.

- ISAIAH 28:16

A FIRM FOUNDATION

When I was a boy, I helped my father pour many foundations. We would dig down to solid ground, making a trench for the foundation. The cement truck would come, and we would pour the foundation. After the foundation was poured, there wasn't much you could do to change it. Once the foundation was hardened, we would build on it.

According to verse eleven of our Bible reading, the foundation of our Christian life has been poured. It is our responsibility to build on that foundation. This foundation is sure and will remain. It's an eternal foundation. The Lord Jesus, who is the Word, is our foundation. "Heaven and earth shall pass away: but my Word shall not pass away."

How deep is your foundation? What is it made of? Is God your foundation? Read the Bible. Pray to the Lord Jesus. Build on the Foundation. It's critical to build. Without building, we fail. We need to use good building materials and build daily. Our attitudes, our thoughts, our actions, and where we look make a difference in our building. We must use good fire-retardant building materials because they will be tried by fire. We are building for eternity on an eternal foundation. Without this foundation we can do nothing.

We can all build on this foundation, so let's encourage each other to stand firm on the Lord Jesus Christ.

Harold R. Troyer, Kiev, Ukraine

The foundation of the Lord stands sure!

February 11

Bible Reading: Judges 16:4-21

One Year Bible Reading Plan: Matthew 26:20-54, Leviticus 13

See then that ye walk circumspectly, not as fools, but as wise.
- EPHESIANS 5:15

WASTED POTENTIAL

Surrounded by the enemy, he submitted to capture and was bound with ropes. But suddenly Samson shook himself, and the ropes binding him burst like burnt flax. His enemies had badly underestimated the power of Samson's God. Taking the jawbone of a donkey, he killed a thousand Philistines.

What strength! No one could stop Samson but he himself. Only a few years later, the same enemy bound him and put out his eyes. He became their slave. How tragic! It all happened because Samson listened to his own desires instead of heeding the godly advice of his parents.

Samson's parents warned Samson, but he repeatedly scorned good counsel. He loved to go in to heathen women and carelessly defiled his Nazarite vows. The Spirit departed from him, and Samson, unprotected, was blinded and enslaved by the enemy. At last he died with them. What a sad ending for a man who could have done so much for his Lord. He failed simply because he was ultimately concerned about pleasing Samson.

We can learn a lesson from Samson's story. It is possible for us to waste our potential because we refuse to do what we know is right. Often our own selfishness, pride, and stubbornness trap us. We accomplish so little for the Lord because we refuse to surrender fully to Him. The good news is that we still have a choice in the matter. We live in the present, when affecting our circumstances is still possible. By the grace of God, we can live a life that is victorious, a life that accomplishes much for our Master.

Craig Eicher, Butler, IN

Wasted potential is the greatest waste of all.

February 12

Bible Reading: Romans 12, Ephesians 4:11-16

One Year Bible Reading Plan: Matthew 26:55-75, Leviticus 14

Can two walk together, except they be agreed?

- AMOS 3:3

ROW TOGETHER

It was a beautiful fall morning to be out enjoying nature. The sun was shining, and the birds were singing joyously to their Maker. We were out to try our hand at canoeing. We had an enjoyable time getting our canoes into the water. Most of the canoes had two people in them with each one using an oar. It was amazing what could be done when we worked together. We were actually going somewhere!

Imagine that a pair of canoeists began arguing whether to go upstream or downstream. Unable to settle the conflict, one of them simply begins to row upstream and the other begins to paddle in the opposite direction. We know that the chances of this pair getting anywhere would not be very great. Such an argument would most likely end in chaos, rather than in the enjoyable time they could have had. What wasted effort!

How is it in the church? Are we pulling together toward one common goal? Together we should "press toward the mark for the prize of the high calling of God in Christ Jesus" (Philippians 3:14). Too often we face conflict because we are determined things must be done our way. We dare never give in to wrong simply for the sake of peace. But neither should we be so opinionated that we cannot see a brother's point of view and go along with it if it does not violate Scripture.

Working toward the same goal includes giving and receiving encouragement, as well as constructive criticism. Do we feel for the weaker brother? Are we doing all in our power to help him on to glory?

It is only as we all look to Christ that we can truly work together. Be faithful until the end!

Philip Cross, Leitchfield, KY

In matter of principle, stand like a rock; in matter of preference, flow like a river. - Abraham Lincoln

February 13

Bible Reading: Proverbs 28:1-14

One Year Bible Reading Plan: Matthew 27:1-31, Leviticus 15–17

Have mercy upon me, O God, according to thy lovingkindness: according unto the multitude of thy tender mercies blot out my transgressions.
- PSALM 51:1

I AM SORRY

When John the Baptist, Jesus, and the disciples began their ministries, the first thing they preached was "Repent ye." The responsibility for repentance was placed on man. God will not repent for us. Only as I see my sin as an affront to a holy God can I clearly say, "I am sorry."

The first point in repentance is to acknowledge a contrite heart that will create within us a desire to live differently.

A teacher asked her students, "What is repentance?" One child answered, "It is being sorry for our sins." Another child added, "So sorry that we quit sinning."

When someone repents, they lay off their wicked ways, evil feelings, and wrong habits. If you cease to do evil and learn to do well, that is repentance.

The psalmist David expressed his sorrow in Psalm 38:4-9. He said, "My wounds stink . . . I am bowed down greatly; I go mourning all the day long . . ." In verse seven, he says he has a "loathsome disease, and there is no soundness in [his] flesh." David gives us a true example of saying, "I am sorry."

Is my sorrow for my sin as evident as what David expressed? Remember, most people know when we are sorry. True repentance says, "I have sinned." "For all have sinned, and come short of the glory of God" (Romans 3:23).

Allan A. Miller, Sarcoxie, MO

We cannot be saved without repentance.

February 14

Bible Reading: Hebrews 12:1-29

One Year Bible Reading Plan: Matthew 27:32-66, Leviticus 18, 19

Looking diligently lest any man fail of the grace of God; lest any root of bitterness springing up trouble you, and thereby many be defiled.

- HEBREWS 12:15

SEEKING DILIGENTLY

Our Scripture reading reminds us to look or seek diligently. This indicates that the casual seeker is in danger of failing of the grace of God. The first verse urges us to lay aside every weight and the sin which so easily besets us. The importance of being diligent in pursuit of salvation cannot be overemphasized.

The story is told of a man who thought highly of his dog that could run very fast. One day the dog was put to the test. He was turned loose with a rabbit to see if he could catch it. The rabbit got away. When the owner was asked to give an explanation, he replied, "The rabbit was running for his life. The dog was only running for his dinner."

Paul speaks of our spiritual journey and refers to it as a race. The Scripture tells us to lay aside every weight so we can run the race successfully. I am afraid that many today are running only for their dinner. Their god is their belly. They are more concerned about earthly or material things than they are about the things of the kingdom. They sacrifice freely on the altars of the idols of fashion, entertainment, and self-indulgence.

Let us ask God for strength and grace to lay aside every weight that we may run the race successfully. Let us rejoice in the Lord and in the task at hand. Christ said, "No man, having put his hand to the plough, and looking back, is fit for the kingdom of God" (Luke 9:62). Let us not look back but reach forward to the eternal prize which we have been offered. While others may only be running after their dinner, let us run for eternal life.

Melvin L. Yoder, Gambier, OH

Are you running on the high road that leads above the clouds?
Or are you running on the low road with the world
and its sinful crowds?

February 15

Bible Reading: Ephesians 6

One Year Bible Reading Plan: Matthew 28, Leviticus 20, 21

Greater is he that is in you, than he that is in the world.

- 1 JOHN 4:4

CAUGHT

I met him in the convenience store as he was checking out. I was behind him and saw that all he wanted was a pack of cigarettes. He smelled of beer, and my heart sank as I remembered how clean and good he had looked at the Thanksgiving dinner. He was a wayward son drawn into the world.

I left the store crying out to God that He would protect me from the world's system and rescue the lost and dying. I prayed that God would somehow keep me faithful. The world has no mercy in its pursuit of man. It is subtle in its approach and masks its true motives with an innocent preview. We are no match for the world's influence. We think we can stand against the tide, but we can't.

That night at home I told the Lord, "I hate the world. Take me as far from it as possible. I'll live in a mud shack in the remotest hills, telling souls about the Savior; just take me away from the world, God!"

Then a sense of calm came over me as I thought of the power of God. God is greater than the world. I have no reason to fear if I trust in Him.

As I knelt to pray that evening, I couldn't stop the tears. *The world and its mastermind may be strong, but I've got Someone even greater I can trust,* I thought as I rose.

Harold R. Troyer, Belleville, PA

Practice the ways of the world and you will have the results of the world.

February 16

I beseech you therefore, brethren, by the mercies of God, that ye present your bodies a living sacrifice, holy, acceptable unto God, which is your reasonable service.

- ROMANS 12:1

A PIG OR A HEN

The story is told of a hen and a pig that felt sorry for a homeless man and wanted to do something to help him.

"I have an idea," suggested the hen. "We could give him a nice breakfast of ham and eggs."

"That's easy for you," replied the pig. "For you it's just a contribution; for me it's a total sacrifice."

Is your Christian walk just a contribution, or is it a total sacrifice? Are you content to give tithes and warm a church pew, or do you go beyond the requirements and focus on meeting the physical and spiritual needs around you?

When Christ came to earth, He did not merely contribute to the good of mankind. He gave His life as a total sacrifice for us.

Many of our forefathers were willing to suffer or to die for the cause of Christ and the good of their fellow man.

We may never have the privilege of literally dying for Christ, but we have a responsibility to die for Him by daily dying to self and by seeking opportunities to serve Him. No, we cannot meet all the needs we see, but we can certainly be available to "Rejoice with them that do rejoice, and weep with them that weep" (Romans 12:15). We can give a word of encouragement or concern to a brother or sister and be open to the Spirit's leading to show us needs we can help meet.

What do we owe Jesus? We owe Him nothing less than totally yielding our lives to Him.

Joseph Jones, Ash Fork, AZ

You are not really living until you are willing to die.

February 17

Bible Reading: 2 Chronicles 26

One Year Bible Reading Plan: Mark 1:23-45, Leviticus 24, 25

Pride goeth before destruction, and an haughty spirit before a fall.
- PROVERBS 16:18

KING UZZIAH'S DOWNFALL

Uzziah was sixteen years old when he replaced his father as king, and he ruled for fifty-two years. He built walls and fortified them, built towers in Jerusalem and in the desert, and dug wells to water his many cattle. He had vine dressers in the mountains and in Carmel because he loved the soil and husbandry. He had a host of fighting men and made war with mighty power. Uzziah prepared shields, spears, helmets, habergeons, bows, and slings to cast stones for his host of soldiers. In Jerusalem he made engines to put on the towers and bulwarks to shoot arrows and great stones. King Uzziah's name spread far. The year of King Uzziah's death was approximately 740 B.C. He died of leprosy for trying to take over the High Priest's duties.

Although Uzziah was generally a good king and his reign was long and prosperous, many of his people turned away from God. Uzziah turned away from God and died a leper. He is remembered more for his arrogant act and subsequent punishment than for his great reforms.

God requires life-long obedience. Spurts of obedience are not enough. Only those who "endure unto the end" will be rewarded (Mark 13:13). Be remembered for your consistent faith, otherwise you, too, may become more famous for your downfall than for your success.

Marvin C. Hochstetler, Napanee, IN

The fear of the Lord is a fountain of life, to depart from the snares of death.

February 18

Bible Reading: Acts 21:7-24

One Year Bible Reading Plan: Mark 2, Leviticus 26, 27

Then Paul answered, What mean ye to weep and to break mine heart? for I am ready not to be bound only, but also to die at Jerusalem for the name of the Lord Jesus.

- ACTS 21:13

FOR THE NAME OF GOD

Matthew Henry was once robbed. In his diary he wrote, "Let me be thankful, first, that I was never robbed before; second, because they took my purse and not my life; third, because although they took my all, it was not much; and fourth, because it was I who was robbed, and not I who robbed."

Matthew Henry's loss was not nearly so important to him as doing God's will. Apostle Paul also showed this attitude when Agabus told him what would happen to him if he would go to Jerusalem. He would be bound and delivered to the Gentiles. Paul was not deterred. His desire was to do God's will and to fulfill His purpose in life no matter what might happen to him. He desired to obey the Lord for His name's sake.

No one knows what the future holds for us. If we seek to do God's will, it may include walking through the valley of the shadow of death. At times we may have to choose the pathway of hardship because we wish to do what is right, rather than what is the easiest. As we go through life making decisions and facing difficulties, we should remember that doing God's will is far more important than what may happen to us or to our material goods. We should do all for God.

Daniel Miller, Dunnegan, MO

What we call adversity God calls opportunity.

February 19

I beseech you, brethren, (ye know the house of Stephanas, that it is the firstfruits of Achaia, and that they have addicted themselves to the ministry of the saints,) . . .

- 1 CORINTHIANS 16:15

ADDICTED

Have you ever heard of Benzedrine? How about marijuana, nicotine, cocaine, or heroin?

There is one characteristic these all have in common. They are addictive to those who make frequent use of them. Folks who are addicted develop a nearly unquenchable craving for these substances. Many addicts will go to great lengths to get their hands on these things. It becomes their obsession–they can think of nothing else.

Now there is one other thing to add to our list of addictive substances–ministry. Not many people get into this addiction.

Some folks in the Bible were addicted to ministry. Stephanas and his household, the first Christians in Achaia, were some of the few believers baptized by the Apostle Paul. In Paul's letter to the Corinthians, they are noted for their ability to see people's needs and to do all they could to meet them.

The church at Macedonia had similar qualities. The reason for their outstanding ministry is found in 2 Corinthians 8:5. They first gave themselves to God, then to others, and to themselves last of all. Even though they were going through great trials and poverty, the joy of the Lord in their hearts compelled them to give willingly all that was in their power to give. If they had an abundance of a certain thing, they shared with someone in need.

Try to follow the example of these early pillars of the church. First give yourself completely to Christ, and then give yourself to others who have needs. Become addicted to Christian ministry!

Lavon Miller, Mack, CO

Jesus first, yourself last, and others in between.

February 20

Bible Reading: Luke 15:3-32

One Year Bible Reading Plan: Mark 3:22-35, Numbers 3, 4

How think ye? If a man have an hundred sheep, and one of them be gone astray, doth he not leave the ninety and nine, and goeth into the mountains, and seeketh that which is gone astray?

- MATTHEW 18:12

REDEMPTION

Picture a shepherd looking for his lost lamb. He may know the general area where his lamb has gone. His lamb made a wrong move in removing itself from the flock. At first, when the lamb made its escape, everything looked so glorious. It continued to walk through the woods and thickets, every step bringing it nearer to its destruction. Scratches and bruises covered its body, and the lamb became weaker each step of the way. Finally it recognized that it was lost and doomed. It was exhausted and didn't know which way to turn. When the lamb finally came to the end of itself, it bleated for help, hoping that the shepherd would find his lamb.

The shepherd was earnestly looking and calling for his lost lamb. He looked for its tracks and listened for its cry. Finally he heard the bleating. In spite of the steep and stony area, he rushed toward it. He picked up his lamb and tenderly carried it back to the fold.

Those who have not given their hearts and lives over to God are like this lost lamb. They are wandering deeper and deeper into sin. It is leaving scratches and scars in their lives. Each person must recognize his lost and sinful condition and cry out to the Good Shepherd. He is ever looking for those who are willing to give their lives over to Him.

Jesus gave His life for me, should I not give Him mine?

Samuel Beachy, Belvidere, TN

Though scratched, torn, and bleeding, Jesus can save my soul.

February 21

Bible Reading: Mark 4:1-20

One Year Bible Reading Plan: Mark 4:1-20, Numbers 5, 6

And he said unto them, He that hath ears to hear, let him hear.

- MARK 4:9

WHOSE PROBLEM IS IT?

Whose fault is it when it seems the sermons don't take root? We would often like to blame the preacher, but let's think it over.

In the parable of the sower, we see that Satan devoured the seed that fell by the wayside. Perhaps we sometimes don't concentrate on the message, and like the birds, the Devil will snatch these seeds before we can even put them into our mind. Perhaps our soil is stony, but the Word takes root and springs up. We may say we were convicted, but like a stony field, the roots do not go down, and the first difficulty will cause our growth to cease and we will die once more.

There is no easy cure for stony soil. It takes sweat, tears, and lots of effort to remove the rocks that are hindering a strong root system. God can help us remove the stones from our lives. He is waiting on us to ask Him. He is able. Thorns are also a problem in our spiritual lives, not unlike the physical world. Again, we must allow God to remove the hindrances Satan uses to bring us down.

Can you imagine raising corn but being unwilling to remove the weeds? What a crop failure that would be! Unfortunately, many church-going people are doing just that in their spiritual lives. How is your soil?

Michael David Yoder, Dundee, OH

When there is no thirst for righteousness, the sermons seem dry.

February 22

Bible Reading: Hebrews 12

One Year Bible Reading Plan: Mark 4:21-41, Numbers 7

Looking unto Jesus the author and finisher of our faith; who for the joy that was set before him endured the cross, despising the shame, and is set down at the right hand of the throne of God.

- HEBREWS 12:2

KNOWING THE AUTHOR

In my collection of books, I had a book about a young missionary who died on the mission field. The book had been given to me as a gift, but it meant very little to me. Its dull, black cover wasn't appealing. I had made several weak attempts at reading it, but somehow couldn't get myself involved in it. It lay dormant on my book shelf for some time. And then . . .

I spent a weekend at a little mission house in a distant town. After an edifying evening of fellowship, I had a lengthy discussion with the people who were hosting the mission. During the course of conversation, I discovered that I was talking with the author of this dull, black book on my bookshelf. I could hardly wait to go home and read the book. The book didn't change, but my attitude toward it did. The difference was that I now knew the author.

When I was growing up, there was always a Bible laying on the desk in our living room. It wasn't very appealing in its dull, black cover. Several times I made weak attempts at reading it, only to put it back on the desk. And then . . .

After a life of sin and self, one evening in my bedroom God gave me a vision of hell and where I was headed. In anguish I cried out to God, and He reached down, touched me, and flooded me with peace.

That dull, black Bible became very precious to me. Its appearance didn't change, and neither did its wording, but my attitude toward it did. I had met the Author.

There are still times when I get distracted and lose my desire to read the Bible. Those are the times when I need to spend time getting better acquainted with the Author.

William J. Miller, Conneautville, PA

Know God or No God.

February 23

And put a knife to thy throat, if thou be a man given to appetite.
- PROVERBS 23:2

RESISTING THE DAINTIES

We live in a sensual world where all activity is geared toward pleasing self. The world says "Eat what you want, drive what you want, live where you want, do what you want. Do it when you want, with whom you want, and as long as you want. And as long as you are not tired of it, keep doing it. When you do get tired of it, try something else."

What we need today is less indulgence and more discipline and instruction. How do we gain and maintain temperance in a splurging society?

Our key verse gives drastic measures in the prevention of overeating. "Put a knife to thy throat." That sounds deadly, but which is worse–dying of gluttony or dying of bloodletting? Neither option would be recommendable. Try restraint.

We are called to crucify the flesh with its affections and lusts. Since we are the temple of God, what we do affects the indwelling of the Holy Spirit. If we sow to the flesh, we will reap of the flesh; if we sow to the Spirit, we will reap of the Spirit.

One practical way to put a knife to your throat is to fast and pray. Skip a few meals and starve the flesh. Pray for temperance and love– not love for self, but love for the Designer of the human body. Always remember that the Designer of your body made no mistake.

Harold R. Troyer, Belleville, PA

A life of ease is a difficult pursuit. - William Cowper

February 24

Bible Reading: Ecclesiastes 7:1-22

One Year Bible Reading Plan: Mark 5:21-43, Numbers 11–13

Blessed are they that mourn: for they shall be comforted.
- MATTHEW 5:4

SORROW

We have all experienced sorrow at one time or another. It is not wrong to sorrow. Jesus sorrowed at the time of Lazareth's death. He also wept over Jerusalem. The Bible tells us that He was acquainted with grief.

Job grieved over his children. In Job's experience it would seem to us that God allowed too many things at once, but His grace was sufficient. This account gives us insight into the spiritual warfare that goes on behind the scenes. The Devil tries to break down God's people, but he cannot go beyond what the Lord allows. The Devil tries similar tactics on us in our times of sorrow. To our load of grief, he might try to add things like family differences, church problems, or financial struggles. With such things the Devil tries to get us to give up in our commitment to Christ.

It is not wrong to think about our problems. But it is wrong to start blaming God, other people, or circumstances for our problems. Job was tempted to do this. Even his wife suggested that he curse God. We see the response of a godly man as he called the idea of blaming God "foolishness" even in the midst of his undesirable circumstances.

We also need to keep in mind that we sorrow not as those who have no hope. "For if we believe that Jesus died and rose again, even so them also which sleep in Jesus will God bring with Him. Wherefore comfort one another with these words" (1 Thessalonians 4:14, 18).

Elvin Fox, Shiloh, OH

What a friend we have in Jesus, all our sins and griefs to bear!

February 25

Bible Reading: Revelation 2:1-7, Matthew 24:3-13

One Year Bible Reading Plan: Mark 6:1-32, Numbers 14, 15

And because iniquity shall abound, the love of many shall wax cold.

- MATTHEW 24:12

WHERE IS YOUR FIRST LOVE?

Are you still thriving on the things of God or has your focus shifted back to the things of the world? Do you use your spare time for God or for yourself? Do you really love the Lord with all your heart? He wants 100 percent of our lives. When we read the Bible, do we read it with true love for the Author and a desire to know Him better, or just because it is what all good Christians do? These are some thought-provoking questions we need to ask ourselves from time to time.

The author says in Hebrews 10:23, "Let us hold fast the profession of our faith without wavering; (for he is faithful that promised)." The Lord will see us through if we totally surrender our life to Him and rely on Him. We cannot just sit back and let everyone else do the work. We have a work to do. We need to pass on the torch of faith to the next generations.

Let us keep pressing onward, striving to stay near the Lord so we can reach that eternal goal waiting for us. "I press toward the mark for the prize of the high calling of God in Christ Jesus" (Philippians 3:14). We need to forget the things behind and reach for the things before us. May we all remain faithful so we can hear those words, "Well done, thou good and faithful servant, enter thou into the joy of thy lord" (Matthew 25:21).

Darin Stoll, Greensburg, KY

Is the fire still burning in your soul?

February 26

Bible Reading: Genesis 22:1-18

One Year Bible Reading Plan: Mark 6:33-56, Numbers 16, 17

Then Peter and the other apostles answered and said,
We ought to obey God rather than men.

- ACTS 5:29

GENUINE OBEDIENCE

When God asked Abraham to take his only son and offer him up for a sacrifice to the Lord, Abraham did not ask God why or try to convince Him of some other way to show his love and obedience. Abraham rose up early in the morning and promptly obeyed God. God likes when we, like Abraham, promptly and willingly obey Him. Would you be willing to offer up your only son?

The Lord will remember those who are obedient to Him. God expects that we obey Him wholeheartedly and follow all His commandments.

Saul, in 1 Samuel 15:22, was not obedient to the Lord when he did not utterly destroy the Amalekites. God punished him by taking the kingdom from him even though Saul repented of his sin.

God must be the object of our goals and endeavors. The imperfect results of even our most strenuous efforts reveal that we need God's grace in our lives. Nothing less than our full obedience and trust in God can make this grace available (1 John 2:1-6).

Christian obedience also includes that of children to their parents (Ephesians 6:1-2). Parents are good examples to their children when they obey the church and other figures of authority God has placed over them.

May we, like Abraham, obey God at any cost.

Joash Yoder, Greensburg, KY

Trust and obey, for there's no other way, to be happy in Jesus, but to trust and obey.

February 27

Bible Reading: Job 37

One Year Bible Reading Plan: Mark 7:1-13, Numbers 18–20

Teach us what we shall say unto him; for we cannot order our speech by reason of darkness.

- JOB 37:19

WRONG FIRST IMPRESSIONS

Recently a trip to town took me into a hardware store I had not patronized before. Approaching the store, I noticed there were no cars in the parking lot. Upon entering, the first thing I noticed was dust and dirt all over the products and shelves. The shelves were lightly stocked and in complete disarray. I remember thinking, *What do I want in here? This store will probably soon shut its doors, as not many people shop here.*

The man in the back of the store cleaning windows looked as if he might be the owner. The front door buzzer and footsteps on the old wooden floor announced the entry of a customer who commented, "It sure looks great!"

What was he talking about? I looked around a little closer at the insides of the long, old store. Finally I asked, "Have you been sanding floors?"

"Yes," he said, "I have been working on it."

As my eyes did further exploration, I noticed an area with new finish and a part that hadn't been sanded yet. It appeared someone had put forth a lot of effort to renew the dark, worn floors.

I was quite ashamed of my earlier thought about this being an undesirable place to shop. Taking another look at the owner, I found myself seeing him in a new light. He appeared to be a young, energetic, and industrious person, willing to pay the price to make his business work.

It is amazing how my whole perception changed. Too often we judge things too quickly and often wrongly. It is much better to evaluate a situation slowly, always remembering that we might not see everything involved.

Roy Keim, West Union, OH

It is better to follow and fail than to fail to follow.

February 28

Bible Reading: Romans 6:11-23

One Year Bible Reading Plan: Mark 7:14-23, Numbers 21, 22

Abstain from all appearance of evil.
- 1 THESSALONIANS 5:22

GRIZZLY BEARS

Most of us would not be comfortable camping in grizzly bear territory unarmed, but Tim Treadwell was. Every summer he went to an Alaskan island to befriend bears, ignoring warnings that grizzly bears are dangerous. He went unarmed and spent days studying and observing bears and their habits. His goal was to get close to grizzlies while being videotaped, and he often ended up within touching distance of half-ton bears. In the winter while the bears slept, he would return to his home in California and show videos of his daring actions. He gave presentations to thousands of school children and became quite popular. Several broadcasters filmed him.

But in Alaska, the bear biologists and park officials were not impressed with his actions. They kept warning Tim to stop his bear play. But Tim refused. In September of 2003, Tim and a friend were camping in bear country again. One evening Tim crawled out of the tent to confront a grizzly that was in their camp. This time his confrontation was fatal. He and his partner were both killed and partly eaten by the grizzly. His camcorder was found later, and it had recorded the final minutes of Tim's life. His desperate cries for help escalated into high-pitched screams as he was mauled. No doubt he regretted that he had tried to befriend bears.

Today many people play with a spiritual grizzly called sin. Often they are warned that it is dangerous, but many, like Tim, ignore the warnings till it is too late. On Judgment Day they will regret it because the grizzly named sin will doom them to eternal destruction. Sin truly is dangerous. Let us not play with it. We must do what we can to keep a distance from it. The wages and consequences of sin are always spiritual death.

Nathan Mast, Sugarcreek, OH

He who plays with fire gets burned.

February 29

Obey my voice, and do them, according to all which I command you: so shall ye be my people, and I will be your God.

- JEREMIAH 11:4

GOD'S WAYS ARE ALWAYS BEST

God made everything after patterns or designs. We go to school to learn about these patterns so we can better understand God's plan. God made special patterns for people. He never makes two people exactly alike. Some people are tall and slim. Others are short and heavy. Some are quick thinkers and others are slow.

A man once wanted to make a special kind of soap. The recipe said to mix some of the ingredients then allow it to harden. After it was hard, it could be cut up, dissolved, and the other ingredients added. But this man thought, *Why go to all the trouble? Why not put all the ingredients in while it is still soft, instead of allowing it to harden then dissolve it again?* He put all the ingredients in the soft mixture, but it just did not come out right.

It was a failure because he didn't follow the directions. In the Christian life, if we don't follow God's instructions, we will not have His blessings. When we speak harshly to someone, it is not according to God's rules. God's Word says, "A soft answer turneth away wrath, but grievous words stir up anger" (Proverbs 15:1). In the same way, all the instructions in the Bible tell us the best way to get along with people and have joy in our hearts.

Eli A. Yoder, Stuarts Draft, VA

If you don't have time to do it right, when will you do it over?

March 1

Bible Reading: 1 John 2

One Year Bible Reading Plan: Mark 8, Numbers 25–27

Love not the world, neither the things that are in the world.
If any man love the world, the love of the Father is not in him.

- 1 JOHN 2:15

FULLY SURRENDERED

Today's Scripture reading warns of the lust of the eye, lust of the flesh, and the pride of life, which is of the world and not of the Father.

History tells us the little town of St. Quentin on the borders of France was attacked by the Spaniards. One day the Spaniards thought victory was within sight. They shot a shower of arrows over the walls with little notes attached promising the inhabitants that if they surrendered, their lives and property would be spared. The governor took a note and wrote on it two words: *Regem habemus*–we have a King. He tied it to a javelin and sent it back over the wall.

Satan constantly tries to tell us that it would be better for us to surrender to his will. If we accept his teachings, we need not give up our carnal nature. We can have our pride and our entertainments. We may go where the world goes, and do whatever the world does, as long as the heart is right. He tries to persuade us that all traditions are wrong. He has persuaded many that church membership and attendance are just necessary traditions. Just surrender those old traditions and be free. Nonconformity and non-resistance are just old-time traditions. You are trying to earn salvation rather than trusting grace. Surrender those old outdated traditions and enjoy the music, sports, and entertainment that you have been missing.

He fails to mention that entertainment is this nation's number one tradition. Going to the ball game has replaced going to church. Business and entertainment have replaced the Wednesday evening prayer service. The golf course, the pool hall, and the bowling alley have all invaded the church which has surrendered the old traditions. They have traded the old-time Bible traditions for the traditions of the world.

Melvin L. Yoder, Gambier, OH

We either surrender the joys of heaven, or the things of this world.
Which will you surrender?

March 2

I am come that they might have life, and that they might have it
more abundantly.

- JOHN 10:10

A MESSAGE IN DUST

All of us have seen dusty, dirty vehicles. The windows and doors
provided an opportunity for some witty person to get their point across
with a message such as, "Wash me."

A number of years ago while traveling along a highway, we drew up
to the rear of a semi. Someone had written in the dust on one of the
rear doors. I don't recall what state we were in, what time it was, what
highway we were on, where we were going, or where we were coming
from, but I do remember the message. All it said was "1 John 1:4." I
immediately turned to the Scripture and found these faithful words,
"And these things write we unto you, that your joy may be full."

Whoever would think that lowly dust could portray so much good!
We would be surprised to know how many decisions have been hinged
upon the use of dust as a quick and handy writing pad. The farmer
wants to remember a certain figure. With a finger he marks the dust
to help him remember. Many people from all walks of life have done it
at one time or other. Layouts of maps in the sand or dust were used
by explorers, armies, and others. Why? So it could be committed to
memory. In our reading, Jesus seemingly used it too, and the scribes
and Pharisees also remembered.

Wayne E. Miller, Rushsylvania, OH

When our bodies have turned to dust,
Will we have left a message good and just?

Bible Reading: Luke 15:11-32

One Year Bible Reading Plan: Mark 9:30-50, Numbers 30, 31

And when he came to himself, he said, How many hired servants of my father's have bread enough and to spare, and I perish with hunger!
- LUKE 15:17

SWEET REASONABLENESS

In this parable of the prodigal son, the younger brother wasn't wayward because he ran away; he ran away because he was wayward. He didn't consider how his father and his brother would feel about his leaving. Notice his words in verse twelve, "Give me the portion of goods that falleth unto me." He was only concerned about his share.

When the younger son received his portion, the older son received his as well. Consider what this cost their father. He was probably not ready to divide his living between his two sons. Then the younger brother left for a far country. Now the father was left with a financial loss and a labor loss. The father was left very short-handed.

The younger son's attitude was, "Give me my portion." This had probably been his attitude for a long time. I find it interesting that it only took the prodigal son two verses to become poverty stricken. That which had taken his father years to save was now gone, and reality set in. He probably started remembering his mother's cooking and the pleasant atmosphere of home. Surely he thought of how his father's camels used to transport him from place to place. He now had none of these. His clothes smelled like pigs, and the Bible says, "He came to himself." When he remembered the goodness of his father, and the plenty that he once had, this young wayward son repented. This change of mind and attitude has been referred to as sweet reasonableness. Now the young man was willing to be just a servant in his father's house.

This story touches my heart because that's how so many of us are in our relationship with God. It's "Give me my portion," when all the while God is waiting for us to come to sweet reasonableness.

Terry Lester, Montezuma, GA

The goodness of God leadeth thee to repentance.

March 4

Bible Reading: Romans 10:1-13

One Year Bible Reading Plan: Mark 10:1-31, Numbers 32, 33

For I say unto you, That except your righteousness shall exceed the righteousness of the scribes and Pharisees, ye shall in no case enter into the kingdom of heaven.

- MATTHEW 5:20

RELIGIOUS OR RIGHTEOUS?

Did you know that the Devil is religious? The Scripture says he "believes and trembles." Is it possible that the neighbor who works on Sunday and rarely goes to church is religious? Yes, he may be a church member and believe there is a God. Could the atheist, who says there is no God, be religious? Yes, again, for is he not zealous and fervent in promoting his belief and persuasion?

Is it possible to be religious without being righteous? Is it possible to be righteous without being religious?

Righteousness and religion are complimentary to each other if the emphasis is first on righteousness. Being found righteous before God, as was Abraham, is a result of saving faith. When salvation by faith works in one's life, then certainly he will be religious. He will be fervent and devoted in living and promoting his belief.

On the other hand, religion without righteousness before God is worthless. Its goals and aims range far and wide. Religion may include satanic worship, earth worship, or idol worship. It may drive men to fanatic suicide missions, self-abuse, or immoral practices.

Closer home, religion may be a prescribed set of forms, modes, or practices. It may be only an heirloom passed to us from a previous generation. It may be present only on Sundays.

God is looking for more than that. He is looking for a heart religion, not just a head religion. God is looking for righteousness that produces "pure religion and undefiled."

Is your religion rooted in and springing from the righteousness of faith? If righteousness is not producing your religion, then neither is your religion producing righteousness.

Delmar R. Eby, London, KY

Being religious requires only reformation.
Being righteous requires regeneration.

Bible Reading: Proverbs 3:1-20

One Year Bible Reading Plan: Mark 10:32-52, Numbers 34–36

My people ask counsel at their stocks, and their staff declareth unto them: for the spirit of whoredoms hath caused them to err, and they have gone a whoring from under their God.

- HOSEA 4:12

GOD IS FAITHFUL

A herd of a hundred cows with their young stock requires an abundant supply of water. When the exclamation came "The well is running dry!" it was due cause for concern. After a plumber verified the plight, it was evident we needed a new well. Our first thought was, *Lord, are we going to be put to a test? Will we have a challenge finding water and be tempted to use a water diviner?*

With the prayer, "Lord, we place the whole matter into Your hands," a call was made to the well drillers. Although they were extremely busy due to the drought, it worked out that they were able to start on our well the same day.

Early in the afternoon the drilling rig pulled in. We showed him the general area where we thought the new well should be located for convenience. The operator asked, "Did you have a diviner locate the new well?"

"No, we did not," came the reply. "We have faith and trust in the Lord to guide us that we will have abundant water where you drill."

The operator replied, "You made a wise choice." He jumped into the drilling rig, backed into the area specified, raised the derrick, and started to drill. By ten o'clock the next morning the drillers hit good water. Shortly after lunch the plumbers came, and by evening the new well was in service.

Where is the Christian to go when he faces the unknown? Our Lord states in His Word that He knows our needs before we ask Him. Heartfelt prayers seeking God's help and guidance will not go unnoticed. Satan has a counterfeit plan, but those who are faithful to God will not be deceived and will be blessed by their faithfulness.

Lester K. Burkholder, Fredericksburg, PA

*The finger that points the way is part of the hand
that supplies the need.*

March 6

Bible Reading: 1 Peter 4

One Year Bible Reading Plan: Mark 11:1-19, Deuteronomy 1, 2

In a great trial of affliction the abundance of their joy and their deep poverty abounded unto the riches of their liberality.

- 2 CORINTHIANS 8:2

THROUGH SUNSHINE AND STORM

When we had a period of nice, warm, dry weather, I thought about how nice it was to have sunshine every day. But then I saw the grass turn brown and flowers and gardens starting to wilt and lose their color.

Then later we had some thunderstorms. During the storm it wasn't as pleasant as before, but afterward we could see it served a good purpose.

During the storm the plants drooped down and looked worse than they did before the storm. But after the rain stopped and the sun shone again, they looked better than they did before the storm, and the grass was growing green again.

That's the way it is with our daily life. If we only had sunny days, we would not appreciate them as much as when we have storms too. In life we need some rain now and then to help us to grow. During the storms we might look worse than before, but after it passes over, we can see that we have gained from it.

As we go through our trials, let's ask God to help us and lead us so we can benefit. When we are back in the sunshine again, we can help someone else who is going through a storm of life. Let's thank God for the trials He has us go through. They will help our roots grow deeper, so we can live a better life for Christ today and receive that reward in heaven.

Melvin Byler, Newaygo, MI

If we want to see a rainbow, we have to endure a little rain.

March 7

Then saith Jesus unto him, Get thee hence, Satan: for it is written,
Thou shalt worship the Lord thy God, and him only shalt thou serve.
- MATTHEW 4:10

IDOLATRY AND THE FLAG

The other night we were at a revival meeting. The topic was on idolatry. My thoughts were turned to God and the American flag. Do we as Christians look to God for our refuge or to the flag? Can the flag save us? Can the flag answer prayer? Do we idolize the flag? Exodus 20:3 says, "Thou shalt have no other gods before me." The flag has been around since 1777, but God has been around since before creation and time.

Do we as Christians look to God the way the world looks to the flag? People around me should be able to see Jesus through my way of life. I must have Jesus flying high in my heart. In times of trials and troubles I must turn to Him rather than to the flag. The flag is only a piece of cloth that will perish with time and has no spiritual value for Christians. We need to remember that God wants us to worship Him, not the flag.

The flag is just one of the many material things that can become an idol to us. The Bible says in 1 Corinthians 10:14, "Wherefore, my dearly beloved, flee from idolatry." Let us keep God in focus at all times, not just when trials and troubles appear, but also when things are going good for us. Let us worship God with all sincerity. Let us lift high the banner of the cross. God our Father is the only One who can help us with our struggles.

Idolatry will only destroy our relationship with Jesus.

Menno H. Eicher, Miami, OK

Live for God, He gave His only Son for us.

March 8

Bible Reading: Acts 17:1-15

One Year Bible Reading Plan: Mark 12:1-27, Deuteronomy 5–7

These that have turned the world upside down are come hither also.
- ACTS 17:6B

TURNING THE WORLD UPSIDE DOWN

One afternoon several years ago, I was visiting with some old-timers from the area who had stopped by the field where I was working. After a few minutes of conversation, one of them turned to me and asked, "So, how old are you?"

"Eighteen," I replied.

"Eighteen!" he repeated emphatically. "Eighteen! Young man, do you know what I would do if I were eighteen?"

"No," I responded, "I don't. What would you do?"

Pulling himself up to his full height and locking his steel gray eyes solidly on me, he hooked his thumbs under his giant suspenders and responded with a measured emphasis on each word, "I'd try to tear the world apart."

As I continued working, I tossed his statement around. With youthful imagination, I decided to do some actual calculations of what it would take to literally tear the world apart and haul the mass volume on an imaginary road to the moon in terms of numbers of truck loads and years to complete the project.

As foolish as man would be to attempt a literal tearing apart of the world, there is a sense in which God calls all of us to help turn it upside down. When Paul and Silas were going about their way, sharing about the risen Savior, they were accused of this very thing. We, too, should not hesitate to share the same message. If our views on creation, salvation, and obedient discipleship cause the world to reject us, then let us thank God for the privilege of being a soldier in His "upside-down Kingdom."

Joshua Eicher, Rosebush, MI

For the battle is the Lord's. - 1 Samuel 17:47

March 9

Bible Reading: Matthew 24:1-28

One Year Bible Reading Plan: Mark 12:28-44, Deuteronomy 8-10

And what I say unto you I say unto all, Watch.

- MARK 13:37

TAKE HEED THAT NO MAN DECEIVE YOU

In Matthew 24:3 the disciples request of Jesus, "Tell us, when shall these things be? And what shall be the sign of thy coming, and of the end of the world?" Why did Jesus answer their question by saying, "Take heed that no man deceive you"? He didn't really answer their question. The way Jesus answered this shows us that it is more important to take heed and watch than to know all the details of His coming and the end of the world.

To take heed means to be alert and watchful. It is indicating that unless we take heed there is a possibility of being deceived, even if we are aware of the signs of His coming and the end of the world.

Deception includes false ideas, beliefs, and opinions that people hold. Satan is the originator of deception. We must be careful of our reading material. "Be not deceived, evil communications corrupt good manners." We need to be watchful and alert as Paul says in 2 Corinthians 2:11, "For we are not ignorant of his devices." Even though Satan is about us as an angel of light and a roaring lion, we can overcome him by the blood of the Lamb.

So let us be in a state of watchfulness, for Jesus said, "Many false prophets shall arise and deceive many." But we also have the wonderful promise in 1 John 4:4, "Greater is He that is in you than he that is in the world."

Eli A. Yoder, Stuarts Draft, VA

No matter how much we deceive ourselves and others,
we never deceive God.

March 10

Bible Reading: Luke 21:5-28

One Year Bible Reading Plan: Mark 13:1-13, Deuteronomy 11-13

While we look not at the things which are seen, but at the things which are not seen: for the things which are seen are temporal; but the things which are not seen are eternal.

- 2 CORINTHIANS 4:18

IT'S GETTING BRIGHTER

It was a cloudy Sunday morning with a light rain falling. A little later the clouds began to break up, and some blue sky appeared. As we were going home after church services, my wife remarked, "It keeps getting brighter the closer home we get." Her comment made me think of the journey of life and our heavenly home.

When I was a youth, heaven seemed rather unreal and far away. I was anticipating years of life ahead of me. Hardly a serious thought was given to leaving this world. Though not yet an old man at fifty years, my perspective of heaven has changed somewhat. Some friends and loved ones have already passed on to that eternal home. I am keenly aware that I'm closer myself. The reality of it is becoming brighter and more attractive.

The Scripture says of Abraham that he sojourned in the land of Canaan. A sojourn is a temporary stay. We know this word describes our life on this earth. It was also said of Abraham that he looked for a city whose builder and maker is God. The phrase "looked for" does not mean searching for, but rather anticipation and expectation. Should we not also be anticipating our heavenly home?

This earthly scene is certainly not becoming brighter. Among the nations there is terrorism, war, and turmoil. Even more alarming is the increased ferocity with which Satan is attacking the home and church. The clouds above us are dark and threatening. But as we focus our eyes on the horizon, we see clear sky. Indeed, the Son is shining. Our longing for yon fair land grows stronger. Can we not say, "It keeps getting brighter the closer home we get"?

John E. Glick, Gap, PA

Heaven will surely be worth it all.

March 11

Bible Reading: Proverbs 15:1-23

One Year Bible Reading Plan: Mark 13:14-37, Deuteronomy 14-16

For we are labourers together with God: ye are God's husbandry,
ye are God's building.

- 1 CORINTHIANS 3:9

COMMUNICATION

Communication is depositing a part of you into another person. Open communication among brothers and sisters relieves tension. When we share our problems with others, they can pray for the situation. By coming together and sharing our thoughts, we can be a blessing to others and they to us. As the saying is, "Two heads are better than one."

We need to listen to others' problems and not voice our opinion until they have said it all. We must understand how to listen and be as James 1:19 says, "Swift to hear, slow to speak, slow to wrath." Good listening includes genuine interest in the good of the other person. Attentiveness is very important. By hearing more than words, we can sometimes read between the lines. Before we can really help a situation, we need to hear both sides.

We need to be careful not to communicate things that are to be confidential. This breaks down confidence more than anything else.

"Then they that feared the Lord spake often one to another: and the Lord hearkened, and heard it" (Malachi 3:16). We shouldn't do all the talking and neither should we clam up and do no talking. When there are differences of opinion, we may need to give up our idea even if it is right. Someone else's idea may also be right. We need to submit to each other in the fear of God in order to be at peace in the church. To have proper order in the church, we need to sit down and communicate.

Love is the overall principle in our relationships. Love will cause us to give up our will for the sake of others.

Eli A. Yoder, Stuarts Draft, VA

One thing you can give and still keep is your word.

March 12

For he is our peace, who hath made both one, and hath broken down the middle wall of partition between us.

- EPHESIANS 2:14

THE MIDDLE WALL REMOVED

What is this middle wall of partition?

In Old Testament times, the only way a Gentile or heathen could become a part of the Israelite nation was through many cleansings and ceremonies over a period of time. Today, because of the grace and mercy of God, that wall of partition is removed. God has removed the barrier between the Jews and the Gentiles through the death and resurrection of Jesus Christ. The Jews were God's people before Jesus came to save all men from their sins. Now, because of His death and resurrection, we too can be a part of God's people. We become a child of God by accepting the atonement of Christ, not by following the Old Testament rituals.

We need to remember who we were before God took away the partition. God's purpose to remove this wall was to make one people of the two people. Now everyone has the same access to God. All must repent and believe on the Lord before they can be one of His. Verses eight and nine of our Bible reading explain that it is not what we have done, but what God has provided for us.

Joe Miller, Hartville, OH

God is no respecter of persons.

March 13

Bible Reading: Psalm 125, Hebrews 11:1-8

One Year Bible Reading Plan: Mark 14:26-50, Deuteromony 20-22

O taste and see that the Lord is good: blessed is the man that trusteth in him.
- PSALM 34:8

TRUST IN THE LORD

"Emmanuel! We are going to visit my parents. Take care of the house. It's all yours." That was my good friend Tony and his wife. We have been friends for more than ten years and have built up trust in one another, so he was not afraid to leave his house and children under my care until he returned. Without maintaining a right relationship over the years, we could not have gained each other's trust.

King David was a man who had seen great afflictions and adversity. The one most important lesson he learned in those moments was to trust in the Lord for deliverance. What does it mean to trust in the Lord? It is not merely being a member of a church, even though that is necessary. It is not making a mere tradition of daily Bible reading and prayer without any change of life.

Trusting in the Lord is based on a close, personal, permanent relationship with God. It is believing in the reliability or integrity of the Lord, depending on Him every moment, regardless of the problems that you may be facing.

David says in Psalm 125:1, "They that trust in the Lord shall be as mount Zion, which cannot be removed, but abideth for ever." Trusting in the Lord pays great dividends. The expression "cannot be removed" in the above text means "cannot be carried away, cannot backslide, cannot be defeated." Mount Zion has stood in its geographical position for thousands of years now. Mighty storms and winds over the years could not move it out of its position.

If you trust in the Lord, you will be like Mount Zion—unmovable, unshakable, unconquerable. The storms of life, adverse situations, circumstances, and people may come against you, but you will not be carried away. You will not backslide. You will not be defeated because the Lord in whom you trust will deliver you.

Emmanuel Dareman, Accra, Ghana

Trust in the Lord, and do good. - Psalm 37:3

March 14

Bible Reading: Psalm 10:11-18, Luke 12:16-21

One Year Bible Reading Plan: Mark 14:51-72, Deuteronomy 23-25

My times are in thy hand.
- PSALM 31:15

THIS IS OUR TIME

Time is something we all deal with. It is forced upon us. We can't refuse it; we didn't seek it; we didn't choose it. But it's up to us how we use it. We must give an account to God how we use it.

We measure time: Seconds, minutes, hours, days, months, years, a lifetime. Do we see time as a gift from God, or is it something we just take for granted? Do we use time selfishly or for the glory of God? We all have only one lifetime, one time allotted, and we don't know how long that will be. What are we doing with the gift of time God has given us? Many want more free time—time when I can do what I want to do and be accountable to no one but myself for my time.

Life is short. Time is short. Psalm 39:5 tells us that our days are as a handbreadth. That's not very big, is it?

We need to remember that time is in God's hands. When God declares that time shall be no more, that's it! When God declares that time shall cease, man is powerless to prevent it. We need to be prepared to go at any time. When God says it is our last minute, we won't have time to make things right. If God would say, "You have one more minute," what would be our response? Sit and watch the clock for one minute. What if it would have been your last? Are you ready?

Marlin Schrock, Stark City, MO

The best way to spend time is to invest it in eternity.

March 15

The sluggard will not plow by reason of the cold; therefore shall he beg in harvest, and have nothing.

- PROVERBS 20:4

SAFE RETREAT IN DISASTER

My son Jason and I were strolling through the woods checking on trees that could be sawed into firewood. We came to a leaning, decaying cherry tree that was hung up in the fork of a neighboring tough, sturdy hickory. We notched deeply into the hickory and then cut into the old cherry. With a cracking, crashing thump, both trees hit the ground.

Suddenly there were flying squirrels everywhere. We had cut down their den! Several scuttled along the fallen trees and made their way into a hollow apple tree. Others were airborne in seconds as they glided downhill and disappeared in another hollow cherry tree. Probably in less than twenty seconds they were all in a safe retreat. But soon Jason detected movement in the hollow of the fallen den tree. We peered in and saw a shivering, bewildered, flying squirrel that didn't know where to turn to in time of disaster. No personal retreats were prepared in advance.

Sometimes we are like that flying squirrel. We settle into the routine of daily living. We are well fed, clothed, and sheltered. Our spiritual needs are met as we follow the pattern of church and family living.

But shouldn't we spend additional quiet time with God, a personal digging into the Word to fortify our spiritual reserves? The sluggard decides not to plow ahead of schedule. It's too cold to be out there. We are too busy to spend time alone with God plowing the Scriptures. We don't see any need for quiet retreats. Why bother?

If we refuse to prepare our hearts ahead of time, we will, like the sluggard, have nothing when disaster strikes.

James Beachy, Sugarcreek, OH

Take time or sometime you will be taken.

March 16

Bible Reading: Matthew 25:1-13

One Year Bible Reading Plan: Mark 15:27-47, Deuteronomy 28

Watch therefore, for ye know neither the day nor the hour wherein the Son of man cometh.

- MATTHEW 25:13

BE READY

Awhile back, we as a family traveled to Honduras. On the way back, we arrived at the border about five minutes after they closed. I asked the guard if there would be some way to pass over into Nicaragua, and he said, "It is not possible. The gate is shut!"

Surely! Surely we could cross the border, we thought, but to no avail. We turned around, a dejected group of people wondering what to do next.

We could easily have hurried more on the way to the border, but we did not think it was that important. Is it not the same way with many people? They could do better, hurry more, and take more seriously the issues of life. But really, is it that important? Yes, it is, my friend. Many times we get caught up with the issues of this world. We think there is plenty of time and we can change this or that later. Procrastination doesn't accomplish anything. There are times when by putting off our spiritual needs they become less important to us. That does not change the situation. God still keeps records. We need to remember, the final moment will finally arrive when there will be no more changing. As the tree falls, so shall it lie. When we heard the words, "The gate is shut!" the scene took on new meaning. The situation could not be changed.

Let's not be like the foolish virgins who, upon returning from buying oil, found the door shut! Today is the time to make changes, not later. May God help us to be ready, watching and waiting!

John Byers, Masaya, Nicaragua

On the bypass of by and by, man arrives at the destination of never.

# March 17

Bible Reading: 2 Peter 3:1-18

One Year Bible Reading Plan: Mark 16, Deuteronomy 29, 30

Let us labour therefore to enter into that rest, lest any man fall after the same example of unbelief.
- HEBREWS 4:11

SET UP YOUR OWN LIGHTHOUSES

For many years, lighthouses served an important place in seafaring safety, especially near the shore. They warned of rocks and reefs and provided guidance for sailors as they came into the harbors. Their importance has diminished in recent years because of electronic guidance and warning systems.

Our lives are often likened to a sea. We are the seafarers. We are grateful for the many times others have warned us of dangerous areas. Our churches, homes, and schools have been lighthouses on the rocky shores of time to spare us from shipwreck.

But there may be particularly dangerous areas of our life that others are not even aware of. There may be rocks we might crash on that are peculiar to our situation. Certain temptations may face us more than others. We need protection from these life-threatening, soul-crashing rocks.

It often becomes our responsibility to set up our own personal lighthouses. We must have light to guide us safely away from and around the rocks of temptation so that we can safely reach our heavenly port. We must set up markers or establish some kind of warning signal when we near the rocks of sin. It may be a Scripture verse posted in our vehicle, house, or business place. It may be a verse so well memorized that certain conditions bring it to our mind.

We must have danger places clearly named. What we want to avoid as wrong, must be named as sin, and clearly marked as such. Meditating on God's Word and marking Scriptures pertinent to our needs is another lighthouse building project.

What rocks threaten you? Where is your ship likely to crash? Build lighthouses of truth to guide you past those rocks.

Delmar R. Eby, London, KY

Lighthouses for life will serve their purpose only as well as we give heed to the light they give.

81

March 18

Bible Reading: John 10:1-18

One Year Bible Reading Plan: Luke 1:1-23, Deuteronomy 31, 32

Because strait is the gate, and narrow is the way, which leadeth unto life, and few there be that find it.

- MATTHEW 7:14

A VISION OF THE NARROW WAY

To enter the strait gate, the people have to leave all their burdens and sins on the outside. Some knock, and the door is opened for them. They enter while others stand outside talking about making money or gossiping.

The ones that enter go into a big room and come out as little children (Matthew 18:3). They continue down the narrow way where a large platform is above them with a lot of people standing on it. As the Christians pass by, the people on the platform throw stones at them and poke fun at them. There are some on the outside building scaffolds. They have ladders and are trying to climb over the top. But they are never able to enter. The ladder or the scaffold breaks and the people fall off and are not able to enter (John 10:1).

Which way are you going? Are you walking the narrow way as little children? Are you trying to get in over the top? Or are you on the platform throwing stones and poking fun at the ones on the narrow way? If you have not entered the strait gate, repent today. Leave your burdens and sins on the outside and enter in. The time is short.

"Jesus saith unto him, I am the way, the truth, and the life: no man cometh unto the Father, but by me" (John 14:6).

Daniel Miller, Dunnegan, MO

Sin can never enter there.

March 19

Bible Reading: Judges 7:9-25

One Year Bible Reading Plan: Luke 1:24-56, Deuteronomy 33, 34

For when I am weak, then am I strong.

- 2 CORINTHIANS 12:10

SPIRITUAL WARFARE

In our Scripture reading, Gideon is likened to a cake of barley bread. A cake of barley bread was probably something of very little value. Gideon was also left with less than 1 percent of the army that he had started out with. How helpless he must have felt to go face the enemy with his own abilities. But the Lord was ready to use him. Gideon didn't march boldly into the camp of the Midianites with a 32,000-man army behind him. He tumbled into the host of Midian like a cake of barley bread.

We, too, are in a battle against a mighty enemy. But we are not fighting with warships or helicopters. Neither are we armed with bombs, grenades, or guided missiles. We are not wearing the military garb or carrying guns with ammunition. "For the weapons of our warfare are not carnal, but mighty through God to the pulling down of strong holds" (2 Corinthians 10:4). The battle is not ours but the Lord's. We have a tendency to get in the Lord's way because we have too high impressions of ourselves. If the battle is lost, it will be because we are too big. "God resisteth the proud, but giveth grace unto the humble" (James 4:6).

Alvin J. Coblentz, Free Union, VA

*The best way to overcome the enemy
is in a prostrate position.*

March 20

Though he were a Son, yet learned he obedience by the things which he suffered; and being made perfect, he became the author of eternal salvation unto all them that obey him.

- HEBREWS 5:8-9

PURIFYING PAIN

As we go through life, we meet with all kinds of experiences. Some experiences are happy. Some are sad. Probably the most difficult experiences are the painful ones—mental pain, emotional pain, spiritual pain, or physical pain. All of us have experienced at least one or more of these and have found it very unpleasant. We find pain to be motivating. It helps change our course or helps break a bad habit. Yet we all long for freedom from pain. We sing about being free from it. We pray for those experiencing pain. We all take measures to avoid it.

Why pain? Consider how self-destructive we would be if we didn't have pain to help us. Carpenters could saw off their hands. Farmers could hurt their sons with the farm machinery. Housewives could burn themselves. What kind of destructive behavior would we have in church life, in home life, and in our social lives if we didn't have pain?

Pain helps us see God's love. God created man with a free will. He knew the pain that we would bring Him—pain of rejection, the horrors of sin, death, hell, and the grave. Yet God saw this path as best and most revealing of His love. So He chose pain. Why? The Bible says that He, being made perfect through the things He suffered, became Author of our salvation (Hebrews 5:9). We are all sinful, and pain is God's way of purifying us. Instead of asking, "Why?" would it not help us to say, "Thank You, Lord. Now I'm more pure, like You."

Owen Shrock, Shreve, OH

He who fears to suffer cannot be His who suffered.

March 21

Bible Reading: John 4:13-42

One Year Bible Reading Plan: Luke 2:1-24, Joshua 46

Then saith he unto his disciples, The harvest truly is plenteous,
but the laborers are few.

- MATTHEW 9:37

NO VISION – WE PERISH

Can you see? Do you have vision? How good is your vision? Is your vision making a difference in your life?

What would you say if someone told you that it has been discovered that humans no longer need eyes? No more blurry vision. You'll have no need for eye glasses or contacts. You will never need to worry about dirt or sand irritating your eyes. There will be new technology and new knowledge, but no eyes.

Just think of the disaster if nobody had eyes. Who would help the blind? Oh, but we would soon learn, wouldn't we? Yes, we would learn, the hard way. We would soon die off.

Many people today have no spiritual vision and the lost are suffering because of it. Not only is the lost suffering, but also those who lack spiritual vision. Jesus had vision. He said, "Lift up your eyes, and look on the fields; for they are white already to harvest" (John 4:35). He knew He had just been talking with someone who had a problem and a need, and He understood both.

Spurgeon said, "You will never make a missionary of the person who does no good at home. He that will not serve the Lord in the Sunday school at home will not win children to Christ in China."

We need to sharpen our vision. We need to see beyond the present, beyond the exterior, and beyond the dirt and grime. If we would meet Christ, we must meet our fellowman.

Harold R. Troyer, Belleville, PA

Where there is no vision, the people perish. - Solomon

March 22

Bible Reading: John 11:11-15, John 11:21-45

One Year Bible Reading Plan: Luke 2:25-52, Joshua 7, 8

*This sickness is not unto death, but for the glory of God,
that the Son of God might be glorified thereby.*

- JOHN 11:4

THE GLORY OF GOD

Jesus stated that Lazarus' sickness was for the glory of God. He even waited two days before He started off to see His friends. By that time Lazarus had died, and Mary and Martha were overcome with grief. When Lazarus was raised to life again, it was God who received the glory. God let Lazarus die to create an awareness of His power and His love. It was "for the glory of God."

We Christians need to be careful that we promote a faith that has the emphasis on the glory of God, rather than on the glory of man. Children need both praise and discipline. When they receive a lot of praise and little discipline, they grow up living for the glory of self rather than for the glory of God. If they can feel love in their parents' discipline, they grow up with a picture of love as part of discipline. When we see God's love in His discipline, we can glorify Him by returning a measure of that love to Him. The Christian life then is lived for His glory, not for our own. If we seek lots of attention from others, our life is concentrated on ourselves rather than on God.

God showed His love for us when He let His own Son die for our sins. That, too, was not for our glory, but for His glory. In 1 Peter 3:18 we read "Christ also hath once suffered . . . that he might bring us to God." The goal of God's love in sending Christ was not to glorify us, but to prepare a way for us to glorify Him forever.

Amsey Martin, Wallenstein, ON

---

*The basis of our faith is not God glorifying man,
but man glorifying God.*

March 23

Bible Reading: Isaiah 40:12-27

One Year Bible Reading Plan: Luke 3, Joshua 9, 10

Behold, the nations are as a drop of a bucket, and are counted as the small dust of the balance.

- ISAIAH 40:15

HOW MANY ON THE ROAD?

My cousin and I were broken down on Interstate 70, westbound out of Denver, Colorado. While we waited for a tow truck, I was amazed by the amount of traffic we saw. We were stopped at a very tight spot with little shoulder and there was a curve right behind us. The many cars sailing close by our window aroused my curiosity. I began to count and found that anywhere from twenty to fifty vehicles went by every minute.

Doing a little math, I discovered that, figuring conservatively, in the twelve-hour daylight period, around 22,000 vehicles exit Denver, Colorado, on westbound I-70 alone. If there were an average of one and a half persons per vehicle, it would add up to 32,400 people.

Now, think of the many other highways and cities in our nation. All those thousands are a drop in the bucket compared to the rest of this great world. To our God all of this is nothing. My mind wandered. Where is everyone going? What are they all doing? And what is their purpose in life? Then I thought of a different road that many more are traveling. It is the road to hell and destruction. On this road many are busy loving money, fulfilling the lusts of their bodies, abusing those around them, and serving their flesh.

In the year 2000, 54,513,000 people died worldwide. That's a staggering 149,350 people per day or 1 to 2 people per second. Look at your clock for a minute, and every time the second hand moves forward imagine another one or two people bowing before the Almighty.

What are we doing for God? Are we a city set on a hill that cannot be hid? May we truly have God's love in our hearts for lost souls on the road to destruction.

Llewellyn Miller, Grand Junction, CO

Those on the road to heaven will not be content to go there alone.

March 24

Bible Reading: 1 John 4

One Year Bible Reading Plan: Luke 4:1-32, Joshua 11-13

Greater love hath no man than this, that a man lay down his life for his friends.
- JOHN 15:13

LOVE ONE ANOTHER

The story is told of a little girl who needed a kidney transplant. After checking around and testing different people, it was discovered that her younger brother's kidney matched hers. Little Brother readily agreed to donate a kidney. They were both prepared for surgery, and while they were lying there waiting, one of the doctors noticed that the young boy looked sad. Going over to him, he asked, "What's wrong? Are you afraid?"

"No," replied the boy, "but can you tell me when I will die?"

This loving young brother had not understood that he had two kidneys, and that they would only be taking one. He thought that once they took his kidney he would die. So great was his love for his sister, that he was willing to die so his sister could live.

Do we have such a love for others? Great love will willingly sacrifice for the good of others.

Another story is told of a young boy who was carrying his little brother. When asked if his little brother wasn't heavy, he replied, "Oh no, he's my brother."

If we love our brother or sister, helping them along will not be a burden to us, whether it is carrying them through a time of trial, or giving of ourselves until we don't expect to survive.

Joe Miller, Hartville, OH

Let brotherly love continue.

March 25

Bible Reading: Ephesians 6

One Year Bible Reading Plan: Luke 4:33-44, Joshua 14, 15

There is therefore now no condemnation to them which are in Christ Jesus, who walk not after the flesh, but after the Spirit.

- ROMANS 8:1

CONVICTION OR CONDEMNATION?

Have you been joyless lately? We probably all have had times when we could have said, "I feel joyless." When we feel joyless, we need to remember the difference between conviction and condemnation.

The feeling of condemnation is a vague, indefinite guilty feeling. It is like a black cloud over your head following you everywhere you go, but you don't know exactly what you feel guilty about. The feeling of condemnation is often untruthful and never edifying. It doesn't cause you to repent and change, because you don't know what you are guilty of.

Satan uses condemnation to steal our faith and confidence in God. For protection we need to take "the shield of faith, wherewith ye shall be able to quench all the fiery darts of the wicked" (Ephesians 6:16).

The feeling of conviction, on the other hand, is definite and specific. It is not vague, and you are not confused about what the problem is. That conviction bothers you until you do what you know you should do. If we feel condemned, we should first of all stop and see if we are trying to avoid God's convicting voice in our lives.

"If we confess our sins, he is faithful and just to forgive us our sins, and to cleanse us from all unrighteousness" (1 John 1:9). Don't trust your feelings; trust what has been promised to us in this verse.

Aaron Miller, Loudonville, OH

Many are seeking feeling instead of healing.

March 26

Bible Reading: 1 Timothy 6

One Year Bible Reading Plan: Luke 5:1-16, Joshua 16-18

A faithful man shall abound with blessings: but he that maketh haste to be rich shall not be innocent.

- PROVERBS 28:20

IN GOD WE TRUST

We see signs at gas stations that say, "One Million Dollar Lottery." All we need to do is pay a dollar and put the right numbers in the right place and we win a million dollars. At least I think that's the way it is done; I never tried it. Sad to say, many people try this, some even using their last dollar in hopes of winning a million dollars.

Suppose I wanted to make a telephone call to someone in another state, but I didn't know the number, not even the area code. But I'd just make a guess at the numbers to see if I didn't happen to get it right. We would consider that foolish. There is only one chance in ten billion that I would get the right number. We could also say it is foolish to use money to play the lottery. There may be only one chance in a million to win a million dollars.

That is looking at it in a natural way. But we, as Christians, should not even want to win a million dollars by luck. Some may even say, "If I'm lucky, I'm going to go to heaven." Nobody is going to heaven by luck. If we go to heaven, it is because we have accepted Jesus as our Lord and Master and are living for Him.

Let us not take any chances in winning salvation or the lottery. God told Adam, "In the sweat of thy face shalt thou eat bread" (Genesis 3:19). We want to work for a living. In John 5:24 it says, "Verily, verily, I say unto you, He that heareth my word, and believeth on him that sent me, hath everlasting life, and shall not come into condemnation; but is passed from death unto life."

Eli A. Yoder, Stuarts Draft, VA

Work as though everything depended on you,
and pray as if everything depended on God.

March 27

Come unto me, all ye that labour and are heavy laden, and I will give you rest.
- MATTHEW 11:28

FEAR BELIEVES THE WORST

Discouragement is one of the Devil's most important tools. When he can get someone depressed, discouraged, defeated, and feeling that life is not worth living, he wins. We don't want Satan controlling our lives. Some may even decide to end it all by taking their own life. Suicide is becoming more common as the pressures of life increase. Doctors, lawyers, business men, movie stars, and quite a few teenagers are dying at their own hands. Notes often tell the story. Frustration, despair, loneliness, and grief are common causes.

The Bible tells us in 1 Thessalonians 5:14 that we should, "Comfort the feebleminded, support the weak." The person that committed suicide was convinced that there was no solution for his problem except death. But suicide is not the solution. It is the gateway to worse troubles, torments, and anguish than ever experienced in this life. The person who takes his own life bars himself forever from peace, happiness, and contentment.

After death there is no forgiveness of sin. No matter what the problem is, Jesus is the answer. Jesus has the power to give us peace and happiness if we obey Him instead of our selfish desires. Let us be careful that we don't let discouragement have an abiding place in us, as that is the beginning of these evil thoughts.

Eli A. Yoder, Stuarts Draft, VA

It is not the greatness of our trouble,
but the littleness of our spirit that makes us complain.

March 28

Bible Reading: Matthew 13:18-32

One Year Bible Reading Plan: Luke 6:1-26, Joshua 21, 22

Casting down imaginations, and every high thing that exalteth itself against the knowledge of God, and bringing into captivity every thought to the obedience of Christ.

- 2 CORINTHIANS 10:5

CHICKENS IN THE GARDEN

It has been three days since we planted our garden. We are having a real battle with the neighbors' chickens. They just love to scratch in the freshly tilled earth and steal the seeds we so carefully placed there. When I wake up at daybreak and hear the roosters crowing, I know it is high time to be checking the garden. Sad to say, the chickens sometimes beat me to it. Out I go, flapping my arms, clapping my hands, and making scary noises. They are learning. Now they take one look at me and head the other direction.

Jesus used the parable of birds picking up the seed that fell by the wayside to explain how the Devil works in our minds. He is always waiting for his chance to steal the truths of God's Word before they can take root in our hearts.

Our key verse exhorts us to control our thought life. Satan's "chickens" are constantly attacking our thought "gardens." He uses the billboards along the road, the newspapers, the music that comes over the store radio, the rampant immodesty, and many other things to scratch out the good seed and plant weeds. We need to be constantly on guard. Let's "cast down . . . every high thing that exalteth itself against the knowledge of God" (2 Corinthians 10:5). Let's ask for God's help today to keep our minds pure and free from Satan's weeds.

Joel Showalter, Choluteca, Honduras

Are Satan's "chickens" scratching in your garden?

March 29

Bible Reading: Matthew 27:24-54

One Year Bible Reading Plan: Luke 6:27-49, Joshua 23, 24

Then said Jesus, Father, forgive them; for they know not what they do.

- LUKE 23:34

IT WAS A GOOD FRIDAY

What was all this commotion? The Roman soldiers were marching some criminals out to Golgotha to be crucified. But it seemed something was hindering their progress. Yes, One was feeble and evidently struggled with His cross. They compelled a curious onlooker to carry the cross for Him.

After getting to Golgotha, they quickly set to work. Two of them were protesting loudly, and it took force to stretch them on the crosses and complete their work. The third was different. He didn't resist. When they drove the nails into His hands and feet, He prayed, "Father, forgive them."

When the crucifying was complete, the soldiers sat down to watch. The Man on the center cross was quiet all the while. It seemed a holy hush. Some priests and chief rulers made mocking remarks about Him being the Son of God.

At noon a deep darkness settled in. Everyone was fearful. All three were in agony. At 3:00 p.m. the Man on the middle cross cried out in a loud voice, "It is finished!" and hung limp on the cross. Dead. Suddenly there was a mighty earthquake that split the rocks. The earthquake shook the city and ripped the veil in the great temple from top to bottom.

The perplexed centurion and those with him exclaimed, "Truly, this is the Son of God!" And He was.

He died for you. He died for me.

Wilmer S. Beachy, Liberty, KY

Think of all the good that came from this memorable day.

March 30

Bible Reading: Luke 23:26-43

One Year Bible Reading Plan: Luke 7:1-30, Judges 1, 2

But God forbid that I should glory, save in the cross of our Lord Jesus Christ, by whom the world is crucified unto me, and I unto the world.

- GALATIANS 6:14

THREE CROSSES, THREE CRUCIFIXIONS, ONE GLORY

Let's look at the three crosses on Calvary. We usually look at the middle cross where Jesus hung. It is right that we do so. But the two crosses with the two malefactors are also significant. Sometimes we liken them to the two categories of people in the world. Some mock and ridicule the provisions of Christ's death, dying in doom and misery. The other represents sinners who look to Jesus and repent, seeking His acceptance and salvation. They die in hope.

Our theme verse recently impressed itself on me in another way. It says the world is crucified to me. Let the scornful represent the world. For us to experience salvation, we must hang the world on the cross. The world must be put to death so it has no influence on my life. It may scorn and mock me even while I am crucifying it. It even scorns the cross of Christ. But it must be crucified.

There is another crucifixion taking place on the other side of the middle cross. I, myself, am being crucified to the world. He who once was my crony must hold no appeal to me. Even if he ridicules and rails, I must give him no attention. I am crucified to the world.

Now I can turn my attention to the One on the middle cross. This is the only One who holds any appeal to me. Not the world, not myself, but Jesus only! I turn to Him and make my appeal, "Lord, remember me when thou comest into thy kingdom." And the gracious words **come** back, "Today shalt thou be with me in paradise!" O glory! Let the world go! Let self die! I will glory in the cross of Jesus Christ! God forbid that I should do otherwise.

Delmar R. Eby, London, KY

The paradox of the three crosses: Two were instruments of death, the third and middle one administered life.

March 31

Bible Reading: Matthew 28, John 20:11-18

One Year Bible Reading Plan: Luke 7:31-50, Judges 35

He is not here: for he is risen, as he said.
Come, see the place where the Lord lay.

- MATTHEW 28:6

RESURRECTION MORNING

"Ah-uh-we-ah-I-we couldn't help it," sputtered the guard to a knot of priests. He and the rest of the guards were pale, restless, and extremely fearful.

"Couldn't help what?" retorted the High Priest.

"Ah-uh-this J-Jesus . . ."

"Yes?"

"He arose!"

The eyes of the priests opened wide, their eyebrows rose to the limit, and their mouths dropped open. "Arose?"

"Yes, we could not prevent it. There was an earthquake and a bright flash. We all fell down and were unable to get up. The stone was rolled away, and Jesus came out of the tomb and walked away.

Mary stood outside the empty tomb, weeping. Oh, the distress! Jesus was gone! As she looked again into the tomb, she saw two angels who asked why she was crying. "They have taken my Lord away, and I don't know where they took Him." She turned slightly and saw someone she supposed to be the gardener. "Sir, if you carried Him away, tell me, so I can go get Him."

"Mary!" That voice she recognized at once.

"Oh," she cried out, "Oh, Teacher!" Now Mary knew that Jesus was alive. "I have seen the Lord!"

Unless we capture this vision with Mary, with a sure knowledge that Jesus lives, we will revert to the lies of the guards.

Wilmer S. Beachy, Liberty, KY

He is not here; He is risen. The greatest truth of all Christianity.

April 1

Did not our heart burn within us, while he talked with us by the way, and while he opened to us the scriptures?

- LUKE 24:32

WE WOULD SEE JESUS

"Brother, what do you think?"

"I don't know what to think." He answered sadly.

"Well, I don't either."

They talked in undertones as they walked along. Suddenly, a stranger came from a side path and walked with them. "What are you talking about? Why are you so sad?"

They stopped short in disbelief, "Well, are you the only stranger in these parts that does not know what things happened in the last days?"

"What things?"

"Well, this man, Jesus of Nazareth, was a very good Man, a mighty Teacher, and highly respected by God and man. The priests and religious leaders hated Him and crucified Him. We had hoped He would deliver our nation from the Romans. To compound matters even more, some women claimed this morning that He resurrected. If He is risen, we wish we could see Him."

Then the stranger began talking from the Scripture, beginning with the writings of Moses and the prophets, all the things concerning Christ.

When they got home, the stranger wanted to go on, but they persuaded Him to stay with them. They sat down for supper and asked Him to bless the meal. He took a small loaf of bread, blessed it, broke it, and gave each a morsel. In a flash, they recognized that this was indeed Jesus, but then He was gone. Amazed, they confessed how their hearts were drawn to Him as He expounded the Scripture.

Unless our hearts warm to the preaching of the pure Gospel truth, we become cold and withdrawn and finally we become reprobates.

Wilmer S. Beachy, Liberty, KY

I wish I could have been there.

April 2

Bible Reading: Genesis 37:18-36

One Year Bible Reading Plan: Luke 8:22-56, Judges 8, 9

And they said one to another, We are verily guilty concerning our brother, in that we saw the anguish of his soul, when he besought us, and we would not hear; therefore is this distress come upon us.

- GENESIS 42:21

FORGIVENESS

The words of our key verse show the remorse of Joseph's brothers. They were the very ones who placed him into the pit and later sold him into slavery. At the time, they showed no remorse. They had refused to see the pain their actions caused Joseph. They had turned a deaf ear to the pleadings of their younger brother. Now, years later, they acknowledged this was hindering them. They confessed they were guilty of the supposed death of their brother Joseph who, unknown to them, was in the room with them.

What was the response of Joseph when he heard his brothers expressing remorse for the grief they had caused him? He wept. He had to remove himself from them, so great was his empathy. The record of Scripture reveals that Joseph wept at five different occasions, most dealing with his brothers' acknowledgment of injustices to him.

What are our own thoughts when a brother or sister acknowledges sin in their life? Do we think less of them? Or do we rejoice in their newfound relief from guilt? If a brother is asking forgiveness, can we freely and willingly forgive him?

When Joseph revealed himself, his brothers were terrified, fearing revenge. But Joseph reassured them and gave them the best Egypt had to offer–an example we can strive for when dealing with a repentant brother or sister. Offer them the Christian hand of fellowship with the past forgiven and forgotten and help them forward in their newfound victory.

Lester K. Burkholder, Fredericksburg, PA

No one is ever stronger nor stands higher than when he forgives.

April 3

Bible Reading: Colossians 3

One Year Bible Reading Plan: Luke 9:1-36, Judges 10, 11

Set your affection on things above, not on things on the earth.

- COLOSSIANS 3:2

YIELD NOT TO SIN

There are many things in this world to get our attention off heavenly things. The world has set up many entertainments to please the flesh. Some things look like they might be okay, but soon distract us from the Christian life. Let us avoid these worldly amusements and ask the Holy Spirit to help us determine right from wrong.

It could be right to have a ball game, or for young folks to get together once in awhile, but this should not have priority in our lives. Social gatherings or sports shouldn't be so important that they take priority over everything else. We see church houses with large entertainment centers to give youth (and maybe some older people too) something to draw them to church.

A buzzard was sitting on a big chunk of ice feeding on something dead that was frozen in the ice. He came closer and closer to the falls, and the people wondered just how close the buzzard would come. He was very close before he noticed that he was in danger and tried to fly away. But alas, he couldn't move! He was sitting on the ice for so long that his feet were frozen fast, and it was impossible for him to fly away. So he fell to his death because he was more concerned about feeding on something dead than he was to save his life, until it was too late. This event was observed by someone at Niagara Falls one winter.

Isn't this the way Satan gets people to feed (enjoy) on dead things (sin) until they are so engrossed or involved that it is very hard to get away? But, thank God, unlike the buzzard which had no way to get loose, there is a way prepared to break loose and come to Jesus.

Daniel Miller, Dunnegan, MO

Yield not to temptation, for yielding is sin.

April 4

Bible Reading: Mark 5:1-20

One Year Bible Reading Plan: Luke 9:37-62, Judges 12-14

Even so it is not the will of your Father which is in heaven,
that one of these little ones should perish.
- MATTHEW 18:14

IS IT WORTH IT?

It was really a senseless loss. When the demons asked Jesus if they could go into the pigs, Jesus apparently didn't do any mental math to see if the end justified the cost. He just said, "Go," and just like that, two thousand pigs charged down the hill to the sea and drowned. Even if the pigs were worth only $50 apiece, it would have been a loss of $100,000. No wonder the men of the city came out and begged Jesus to leave.

But it is a fascinating thought–how many pigs does it take to equal the value of one man? It seems Jesus thought a man was worth more than two thousand pigs. But what if there were twenty thousand pigs? Or what if there were two hundred thousand? Would Jesus maybe have thought it better to lose one man than so many pigs?

The fact is, you cannot compare a man with a pig. When a pig dies, the only loss is a little money–whatever one animal is worth. When a man dies, his soul still lives in heaven or in hell. Man is immortal; that is, he simply cannot cease to exist. So the dollar we use to measure pigs just doesn't work for people.

How often are we guilty of measuring the value of souls in dollars? Do we think it's too expensive to make peace with an unreasonable neighbor? Does it take too much time off work to pass out tracts? Is it a loss to sell our business so we can serve God on the mission field?

Next time you wonder, "Is it worth it?" just make sure you're using the right unit of measure.

Rodney Yoder, Union, WV

You will never win the world for Christ with your spare cash.

April 5

Bible Reading: Ephesians 6:1-9, Matthew 23:1-12

One Year Bible Reading Plan: Luke 10:1-24, Judges 15-17

And whatsoever ye do, do it heartily, as to the Lord, and not unto men.
- COLOSSIANS 3:23

GOOD DEEDS FROM A LOVING HEART

A father and son were talking. The son asked, "Dad, can I go help the neighbors put in hay tomorrow?" The father answered, "No, we need to get the barn cleaned up. Maybe you can get started until I come back from town."

Tomorrow came and the boy went and helped the neighbors put in hay even though his father had told him not to. The father came home and learned that the son had gone to help the neighbors with their hay. When the son came home, the father asked him why he hadn't listened. The son's reply was, "I only meant it good to go help them." Was the son's good deed, done in disobedience, right or wrong?

Do we practice good deeds for the right reasons? When I lend a helping hand to someone, is it for personal gain? Do I do good deeds to the point of disobedience? Do my good deeds flow from a loving heart, or am I only hoping for something in return? When we disobey in order to do a good deed, our motive is sinful and displeasing to the Lord. Even we as parents must be sure we have the Lord's blessing before doing good deeds.

Good deeds are good if we do them with a loving heart. When doing something we think is good, let's remember to make sure that it is okay with Dad and Mom, with the church, and, most importantly, with God.

Menno H. Eicher, Miami, OK

The road to hell is paved with good intentions.

April 6

Bible Reading: James 3

One Year Bible Reading Plan: Luke 10:25-42, Judges 18, 19

Even so the tongue is a little member, and boasteth great things.
Behold, how great a matter a little fire kindleth!

- JAMES 3:5

THE POWER OF THE TONGUE

In the summer of 2002 there were many forest fires in the Western U.S. Because of dry weather conditions, record-breaking acreage was scorched to charred destruction by massive forest fires.

One of these fires began when an angry man wrote a letter to his former wife. The letter embittered the woman to the point that she took the letter out into the woods and burned it. The fire got out of hand and ended up burning over 300,000 acres of forest. Just think—the words written in this letter resulted in millions of dollars' worth of loss. The power of words!

Many hurts and damaged feelings have been created by the tongue—damage that far exceeds 300,000 burnt acres and millions of dollars. We all can remember an incident in our past when harsh words crushed our spirit. Maybe someone snapped at us or cut us off by a curt word or two, or even a tongue lashing. But if we stop to consider, the words that stick in our minds and hurt the most may be only a few.

On the other hand, we all can remember small words of encouragement at the right time that gave us a lift and courage to move on. Those words that stick may also be only a few.

Let's never underestimate the power of the tongue. Truly it is but a small member of our body, but it rules our being and all we possess.

Most of us have a functioning tongue. Let's remember that we need to use our tongue in a guarded manner. We must think before we speak and not let any of our words be wasted. This takes the power of God. We need to keep our hearts in tune with God's Spirit. Only when our hearts are right with God can we use the power of our tongue to relate to our fellow man in a kind and selfless manner.

Stephen Miller, McBain, MI

The tongue—small but mighty.

April 7

Bible Reading: Romans 1:1-16

One Year Bible Reading Plan: Luke 11:1-28, Judges 20, 21

For God so loved the world, that he gave his only begotten Son, that whosoever believeth in him should not perish, but have everlasting life.

- JOHN 3:16

GOOD TIDINGS FOR ALL

There were hundreds of people walking through the station; so many people going somewhere, seemingly in a big hurry. They were all dressed differently. They all looked different. What about their families? What about their fathers or mothers? What about their children? There were many, many people with many families represented and they kept coming and coming. Would they ever stop coming? As long as I sat and watched, the flow of people never stopped.

In Revelation, John says, "And I beheld, and, lo, a great multitude, which no man could number, of all nations, and kindreds, and people, and tongues, stood before the throne and before the Lamb, clothed with white robes, and palms in their hands." I wonder how many of those people at the station will be in that multitude up there in heaven? How many of those souls know Jesus Christ as their personal Shepherd?

The people I saw were only a small part of the population on earth. Even every person in every train station on the earth is only a few. Four million people live in the city where I sat and watched.

I read recently that 80,000 people die every day without Christ. As Jesus said, "The harvest truly is great." There are many people going somewhere, and they're going there in a big hurry! We should hurry and tell them the Good News. We can say as the angels told the shepherds on the hills of Bethlehem, "Behold, I bring you good tidings of great joy!"

Harold R. Troyer, Kiev, Ukraine

God has given the unbeliever the right
to look in upon our fellowship.

April 8

Bible Reading: Romans 6

One Year Bible Reading Plan: Luke 11:29-54, Ruth 14

For the wages of sin is death; but the gift of God is eternal life through Jesus Christ our Lord.

- ROMANS 6:23

WHERE WILL YOU BE PAID?

The story is told of a mining community which had two distinctly different mines. One mine had a vein of very pure and rich ore. Here the employees got good wages, and the mine owners prospered. The other mine was struggling. The ore was of poor quality, and the employees received meager wages. A man who worked at the poor mine decided to turn his time in at the other mine in order to receive better pay. But despite all his pleading he was turned away. He was told, "If you wish to have better pay, you must also work here." He left disappointed. He had been working for the wrong mine.

Verse sixteen of our Scripture reading reminds us that where we serve, there we will also receive our pay. "Know ye not, that to whom ye yield yourselves servants to obey, his servants ye are to whom you obey; whether of sin unto death, or of obedience unto righteousness?"

Many today hope to serve God without any self-sacrifice. They love to run after the world's entertainments, dress to meet the world's approval, and leave God out of their daily walk. As the women of Isaiah 4:1, many today are saying, "Let us eat our own bread and wear our own apparel, only let us be called by thy name, that the reproach may be taken from us." Today it is popular to claim the name of Jesus but still do our own thing.

I must ask myself, how does my walk of life appear in the eyes of God? How much redemptive value is there in the things I do and in the places I go?

Will I be told on Judgment Day that I have been working in the "wrong mine"? "You have enjoyed the pleasures of sin for a season. Depart from me, I never knew you."

Melvin L. Yoder, Gambier, OH

If you play with the world, you will reap with the world.

April 9

Bible Reading: Psalm 8, Matthew 14:13-23

One Year Bible Reading Plan: Luke 12:1-34, 1 Samuel 13

And Isaac went out to meditate in the field at the eventide.

- GENESIS 24:63

COME YE YOURSELVES APART

Somewhere we have become afflicted with the idea that we must always be working or doing something to occupy our minds. I am confident we would be better Christians if we were more alone, attempted less, and spent more time in meditation. The attraction of the things of this world is constantly begging for preeminence in our being. Someone has said, "We believe in having all our irons in the fire, and consider the time spent between the anvil and the fire as lost, or much the same as lost."

Jesus Himself saw the need to withdraw when He told His disciples to "Come ye yourselves apart into a desert place and rest awhile." Many times Jesus would retreat from the crowds, the heat of the day, the noise, and the confusion to commune with the Father. If Jesus needed this, how much more do we?

Go ahead and take a walk, sit beside a rippling brook, watch the sunset in the evening, stroll through the meadow and look for flowers, or listen to the birds singing. When we let nature speak to us, it will have a calming, healing effect on us. No time is better spent than to meditate on the things of God.

Time thus spent is not lost time. It will give you a fresh perspective of the things that are most important. It will also give you new zeal and joy in your life.

Robert Burkholder, Brooksville, KY

We must at times come apart so we do not fall apart.

April 10

Bible Reading: Genesis 32:1-30

One Year Bible Reading Plan: Luke 12:35-59, 1 Samuel 46

O worship the Lord in the beauty of holiness: fear before him, all the earth.

- PSALM 96:9

PERSONAL ALTARS

Esau and Jacob were not only brothers but twins. Just why these two were so opposite in their natures we may never fully understand. We know, however, that man was created with a capacity to choose right or wrong. Esau, being the first-born, never built an altar, never prayed to God, never spoke about God, it seems. He was a Godless character and produced a generation after his kind.

Jacob, though he was not without faults, sought God. The Bible often mentions Jacob's altars. The first one was between Beer-sheba and Padanaram. He made a commitment after which he received step-by-step directions from the Lord, which he followed. Again he had contact with God on his return trip to Canaan when he earnestly sought divine protection from harm because he vividly remembered his brother's hatred toward him. That night Jacob wrestled with an angel of the Lord. After that experience, Jacob testified, "I have seen God face to face, and my life is preserved."

Later, as an aged man who had experienced many trials, he was traveling by divine appointment to sojourn in Egypt. Along the way he stopped to offer sacrifices to God Who gave him further directions concerning that most unexpected move of his life. Jacob was comforted with the assurance of God's presence.

Do I have a personal altar? Is my altar a meaningful one where true adoration and worship is experienced? Is my altar a place where I come to the end of myself and pray honestly, "Lord, not my will, but thine be done"? Our altars don't need to be built of tangible material such as stone or wood, but the main point is to meet God Who made salvation possible through Jesus Christ. It was love that moved Him to do it for us. Let us ever love Him and serve Him!

Willis Halteman, Carlisle, PA

Vital personal altars and victorious Christian living go together.

April 11

Bible Reading: Esther 6, 7

One Year Bible Reading Plan: Luke 13:1-21, 1 Samuel 7-9

Pride goeth before destruction, and an haughty spirit before a fall.
- PROVERBS 16:18

THE DECEITFULNESS OF PRIDE

The fable is told about a turtle who consulted with two geese to take him across the lake. He thought of this grand idea that the two geese would hold a stick in their bills. One goose would hold one end of the stick and the other goose the other end. The turtle would clamp onto the center of the stick with his mouth. Finally they were ready for take-off.

Air travel was going great for the three animals, and the turtle was filled with pride when he saw how well his grand idea was working.

A lad saw this queer mode of transportation and asked, "Who came up with that good idea?"

"I did," said the turtle.

Did you hear the splat? The turtle was so proud of his good idea that he forgot to keep his mouth shut and he fell to his death.

Pride works subtly. It ruins many lives if it is not dealt with properly. A proud look can be very harmful. People who think their way is always best are not enjoyable to be around. As we consider others' viewpoints, may we also consider what God would want us to do.

May God grant us grace and strength to live a life of humility.

Samuel Beachy, Belvidere, TN

Humility will keep pride out of your life.

April 12

Bible Reading: 2 Corinthians 4:14-18; 5:1-10

One Year Bible Reading Plan: Luke 13:22-35, 1 Samuel 10-12

I have learned, in whatsoever state I am, therewith to be content.

- PHILIPPIANS 4:11

HOME SWEET HOME

We had a farm of our own for over fifty years. Now the farm, livestock, and machinery are sold, and all we have is a house to live in and a few acres of land to care for. It is a drastic change. Not only did the farm sell, but our son and family who lived on the farm moved five hundred miles away. The Bible does say we should be thankful in all things and that all things work together for good to those who love God. So we want to thank the Lord for this and trust that some good will come from it. We realize we can't take these material things along to Glory Land.

It reminds me of something that happened some years ago. One of my sisters was on her deathbed. She didn't respond anymore. We and some of the family were standing around her bed. We read the Bible and prayed while she just lay there with her eyes closed. All at once we noticed tears coming from under her eyelids and running down her cheeks. We believe she heard what we were saying even though she couldn't as much as open her eyes.

It was a few years before this that this sister, a widow, had an auction. It surprised me that she would sell some of the keepsakes that we had at our childhood home. Later I realized that my sister probably thought she wouldn't be here much longer, so she might as well let someone else have these things.

I thought about the farm that is now sold. We know that, at our age, we are not going to be here much longer. Many leave this life even at a younger age. We should lightly hold the material things of this life, remembering that it all belongs to our Creator anyway. We are only His stewards.

Eli A. Yoder, Stuart's Draft, VA

As Noah's dove found no footing but in the ark, so a Christian finds no contentment but in Christ.

April 13

Bible Reading: Mark 4:1-20

One Year Bible Reading Plan: Luke 14:1-24, 1 Samuel 13, 14

Be not deceived; God is not mocked: for whatsoever a man soweth, that shall he also reap.

- GALATIANS 6:7

THE GARDEN OF OUR LIFE

In spring people start getting their gardens ready to plant. The soil needs to have the proper water content so it will work down properly. After the ground is worked, we can go ahead and plant the seeds, but gardening does not stop there. The weeds need to be hoed and tilled out, and the plants need proper fertilization. God controls the two important elements of sunshine and rain. Without God's help, gardening would be a failure. With the proper weeding, fertilizing, sunshine, and rain, we can expect to gather the fruit of our labor.

How is the garden of my life? Is God pleased with it? God had many benefits waiting for us when we were born into this world. Jesus died on the cross and rose from the dead. He returned back to the Father and now He intercedes for us. He sends the Holy Spirit to comfort and direct us through life. He takes special interest in each person. He has done so much for me. What am I doing in return?

Jesus looks in the garden of my life. He wants to plant good seeds in my life that will produce good fruit such as love, joy, peace, longsuffering, gentleness, goodness, faith, meekness, and temperance. He wants me to grow up to be a strong plant for Him.

Those who obey God can reap a good harvest. What kind of seeds are we sowing? If we desire to reap good things, we must also sow good things.

Samuel Beachy, Belvidere, TN

In the harvest of life, we will reap what we have sown.

Bible Reading: Psalms 61, 62

One Year Bible Reading Plan: Luke 14:25-35, 1 Samuel 15, 16

For thou hast been a shelter for me, and a strong tower from the enemy.
- PSALM 61:3

STORM SHELTERS

Some people are concerned that they will not be safe when a tornado hits. They may even purchase a storm shelter. This provides them a safe place to be if a storm hits. Proper maintenance must be kept on the shelter so it will perform as expected. It is important that the door hinges are not rusted and the vents are open. It should not be full of stored junk. When a tornado comes, we don't want to clean out the storm shelter first and then expect to have enough time to get inside. The shelter does not protect us if we don't use it. If someone would decide it's not worth their effort to run out to the shelter, they could be consumed in the storm and would not be using the benefits they could experience.

"God is our refuge and strength, a very present help in trouble" (Psalm 46:1). In God we can find refuge and strength as we face the storms of life. Like the storm shelter, our relationship with God needs continual maintenance. We need to stay in tune with God, serving Him through sunshine and storm. Let us build up our lives in the good times. Then when the storms of life come, we can be "steadfast, unmovable, always abounding in the work of the Lord" (1 Corinthians 15:58).

The Christian life takes effort on our part. The storm shelters don't do us any good if we don't use them when the storm hits. God's spiritual protection does not help us unless we commit our whole life to Him.

Samuel Beachy, Belvidere, TN

Keep your spiritual storm shelter well-maintained.

April 15

As obedient children, not fashioning yourselves according to the former lusts in your ignorance. But as he which hath called you is holy, so be ye holy in all manner of conversation;

- 1PETER 1:14-15

TRAPPED

I recall when I was a boy, if we had unwanted stray tom cats in our barn, we used a simple trap to catch them. We took a discarded gooseneck silo pipe with a burlap feed bag tied on one end with baler twine. One of us boys held the trap at a hole where a board was broken on the bottom of the barn door–the only access for cats going in and out of the barn. Another boy went into the barn's straw mow and chased out the cat. With a flash the cat streaked across the barn floor. A scratching of claws could be heard as it hit the steel pipe and the bag became alive with a bouncing and meowing cat inside. It was hopelessly caught by a grinning boy with a tight hold on the top of the bag.

This reminds me of our pilgrimage here below. Do we, like the cat, desire to go places where we do not belong or that are unfitting for Christians? If we enjoy walking past book racks with questionable material, or if we let our wondering eyes observe scantily dressed society during the summer months, are we not like the curious cat, wondering what is inside the barn door? We may even have walked in and out of the door several times without noticing any obvious adverse effects. Be assured though, if we continue on into sin, we will also be caught firmly in the Devil's trap.

Praise the Lord, our situation is not hopeless even then. We can be delivered from the Devil's clutch if we allow the blood of Christ to cleanse us and we repent and change our ways.

David S. Leid, Big Prairie, OH

God formed us. Sin deformed us. Only Christ can transform us.

April 16

Bible Reading: Matthew 6:6-34

One Year Bible Reading Plan: Luke 15:11-32, 1 Samuel 19-21

No man can serve two masters: for either he will hate the one, and love the other; or else he will hold to the one and despise the other.
Ye cannot serve God and mammon.

- MATTHEW 6:24

ATTAINING ETERNAL LIFE

A wise old sage once said, "If you concentrate on two rabbits, they will both escape." It becomes very clear that we cannot love the world and love God at the same time.

It is quite evident that our church pews are being warmed by many who are concentrating on two rabbits. By this I do not mean to say that we are a bunch of grossly wicked infidels. We are, for the most part, a kind, loving people who love the Lord, and we certainly want to serve Him. But perhaps we love the world more than we want to admit. God is asking for our complete, undivided love and loyalty.

We are asked not to lay up for ourselves treasures here on earth which rust, corrode, and are stolen. In the end, such treasures all vanish away with the world. We are living in prosperous times. We have more than we need, but we still tend to concentrate more on material gain than on the things of the kingdom. We find more time for the entertainment world and less time for study. We pray, "Thy will be done," then we go on and do as we please. We pray, "Lead us not into temptation," then we buy tickets for the next attraction and temptation that Satan wants to set before our eyes. We say we are dead to the world, yet we cannot die to sports for a season. We pray, "Forgive us our debts, as we forgive our debtors," then we lose sleep over the way someone has wronged us.

We already know that the one rabbit will escape us. The world with all its allurements will vanish away. Why not concentrate on the other rabbit? Eternal life is attainable. It is offered to us freely. Let us concentrate on the things of the kingdom.

Melvin L. Yoder, Gambier, OH

Let us concentrate on the things of the kingdom, and whatever else is needed will be added to us.

April 17

Bible Reading: Matthew 18:15-35

One Year Bible Reading Plan: Luke 16:1-18, 1 Samuel 22-24

Now unto him that is able to do exceeding abundantly above all that we ask or think, according to the power that worketh in us.
- EPHESIANS 3:20

ONLY ONE THING TO DO

Too often when we try to forgive someone, we try to be God without realizing it. We try to carry out justice, either literally or mentally. We try to get even or make the other person pay. Before we know it, we are bitter. In our mind we have two or three well-planned speeches that we would tell that person if the occasion would present itself again.

We need to let God be God. We need to realize there is nothing we can do to change the past or change the people around us. God works in people in ways we do not understand. We need to accept the fact that there really is nothing left in our power to do but to accept things as they are and allow God to move people the way He sees fit.

If we truly believe this in our hearts, we then can release the people who hurt us to God and forgive them from our hearts. We allow God to cleanse our hearts from all bitterness. We keep our focus on our own shortcomings so that we, through God's help, can respond humbly to those who hurt us.

Think of the people you need to forgive. Say the names of each one and tell God how you felt the hurt each one gave you. Tell God everything. Then mentally picture yourself handing each person over to God and ask God to take him from you. Ask God to forgive you for what you have done wrong in this situation, and ask Him to fill your heart with love that you can share with each person who wronged and hurt you.

Stephen Miller, McBain, MI

Forgive us our debts, as we forgive our debtors.

April 18

Bible Reading: Matthew 25:14-46

One Year Bible Reading Plan: Luke 16:19-31, 1 Samuel 25, 26

She hath done what she could:
she is come aforehand to anoint my body to the burying.

- MARK 14:8

FAITHFUL SERVANTS

"How many shoes have you shined?" I asked the old shoe shiner.

"Huh-huh, I don't keep track," he chuckled. "I done lost count."

"Well," I said, "if you could tell me how many shoes you have shined, I could tell you how many people you have met."

"I just don't know," he said. "What I do is count the money at the end of the day and find out how much I made. Then I know whether I've had a good day or not. That's what counts. It's very sporadic. Sometimes I'm busy. Other times it's slow."

It is much the same in the Christian life. Sometimes we are very busy with Christian service. We meet many people and do a lot of good. Countless hearts are affected by our service. Other days there is not so much to do. Perhaps it's discouraging. We almost feel alone. With not much to do, we almost feel forgotten.

But God has it planned just right. We do just what He has planned. Sometimes He gives us much work and other times not so much. What's most important is that we do what God wants when He wants. We can't expect to do everything because God uses many workers. Some do a lot. Some do a little. Yet all the work is important. The little note given to the sick or the profound message delivered to large audiences are both needed. Someone must do it. Let's be available when God calls us for an errand. Possibly it only will be to shine someone's shoes.

Harold R. Troyer, Belleville, PA

God doesn't ask us to do everything;
He only asks us to do something.

April 19

Bible Reading: Job 5:6-21

One Year Bible Reading Plan: Luke 17:1-19, 1 Samuel 27–29

I waited patiently for the Lord; and he inclined unto me, and heard my cry.
- PSALM 40:1

GOD IS IN CONTROL

We attended the funeral of an older grandmother. Like all funerals, this was a sad occasion. Yet in one sense we could rejoice because we had a lively hope that she was ready to meet Jesus. The graveyard was right beside a pasture field. When we came to the graveyard for burial, a group of goats was right up by the fence looking across the fence to where the people were gathering for the burial. It seemed they were all bleating at once. It was kind of a mournful bleating. It just seemed they wanted to mourn with the family and friends. When we were ready for the grave-side service, the goats suddenly walked away. It seemed God had a hand in this.

Clouds appeared and a storm was brewing. It seemed to come closer and closer as the grave-side services began. I believe a lot of people were praying that God would hold back the rain until the service and burial were over. The rain and storm seemed to stand still until that time. Many thanksgiving prayers went up as we left. God still hears and answers prayers. Sometimes He sees fit to answer in a different way. Then we need to remember that all things work together for good to them that love God. God knows much better what is good for us than we do. We always need to remember when we ask God for a certain thing to say, "Not my will, but thine be done."

Eli A. Yoder, Stuarts Draft, VA

When prayer is answered, forget not praise.

April 20

Bible Reading: Matthew 6:19-34

One Year Bible Reading Plan: Luke 17:20-37, 1 Samuel 30, 31

But my God shall supply all your need according to his riches
in glory by Christ Jesus.
- PHILIPPIANS 4:19

THE LORD WILL PROVIDE

Jehovah-Jireh means "The Lord will provide." It is used only once in the Bible (Genesis 22:14), and yet the theme is evident throughout the Scriptures. What a wonderful promise that the Lord will provide for His people! I consider it a blessing that I was raised in a poor home that was spiritually rich. We learned to trust God for our daily needs rather than a good-paying job or a padded bank account.

One account that stands out in my mind was when two of my brothers wanted to go on a school field trip that required each student to provide ten dollars. Since my parents didn't have the money, we all made it a matter of prayer. On the morning of the field trip, as we went out to catch the school bus, we discovered two ten dollar bills lying in the gutter by the road—exactly the amount that was needed. God had left no doubt as to Who had provided the money. Oh, the blessing we would have missed that morning if we had had the means to do it on our own. What an opportunity to praise God!

God still longs to be Jehovah-Jireh in the lives of His people. But how many of us have become too self-sufficient? It is so easy to put our own perceived needs above the needs of others. We have a wonderful promise in Malachi 3:10, "Bring ye all the tithes into the storehouse, that there may be meat in mine house, and prove me now herewith, saith the Lord of hosts, if I will not open you the windows of heaven, and pour you out a blessing, that there shall not be room enough to receive it."

Joseph Jones, Ash Fork, AZ

*Deposit your money into God's account,
and it will pay great dividends.*

April 21

Not that I speak in respect of want: for I have learned, in whatsoever state I am, therewith to be content.
- PHILIPPIANS 4:11

CONTENTMENT

Soon after the Israelites left Egypt, they murmured. God sent them manna to eat. Soon they were tired of that and wanted meat. They remembered all the good things they had to eat back in Egypt. The Lord had just punished them for complaining with fire that consumed some of them. Every man was weeping at the door of his tent. Moses was very displeased with their complaining. God promised them meat–not for only a few days, but for a whole month. Moses was doubtful that God could do it. God again showed His great power by sending quail. He sent so many that they were piled up three feet deep, a day's journey each way from camp. The ones who gathered the least gathered sixty-five bushels!

God had predicted that they would eat meat until it came out of their nostrils and became loathsome to them. Before it was chewed and yet in their teeth, the wrath of God was kindled against them and smote them with a great plague. We would think the Israelites would have learned a lesson by then and would have quit complaining.

But wait, are we any better than they? If things do not go just the way we think they should, we start complaining. In our fast and instant way of life, when an appliance or a vehicle breaks down or doesn't start, we complain and get upset.

When things do not go as planned, we should thank the Lord instead of complaining. He may be trying to teach us something. "And having food and raiment let us be therewith content" (1 Timothy 6:8).

Daniel Miller, Dunnegan, MO

God is greater than any problem I have.

April 22

Then spake Jesus again unto them, saying, I am the light of the world:
he that followeth me shall not walk in darkness, but shall have the light of life.
- JOHN 8:12

DO YOU HAVE AN ESCORT?

For the last 25 years I have traveled the same route to work every day. Since there is a truss factory in our area, I often follow a truckload of trusses. Many of these loads are extremely large and dangerous and are led by an escort. With an escort, the truck driver can safely travel the two lane county road. However, without an escort, it would be nearly impossible to travel the road without causing an accident. When people see the amber light flashing, they immediately sense danger and pull over for the large load.

One morning when I was following a load of trusses, I thought of our spiritual walk. As we walk through life's journey facing temptations, trials, and Satan's snares, we must have Jesus as our escort. "Jesus saith unto him, I am the way, the truth, and the life: no man cometh unto the Father, but by me" (John 14:6).

We must be born again and accept Him as our Savior. "Verily, verily, I say unto thee, Except a man be born of water and of the Spirit, he cannot enter into the kingdom of God" (John 3:5).

We are rapidly approaching our eternal destination, and we must have Jesus as our Saviour, Guide, and Escort to reach heaven safely.

Hand in hand we walk each day,
Hand in hand along the way,
Walking thus I cannot stray,
Hand in hand with Jesus.
- Selected

Stephen Stoll, Loogootee, IN

Follow Jesus every day.

April 23

I exhort therefore, that, first of all, supplications, prayers, intercessions, and giving of thanks, be made for all men.
- 1 TIMOTHY 2:1

PRAY FOR ME

I stopped at the red light. Just then a sheriff's cruiser stopped along my left side. A commotion in the back seat caught my attention.

A man was pointing at me. He then held his hands in a praying gesture in front of a bowed head and then quickly pointed at himself. He quickly repeated the motions. Then I got it. He was asking me to pray for him! He was handcuffed and obviously on the way to some detention center. The light changed and we were off.

He was looking for someone he could trust, someone whose prayers would get through to God. What is my response to such a plea? Do I shrug it off with, "Well, if you had acted right, you would not be where you are"? Apart from the grace of God, I might easily be in the same shoes. Sure, it is easy to pray for aged parents, the sick, our ministers, our families, and loved ones. But pray for criminals? He keenly felt the need of prayer. Perhaps his greatest need was a change of heart. But why did he ask me to pray for him?

I may never see the man again. We could not talk. I do not even know his name, but the scene stays with me. A soul is at stake. I do not know his offense, but he is trusting me to pray for him. May I be worthy of that trust.

Wilmer S. Beachy, Liberty, KY

The light grows dimmer as the saints pray less.

April 24

That ye might walk worthy of the Lord unto all pleasing,
being fruitful in every good work, and increasing in the knowledge of God.
- COLOSSIANS 1:10

HALF EMPTY LIFEBOATS

Over 1,500 lives were lost when the *Titanic* sank many years ago. In Halifax, Nova Scotia, there is a graveyard where 121 passengers of the doomed vessel are buried. Shortly after the *Titanic* sent the message, "Have struck iceberg," three telegraph cable repair ships were dispatched from Halifax, Nova Scotia, to the collision site to pick up the victims.

The ship, *Carpathia*, rescued hundreds from lifeboats and took them to New York City. The *Mackay Bennett*, the first of the funeral ships to arrive, found 328 bodies floating in their life jackets. The first to be picked up was a two-year-old boy. These would not have had to die. As they floated in the cold water crying for help, the half empty lifeboats just kept rowing away. There was adequate room in the lifeboats for the 328 people found in life jackets.

Those people in the water with life jackets died, not because the *Titanic* sank, but because those in the half empty life boats refused to go back and rescue those in the water. It was a sad situation, which caused the sailors of the ship *Mackay Bennett* to shed many tears.

I trust most of those who take the time to read this are already in the lifeboat of the shed blood of Jesus Christ. We are safe in His lifeboat, but we are surrounded by lost and struggling souls. Do we care enough to come alongside and offer rescue?

Lester K. Burkholder, Fredericksburg, PA

What are you doing with your lifeboat?

April 25

Bible Reading: Romans 12

One Year Bible Reading Plan: Luke 20:1-26, 2 Samuel 13, 14

Blessed are the peacemakers: for they shall be called the children of God.
- MATTHEW 5:9

NON-RESISTANCE IN ACTION

A family moved onto a small farm and soon noticed there were stray dogs roaming in the area. They built a pen with a sturdy fence, five feet high, to keep their goats safe.

One morning the father heard dogs barking and goats bleating. As he rushed outside, he saw dogs inside the pen attacking the goats. When the dogs saw the man, they ran out of the pen and left. He assumed they were stray dogs. That evening he set humane, toothless traps that would clamp onto a dog's foot, but would not damage the foot. The next morning he again heard a commotion. When he rushed out, he saw dogs outside the goat pen, and one was caught in the trap. Then he saw they were his neighbor's dogs. About that time a pickup came in the driveway at high speed. The driver stopped at the goat pen and jumped out. He rushed toward his dog that was caught in the trap. "This is my dog and this is going to cause hard feelings with your neighbor," he snapped. "I moved out to the country so my dogs could roam freely."

The owner of the goats thought, *I moved to the country so my goats could roam freely,* but he didn't say it. He also thought, *If you keep your dogs at home, I'll keep my goats at home,* but then he thought of Jesus' words—to turn the other cheek. So he said, "I'm open for any suggestions."

Then the neighbor said, "If you'd run an electric wire over the top and bottom of your fence, it would probably keep the dogs out."

The man said, "I'm willing to do that in order to have peace."

Eli A. Yoder, Stuarts Draft, VA

---

*Loving kindness has converted more sinners than zeal,
eloquence, or learning.*

April 26

Bible Reading: 1 Peter 5:1-11, James 4:1-8

One Year Bible Reading Plan: Luke 20:27-47, 2 Samuel 15, 16

Be sober, be vigilant; because your adversary the devil,
as a roaring lion, walketh about, seeking whom he may devour.
- 1 PETER 5:8

GRIPPED BY AN OCTOPUS

A man dove beneath the water to work on the underside of a boat. He had a rope tied around him, which was connected to the boat above him. While he was working, a huge octopus attacked him, and wrapped its arms around him. The man pulled on the rope; which was a signal to the man above to pull him out of the water. He pulled man, octopus, and all up out of the water. The octopus had a tight grip on the man, and they had to cut its arms off to release him. If no one had been there to save him, the man would have been doomed to death. The octopus would have carried him away to his destruction.

Before we were converted, we were ensnared by the Devil. He was wrapping us up with sinful allurements. He wanted to devour us by pulling us farther and farther away from God. We recognized that we were lost and that we needed God's help to live a pure and holy life.

We should pull on the rope of prayer and ask God to save us from the octopus called sin, which still tries to destroy and devour us. As we give our life over to God, we can experience peace, joy, and victory in Jesus. We also have the hope of eternal life. Hell is a prepared place for an unprepared people. Heaven is a prepared place for a prepared people. Let us be prepared to meet God at all times.

Samuel Beachy, Belvidere, TN

Only God can loosen us from the Devil's grip.

April 27

Bible Reading: 2 Corinthians 10:1-18

One Year Bible Reading Plan: Luke 21:1-19, 2 Samuel 17, 18

For we dare not make ourselves of the number, or compare ourselves with some that commend themselves: but they measuring themselves by themselves, and comparing themselves among themselves, are not wise.
- 2 CORINTHIANS 10:12

THE NARROW WAY

We are creatures of habit and can easily fall into a certain pattern of doing things without considering why we do them. In the setting of today's Scripture reading, there seems to have been some problem with simply following habits or customs set by others. Paul warns that we dare not measure ourselves and compare ourselves with others. The only safe rule is God's Word.

The story has been told of a young bride who asked her mother why the ham must be cut a certain way before being placed in the roaster for roasting. The mother replied, "Well, Grandma always did it this way."

They decided to ask Grandma. She replied, "When we were young, I did not have a roaster large enough to hold the ham without cutting it and placing the pieces side by side." The mystery was solved.

J. Henry Fabre tells of having done an experiment with a group of Pine Processionary Caterpillars. He set a group of them on the edge of a flowerpot. They followed one another around the rim without deviating for seven days and nights. They did this even though he had placed a pine branch, their favorite food, right beside the pot.

Now I must consider. Am I so busy following others that I fail to see God's will for me? Why do so many blindly follow the styles, fads, and dictates of the world's value system while starving their spiritual bodies? Christ said, "The way is narrow and few there be that find it." Do they perhaps miss the way simply because they are following the crowds?

Melvin L. Yoder, Gambier, OH

If we follow the world, we will arrive at the same destination.

April 28

Bible Reading: Philippians 2:1-18

One Year Bible Reading Plan: Luke 21:20-38, 2 Samuel 19, 20

Let your loins be girded about, and your lights burning.

- LUKE 12:35

LIGHTHOUSE CHRISTIANS

I had the privilege of touring the St. Augustine Lighthouse in Northern Florida. I climbed the spiral stairs to the top of the 165-foot lighthouse. When I stepped out onto the observation deck, the awesome, breathtaking view of the Atlantic Ocean and the surrounding coastline quenched all apprehension and doubt. As I made my way around the deck, not once was I concerned that the platform would not support my weight. I had full trust in the supporting braces, that they would fulfill their duty of supporting the observation deck. Anyone who stepped out onto the deck could view the light up close and experience the majestic view of the surrounding area.

The role of the light is to be an unwavering source of direction to all who are within viewing distance. At night it guides with a 1,000 watt bulb. With the aid of prisms and magnifying lenses, the light can be seen 19 to 25 miles away, guiding sailors to a safe harbor during their darkest hours at sea. During the day it can be seen as a stately figure. It stands tall, erect, and bold in its surroundings, leaving no doubt as to what it stands for and what its purpose is.

As Christians, we can get close to the true Light, Jesus. Are we standing tall and upright, unwavering in our faith? All who come in contact with us should clearly see what we stand for and what our purpose is–to share the gospel here on earth. We can learn a valuable life lesson from the lighthouse. Are we keeping our wicks trimmed and free from sin, so our light can burn brightly to guide the weak and faint of heart? Sin will corrode our wicks until there is only a small flicker of light, casting a shadow of confusion, doubt, and lack of direction to those who travel around us on the sea of life.

Vernon Hershberger, Dundee, OH

The path of the just is as the shining light, that shineth more and more unto the perfect day.

April 29

Bible Reading: Luke 16:19-31

One Year Bible Reading Plan: Luke 22:1-30, 2 Samuel 21, 22

For the wages of sin is death; but the gift of God is eternal life through Jesus Christ our Lord.

- ROMANS 6:23

THE COFFIN

Man is depraved, which means he is corrupt and wicked, destitute of holiness or good principles. The Bible describes the wicked as abominable, filthy, workers of iniquity, that will not depart out of darkness, and hypocrites. What a horrible condition man would find himself in if God would have turned His back and said, "Too bad, you have made the choice, now you must just suffer the consequences. Goodbye." Without God, we are lost.

The flower-covered coffin stood in front of the platform from which the fist-waving, pulpit-pounding evangelist exhorted a wailing audience to true repentance. He spoke of the horror of hell. There were not just a few tears from his listeners, but also some hysterical cries.

The service was announced in the newspaper as a funeral service. The dead one in the coffin had committed every conceivable sin. The evangelist chanted no eulogy over the coffin. The man had lived a very wicked life and would be banished into eternal torment.

When the sermon was finished, the audience was invited to file past the casket and take one last look at the horrible sinner. Each man and woman filed by and peered into the casket. In the casket was a mirror that reflected the face of every person who stared into it.

What a grim reminder of the truth! Only by true repentance and the washing of our sins in the blood of the Lamb, Jesus Christ, are we cleansed from sin. Instead of being forever banished from God in eternal torment, we can be accepted by Him.

Will you come to Him today? God can make us holy and acceptable.

Wilmer S. Beachy, Liberty, KY

Sign on a tombstone: I expected this, but not just yet.

April 30

Prepare to meet thy God.

- AMOS 4:12

HARVEST TIME IS COMING

At the greenhouse where I work, we plant poinsettias about four months before we expect to sell them. Someone may ask why we plant them so early. That is the way it is with many plants at greenhouses, especially in the spring. We start planting some plants the last week of January so they are ready to sell by early spring. It takes a lot of planning at the greenhouse in order to have the plants ready for the customers at the right time.

We, as God's children, also need to do a lot of planning so we are ready when God calls us home. Many people put off planting good seeds for eternity. They want to have a pleasure-filled time first and follow the lusts of the flesh and the pride of life, and then later they think of getting ready. But the Lord may call them at an hour they think not, then it will be forever too late.

D.L. Moody had plans to hold a meeting in a certain town. Many people came from other areas for this meeting. When Mr. Moody got to the town, he went to his room at the hotel. A lady came to him and asked, "How did you manage to get a room? We looked everywhere and all the rooms were already filled."

Mr. Moody said, "I made arrangements ahead of time." Unless we make preparations ahead of time, we will not enter the kingdom of God.

Eli A. Yoder, Stuarts Draft, VA

Have you made arrangements for your stay in Heaven?

May 1

He said unto Simon, Launch out into the deep,
and let down your nets for a draught.

- LUKE 5:4

LAUNCH OUT INTO THE DEEP

In our Bible reading today, the children of Israel were instructed to break camp, pack their belongings, form a line, and be ready to march. The priests who carried the ark were commanded to proceed into the Jordan River until their feet were wet. Upon that step of faith the waters were cut off, allowing them to cross over safely.

Christopher Columbus gave this world a tremendous lesson in persevering even in difficult circumstances. It took courage to leave the shores of Portugal and sail into uncharted waters. Popular reasoning at that time said the earth was flat, and if you sailed too far you fell over the edge to be eaten by sea monsters. His seafaring companions threatened to revolt and wanted to turn back. Always his answer was, "Sail on!" When before them lay only shoreless seas, and it seemed like all hope was gone, it was, "Sail on!" Finally through the darkness the call came, "Land, ho!"

God called Abraham to leave his home country, his kindred, and his father's house. Hebrews 11:8 tells us that "He obeyed and went out, not knowing whither he went."

Sometimes God calls us to leave our comfort zones and to "launch out into the deep." He does not say how deep. That depends upon how ready we are to give up the shore. The fish are in the deep, not in the shallow waters. Our needs are met in the deep things of God. We cannot be in the depth of His will and purpose until our whole being is yielded in obedience to Him.

We must learn to take God at His Word as Abraham did and launch out. The key to Abraham's faith was that "He looked for a city which hath foundations, whose builder and maker is God" (Hebrews 11:10). May we have the same vision.

Robert Burkholder, Brooksville, KY

A ship in harbor is safe, but that is not what ships are for.

May 2

Bible Reading: Judges 7

One Year Bible Reading Plan: Luke 23:1-26, 1 Kings 3–5

So faith without works is dead also.

- JAMES 2:26

FAITH TESTED

How big is your faith? Is it as large as a mustard seed? In Matthew 17:20 we read that if we have faith the size of a mustard seed, which is very small, we will be able to move mountains and nothing will be impossible for us. The next verse gives us the key to attaining this faith: "By prayer and fasting."

While reading about Gideon and his three hundred men, I was blessed and challenged by their faith. They stepped out in faith and obedience, and God worked through them to His glory. In order to have this faith, we need to exercise it when God sets a difficult task in front of us. Don't we too often think we have to have a direct sign from God before we step out and take our responsibility?

Gideon was only human. He also wanted a sign, and God granted that wish. God chose 300 men to fight against 135,000 (1 for every 450). Can you imagine how futile it seemed to the men of Gideon? They probably thought it was like an ant bothering a camel in comparison. Yet I believe they were God-fearing men or they would have turned back long before they got to the Midianite camp.

A mustard seed is very small, yet when it is watered and nourished it can grow to a tree that is big and useful (Luke 13:19). In the same way, when we exercise our faith, taking opportunities to strengthen it, it will grow and flourish to the glory of God.

Marlin Schrock, Stark City, MO

---

*Faith and works go together like two oars in a boat—
use only one and you go in circles, getting nowhere.*

May 3

But the day of the Lord will come as a thief in the night; in the which the heavens shall pass away with a great noise, and the elements shall melt with fervent heat, the earth also and the works that are therein shall be burned up.
- 2 PETER 3:10

BETRAYED

Jesus was betrayed by one of His own disciples. This disciple was chosen by Jesus to follow Him (Matthew 10:1-4). Yet he was not willing to give up self and follow his Lord with a clean heart.

How many times do I betray my Lord Jesus with my speech, actions, or walk of life? When we give our hearts to Jesus, we need to live for Him. If I tell people that I have Jesus in my heart and then try to hide sin, I am betraying Him. What I try to hide from the church, family, and friends, Jesus still sees. It is so easy to forget that Jesus sees everything that we do, whether good or bad.

We will be rewarded for our deeds. "For the Son of man shall come in the glory of his Father with his angels; and then he shall reward every man according to his works" (Matthew 16:27). Do I want to receive a reward for the good or the bad in my life? My desire is to receive the reward for the good that I do. I hope that is every Christian's desire. If there is any bad in us, we should take care of it now. If we wait, it will be too late, for our Lord will come like a thief in the night.

Menno H. Eicher, Miami, OK

Honesty brings happy living.

May 4

For I am the Lord, I change not; therefore ye sons of Jacob are not consumed.
- MALACHI 3:6

DOES GOD CHANGE?

One quality of God is that He does not change. He is always the same. "Every good gift and every perfect gift is from above, and cometh down from the Father of lights, with whom is no variableness, neither shadow of turning" (James 1:17).

Through a recent conversation, I was reminded that many churches believe that some of the Holy Scriptures aren't for us today. They squirm around plainness, non-conformity, modesty and the permanency of marriage. It seems that man in his unsaved condition somehow thinks God will change to what the majority of people do or think even though it's not in accordance with His Word.

"Others are doing it," they say, "so it must be okay and acceptable with God." It burdens me to see this even among our plain churches. We compare ourselves among ourselves as individuals, or even as churches, instead of comparing with God's Word.

Isn't it encouraging, in our changing world, with changes in fashions, vehicles, and building decor, that we as Christians don't have to change?

Because God doesn't change, His Word is also unchangeable. With this confidence in God, we can have the assurance that He will judge us according to His Word at the end of our life. We need not fear that God may judge differently than He says in His Word.

God will always love righteousness and hate unrighteousness. Even Moses, the meekest man, and David, a man after God's own heart, had to reap for their wrongdoing after they repented.

Steve Hershberger, Monticello, KY

I know Whom I believe and am persuaded that He will not change.

May 5

Bible Reading: Proverbs 23:15-35

One Year Bible Reading Plan: Luke 24:1-35, 1 Kings 10, 11

Then saith he to the disciple, Behold thy mother! And from that hour that disciple took her unto his own home.

- JOHN 19:27

BEHOLD THY MOTHER

Jesus spoke these words to "the disciple," believed to be the Apostle John, in the final hours of His life as He hung on the cross. John understood this somewhat cryptic request as a charge to care for Mary, and from that hour he took her into his own home.

John was one of the chosen twelve who had personally known Jesus and had heard His teaching first hand. In a few short weeks, the Holy Spirit would come and the church would be established. John's time and energy would be needed to preach the Gospel to the end of the world. His knowledge of Christ's teaching would be invaluable to instruct the new believers. He also had epistles and the book of Revelation to write. Did it make any sense to waste his resources to care for a dependent old woman? Jesus charged His beloved disciple with this task.

Christian children have a responsibility to provide care for their aged parents. This is one way we can repay them for the care they gave us during our helpless childhood years. Once they sacrificed their time and pleasures for our needs; now we can care for them even though other duties are pressing. Once they nursed us during our childhood sicknesses; now we can care for them in the infirmities of old age. Once they pushed our stroller; now we can push their wheelchair.

Modern rest homes are useful in providing care for elderly who do not have others to care for them, or for those who need constant supervision. While children may place their parents there for many valid reasons, rest homes can make it easy to dodge the responsibility to care for parents. May we never be guilty of despising our parents when they are old (Proverbs 23:22).

Gardell Strite, Warrensburg, MO

Time spent on another person is never wasted time.

May 6

Bible Reading: Matthew 23:23-28, Revelation 3:14-22

One Year Bible Reading Plan: Luke 24:35-53, 1 Kings 12, 13

Verily, verily, I say unto you, He that entereth not by the door into the sheepfold, but climbeth up some other way, the same is a thief and a robber.

- JOHN 10:1

THE DITCH OF FORMALITY

We live in a day when people are so caught up in formality and the keeping of their culture that they miss the purpose of the church—serving Jesus Christ. The church leaders become a god. People in this ditch of formality have lost their focus on Jesus Christ. "Do good," they say. "Abide by the church standards, and when Christ returns, hopefully you will be good enough for Him to accept you." This is false teaching. Jesus said, "Verily, verily, I say unto you, He that heareth my word, and believeth on him that sent me, hath everlasting life, and shall not come into condemnation; but is passed from death unto life" (John 5:24).

Often we hear, "Well, it was good enough for our grandparents, so surely it is good enough for us." My friends, before we claim such a phrase let's first see if it is right or wrong. If it is right, it is more than good enough. If it is wrong, it is sin and we don't want to do it. Jesus said, "He that loveth father or mother more than me is not worthy of me: and he that loveth son or daughter more than me is not worthy of me" (Matthew 10:37).

Claiming your salvation because of your good works gives you a false hope. We confess our sins, dedicate our life to our Savior Jesus Christ, and then good works do follow. The works don't save us, but Christ does.

Andrew M. Troyer, Conneautville, PA

Satan loves when people jump out of the ditch of formality into the other ditch, which is false spirituality.

May 7

Bible Reading: I Timothy 3

One Year Bible Reading Plan: John 1:1-28, 1 Kings 14, 15

For many shall come in my name, saying, I am Christ; and shall deceive many.
- MATTHEW 24:5

THE DITCH OF FALSE SPIRITUALITY

Every road has two ditches. The ditch on the opposite side of formality is the ditch of false spirituality. People cling to certain commandments, or issues, focusing so hard upon them that they miss the whole picture of Christ's teaching concerning His church.

What is found in this ditch? Individualism, a "better than thou" attitude, "If the heart is right, nothing else matters." a puffed up, "I know it all" attitude, people who claim to be Christians but don't deny self, No submission to the church, "I'm free; my heart is right with God, so I don't need any church standards based on Bible principles," people who are not easily entreated, "It feels so good to be right with God that nobody can tell me differently." Those in this ditch often allow feelings to override the facts, instead of letting the facts override the feelings.

In the garden when Eve was deceived, the serpent used some truth and some untruths. "And no marvel; for Satan himself is transformed into an angel of light" (2 Corinthians 11:14). "And Jesus answered and said unto them, Take heed that no man deceive you" (Matthew 24:4). In this ditch there is much truth, but the truth is muddied with deceptive untruths.

Andrew M. Troyer, Conneautville, PA

Some can't see the forest because their focus is only on a few trees.

May 8

Bible Reading: 1 Thessalonians 4:13-18; 5

One Year Bible Reading Plan: John 1:29-51, 1 Kings 16–18

Search me, O God, and know my heart: try me, and know my thoughts: and see if there be any wicked way in me, and lead me in the way everlasting.
- PSALM 139:23, 24

SEEK FIRST THE KINGDOM OF GOD

Today is a day that has never been before and will never come again. We must be careful what we do today–it will affect our eternal destiny.

Every morning when we get up, we should think that this may be the last day for us in this world or that today may be the day Jesus will return. In the evening when we go to bed, we should think about what we have done today. Did we do some good for someone? Did we do a kind deed or speak comforting words? Or did we do or say something we know we shouldn't have? Jesus may come at midnight, so let's not go to bed unless we have peace with God and man.

Think of the song, "Jesus is coming, we know not how soon, coming at midnight, at morning, at noon." Or, "When the trumpet of the Lord shall sound and time shall be no more."

It is important to read and study the Word of God and spend some time on our knees every morning in prayer. Thank God for a good night's rest and that He has given us another day to prepare for eternity. Ask Him to be with us throughout this new day He has given us and to keep us from all appearance of evil. Every evening before going to bed, we need to spend time on our knees asking God to forgive us where we have failed and thanking Him for His protecting hand and His goodness throughout the day.

Eli A. Yoder, Stuarts Draft, VA

The Christian is he who can truly say,
"Thy word have I hid in my heart."

May 9

I have no greater joy than to hear that my children walk in truth.

- 3 JOHN 4

OBEDIENCE-THE GATEWAY TO JOY

While visiting another community recently, we had the privilege of spending the night at the home of a young Christian family. The next morning I could hear voices in the kitchen as the mother prepared breakfast. Her gentle voice could be heard instructing the two small children. "Leave that alone now. Come over here, please, where Mama can see you." I thought of how children, especially small children, are in need of almost constant direction and supervision.

Older "children," even Christians, are also in need of direction to stay away from danger and things that may stunt their growth or hinder their usefulness as children of God. God has graciously provided His Word, the Holy Spirit, and the Church to give that direction and supervision. As children become older and have taken heed to the parental voice of correction, they generally don't need that constant supervision anymore. In the same way, as we recognize our need of direction and respond properly to it, we learn more and more what pleases the Father and brings a good relationship with Him.

Soon I heard a childish voice, "J-O-Y, J-O-Y, J-O-Y." The rest of the song was not sung, but this sounded beautiful! There was plenty of evidence that there was joy, as well as peace, in this home.

May we praise the Lord for His wisdom in providing blueprints in His Word for Christian homes and biblical churches to provide the shelter and direction that all of us need. It brings joy to everyone involved when we follow it.

Daniel Schrock, Stark City, MO

Trust and obey, for there's no other way to be happy in Jesus, but to trust and obey.

May 10

Bible Reading: Romans 10

One Year Bible Reading Plan: John 3:1-21, 1 Kings 21, 22

That if thou shalt confess with thy mouth the Lord Jesus. . .
thou shalt be saved.

- ROMANS 10:9

WITNESS TODAY

If you are at work, in the office, in the home, on the job, at the shop, traveling, shopping, or in the hospital, witness to someone today. Don't wait for the opportunity; take the opportunity. Go out of your way if you have to. Do it today and you will be blessed. Others will also be blessed, and you will want to do it daily.

There are numerous reasons we need to witness. The Scriptures command us to do it. There are always those who need our testimony. It will give honor to our Lord.

When Jesus was here on the earth, He talked and ministered to people. When Jesus went to the Father, He said He would send the Holy Spirit. The Holy Spirit empowers us to be witnesses for the Lord. He wants to use us to carry on His work on earth.

When you see that rough-looking person on the street corner or in the cafe, talk to him of the love of God. Their appearance is a cry for help. They will be lost unless someone rescues them. They are often the product of a broken home and lack the love they crave. It is your opportunity.

Jesus said, "All power is given unto me." Jesus then graciously endows us with His power. He would have us use that power for the sake of His kingdom. All the needy people we see have potential to be a part of the Kingdom of God.

James Yoder, Lewisburg, PA

Sow the seed today for a harvest tomorrow.

Bible Reading: Matthew 15:1-20

One Year Bible Reading Plan: John 3:22-36, 2 Kings 13

Out of the same mouth proceedeth blessing and cursing.
My brethren, these things ought not so to be.
- JAMES 3:10

FAITHFUL LIP SERVICE

A father was asking the blessing at the breakfast table. After he was done, his little daughter asked him, "Daddy, do you really think the Lord hears our prayers?"

"Why, sure God hears our prayers and thanksgiving," the father said with confidence in his voice. Satisfied with her daddy's answer, the little girl started eating her breakfast.

Soon though, the father found that the eggs were not done right and started complaining about the food. When the mother served the coffee, it was rather weak and not very hot. "What's wrong this morning? You know I like my eggs well done and my coffee good and hot," complained the father.

As the little girl listened to her father's critical remarks, she finally asked, "Daddy, do you think the Lord hears what you are saying about the food?"

The father thought a little and finally answered, "Aw, well, yes, I suppose He does."

"What do you think the Lord is going to believe?" asked the innocent little girl.

Like this father, sometimes we need to take inventory of our attitudes and ask ourselves, "Can God believe everything we say?" Jesus had to work with people of whom He said, "This people draweth nigh unto me with their mouth, and honoureth me with their lips; but their heart is far from me" (Matthew 15:8). James 3:11-12 says, "Doth a fountain send forth at the same place sweet water and bitter? Can the fig tree, my brethren, bear olive berries? either a vine, figs? So can no fountain both yield salt water and fresh."

Let's be careful that our words don't contradict our deeds or our prayers. God knows what to believe.

Ben J. Troyer, Baltic, OH

Our deeds speak so loudly that our words cannot be heard.

May 12

Bible Reading: James 3

One Year Bible Reading Plan: John 4:1-30, 2 Kings 4, 5

But if ye have bitter envying and strife in your hearts, glory not, and lie not against the truth.

- JAMES 3:14

A LIE OR A MISUNDERSTANDING?

There is a difference between telling a lie and being misunderstood. How often do we try to hide a lie by calling it a misunderstanding? To tell a lie is sin. We can try to hide it, but it will always find its way out. The most common way a Christian tries to hide a lie is behind a misunderstanding.

When we are caught in a lie, it is easier to say there was a misunderstanding than to be embarrassed. It is very embarrassing for a Christian to be caught in a lie. To lie is a sin and requires repentance. The Ninth Commandment reminds us not to bear false witness against our neighbor, meaning not to lie against him.

Once we start telling lies, they just keep getting bigger. To be misunderstood is one thing, but to tell an untruth and call it a misunderstanding is another. This is what God says in Revelation 21:27, "And there shall in no wise enter into it any thing that defileth, neither whatsoever worketh abomination, or maketh a lie: but they which are written in the Lamb's book of life." A lie, if not repented of, will keep us from the presence of our Lord and Saviour, Jesus Christ.

The next time you are tempted to turn a lie into a misunderstanding, remember, we cannot hide anything from God.

Menno H. Eicher, Miami, OK

Lying robs our peace of mind.

May 13

Bible Reading: Job 21

One Year Bible Reading Plan: John 4:31-54, 2 Kings 6–8

For he maketh his sun to rise on the evil and on the good, and sendeth rain on the just and the unjust.

- MATTHEW 5:45

JOB'S RESPONSE

In our Bible reading Job contradicts Zophar's statements. Zophar the Naamathite said the wicked are always cast down in this life. Job clearly states that the wicked often live a prosperous life with even an honorable burial.

Perhaps we tend to assume that if someone faces tremendous obstacles and hardships in life, they must have hidden sin. Jesus' own disciples assumed that since a blind man was blind that someone had sinned. Either he or his parents had failed somewhere. But Jesus said that neither this man nor his parents had sinned. The man was blind so that the works of God should be made manifest in him.

We cannot gauge a person's relationship with God by prosperity or adversity, because God rains on the just and on the unjust. Actually, what proves our relationship with God is our response to prosperity and adversity. The Christian will give as God has prospered, but the ungodly will spend the increase on himself. The Christian will sing praises through adversity while the ungodly will complain and even curse God.

In verse twenty-six, we read that both the blessed and the cursed shall return to dust. Whether we are ungodly or righteous, we will experience physical death.

May God give us grace to remember that Christians are not promised easy lives. In fact, being a Christian almost insures hardship and adversity. Hebrews 12:6 says, "For whom the Lord loveth he chasteneth." May we, like Job, respond with an attitude of worship.

Harold R. Troyer, Belleville, PA

We learn more from adversity than from prosperity.

May 14

Bible Reading: Acts 8:5-25

One Year Bible Reading Plan: John 5:1-24, 2 Kings 9–11

And ye shall know the truth, and the truth shall make you free.

- JOHN 8:32

TRANSFORMED HEARTS

The Samaritans were a people sent by the king of Assyria to inhabit the land of Israel after the Jews were conquered. The situation caused the Jews to despise the Samaritans. The Samaritans did evil in the sight of the Lord. They built high places and made a temple for Baal. They made it a light thing to walk in sin. They did not heed the voice of God. Samaria, capital city of Israel, should have been a role model instead of a hub of evil, inviting others to join in the reveling in sin. God must have been saddened by what He saw. The Samaritans did not have a very good record.

What was the chance of reconciliation between God and Samaria? Did they stand a chance?

In Acts chapter eight Philip preached Christ to the despised Samaritans. They turned to God and heeded what they heard. There was great rejoicing. But wait; didn't these Samaritans have a bad record? Their fathers of years gone by definitely were not serving God. Didn't the influence of their ancestors keep them bound in its grip?

No, of course not! God breaks chains. He does not fix our sinful heart, but gives us a new one, transforming us completely, no matter what our record may be. He delights in making a new, beautiful creation out of something that wasn't so nice to begin with. And then He calls it good!

John Hochstetler, Worthington, IN

Christian character is not an inheritance.

May 15

Bible Reading: Psalm 73

One Year Bible Reading Plan: John 5:25-47, 2 Kings 12-14

But thou, O man of God, flee these things; and follow after righteousness, godliness, faith, love, patience, meekness.

- 1 TIMOTHY 6:11

ARE YOU CAUGHT IN THE WEB?

In one of our old buildings, my attention was drawn to a moth that was caught in a spider web. It struggled desperately to free itself, going around and around in circles. I don't know how it happened, but all of a sudden it broke free. It took a dive and flew out a hole in the wall of the old building.

As I observed that spider web, I noticed a few interesting things. It was put in a place where insects would likely pass through. It was woven attractively. Often when an insect was caught and struggling, the spider would be right there trying to wrap it up tighter, spinning silk threads around its legs.

Isn't this the way Satan works? He sets traps at the weakest areas of our life and makes sin look just as attractive as possible to our human eyes. Sometimes we find ourselves, like the moth, almost caught in Satan's trap. Do we see the danger? Do we ask God to help us overcome? Satan will see us giving in and, like the spider, he'll be right there to drag us in further.

When we recognize our sin, do we play with it and kind of hang around, or do we, like the moth, quickly flee from it? When we are freed from sin we should thank God for sparing us and renew our commitment to live for Him.

Today let's ask God to reveal any deception. Let's be open to God's prompting when He reminds us and ask Him to help us flee from sin.

Steven Farmwald, Cynthiana, KY

Lord, steer us far from sin.

May 16

Bible Reading: Numbers 14:25-45

One Year Bible Reading Plan: John 6:1-21, 2 Kings 15–17

And the Lord said, I have pardoned according to thy word:
But as truly as I live, all the earth shall be filled with the glory of the Lord.
- NUMBERS 14:20-21

MY WAY OR GOD'S WAY

After the twelve spies returned from spying out Canaan, the children
of Israel chose to believe the negative report that the ten gave, rather
than "a land that floweth with milk and honey" report, that Joshua and
Caleb brought. For that decision, God told them that anyone over the
age of twenty would not see the Promised Land nor enter it. Because
of their sin of not believing that God could do what He had promised,
they were to return to the wilderness to die.

As man so often is today, once the Israelites were told they couldn't
enter the Promised Land, suddenly their focus changed and they
decided they would go in after all. Even though Moses warned them
not to attempt entering Canaan, they took their own way and suffered
great ruin.

The beautiful picture to us is that God still extended mercy. He
showed mercy to Caleb and Joshua who were promised that, because
of their trust in God, they would enter Canaan in the future. He also
showed mercy to the children of these disobedient people and
preserved them so that a remnant would remain.

How much better it is to believe and trust God the first time. God has
a plan for each of us, for our families, and for our churches. He wants
us to trust Him to carry it out in His own way and in His own time. At
times we think in our human minds that certainly God is missing a
perfect window of opportunity. *If I were God, I would do this or that.*
Isn't it true, though, that if we follow God's timing, we find His plan was
so much better than our own? Let's learn to trust Him more.

Steve Burkholder, Nappanee, IN

*Although God's plan for my life is often somewhat hidden,
it is always worth searching out!*

May 17

Bible Reading: Galatians 6

One Year Bible Reading Plan: John 6:22-44, 2 Kings 18, 19

Be not deceived; God is not mocked: for whatsoever a man soweth, that shall he also reap.

- GALATIANS 6:7

DECEIVED?

In his book, *Bones of Contention,* Professor Marvin Lubenow tells the story of Sir Arthur Keith, one of the greatest anatomists of the twentieth century. According to Keith's autobiography, he attended evangelistic meetings in Edinburgh and Aberdeen when he was young and watched students make commitments to Christ. He himself was often on the verge of conversion, yet he resisted, rejecting the Gospel because he felt the Genesis account of creation was just a myth and the Bible was merely a human book.

Later, after Keith was a scientist, he became greatly intrigued by a famous discovery in England. In 1908, in a gravel pit near the village of Piltdown, some bones were discovered including portions of a human skull, a molar, and a lower jaw. For Sir Arthur Keith, the discovery of the Piltdown man was a validation of his evolutionary beliefs. His famous work, "The Antiquity of Man," centered on Piltdown. Much of his life was spent studying and proclaiming the wonders of this discovery.

It was not until 1953 that the fraud was exposed. The bones had been treated with iron salts to make them appear old. Sir Arthur Keith was 86 years old when his colleagues visited him at his home to break the news that the fossil he had trusted in was a hoax. A great scholar had placed a lifetime of faith into what proved to be a fake.

Many today place great faith and trust in their own insights and intellect. They feel little or no need for God-given authority. Our Scripture reading says in verse three, "For if a man think himself to be something, when he is nothing, he deceiveth himself." The carnal minded man will awake too late and find that he has spent his life trusting in a false message.

Melvin L. Yoder, Gambier, OH

Make sure your faith is secure in Jesus, and you need not be disappointed.

May 18

Bible Reading: Proverbs 15:1-26

One Year Bible Reading Plan: John 6:45-71, 2 Kings 20–22

Let the words of my mouth, and the meditation of my heart, be acceptable in thy sight, O Lord, my strength, and my redeemer.

- PSALM 19:14

ACCEPTABLE WORDS

Do we realize the impact that our words have on us and those about us? We reveal our character and the intents of our hearts as we speak. In the Judgment, we will be accountable for all that we have spoken. "For by thy words thou shalt be justified, and by thy words thou shalt be condemned" (Matthew 12:37).

We are probably all guilty of using vain or idle words. How do we respond when things go wrong or the weather isn't cooperating with our plans? We should praise the Lord for all the good things of life rather than leave a poor testimony with our complaints. "A man hath joy by the answer of his mouth: and a word spoken in due season, how good it is!" (Proverbs 15:23).

We declare in our speech the depth of our convictions. When we speak vain words, we show to others that we have not laid all on the altar. The Devil has used the television as a channel to defile the language of many. Through the influence of the world he is finding a foothold in our own circles or even in our own lives. A lot of the vain words of society take the name of the Lord in vain. "Thou shalt not take the name of the Lord thy God in vain; for the Lord will not hold him guiltless that taketh his name in vain" (Exodus 20:7). May we, with the help of our brethren and God's Word, build conviction and rise above vain and idle words.

"For in many things we offend all. If any man offend not in word, the same is a perfect man, and able also to bridle the whole body" (James 3:2).

Elvin Fox, Shiloh, OH

---

*Kind words, How little they cost;
Scatter them freely, That none may be lost.*

May 19

Bible Reading: Ephesians 6

One Year Bible Reading Plan: John 7:1-31, 2 Kings 23-25

Lord, make me to know mine end, and the measure of my days, what it is; that I may know how frail I am.

- PSALM 39:4

TRAGIC MIDNIGHT CRASH

Kevin asked Judy to attend a party with him one night. Judy's parents didn't allow Judy to go to the party but did give her permission to go to her friend's house. Kevin picked her up there and they went to the party. There was drinking and merry making, and afterwards a midnight ride. Judy insisted Kevin take her home. Kevin sped angrily down the road at a high rate of speed. Judy begged him to slow down, but Kevin wouldn't listen. There was a blinding crash and intense pain.

Judy regained consciousness in the hospital, and a nurse told her she had only minutes to live. She was told Kevin didn't make it and the people in the other car were both dead. The nurse asked if she wanted to say something yet. She begged the nurse to tell her parents how sorry she was for not listening to them. The nurse didn't respond, and Judy drew her last breath. The doctor asked the nurse, "Why didn't you tell Judy that you would tell her parents? It was her last wish."

The nurse replied with tears, "The people in the other car were her parents."

It is so much better for young people to obey their parents even if they can't see the danger. Parents have more experience, and it is God's plan for children to obey their parents. "Let us hear the conclusion of the whole matter: Fear God, and keep his commandments: for this is the whole duty of man. For God shall bring every work into judgment, with every secret thing, whether it be good, or whether it be evil" (Ecclesiastes 12:13-14).

Daniel Miller, Dunnegan, MO

You can't sow iniquity and reap life everlasting.

May 20

Bible Reading: Luke 8:4-15

One Year Bible Reading Plan: John 7:32-53, 1 Chronicles 1, 2

So then faith cometh by hearing, and hearing by the word of God.
- ROMANS 10:17

HOW ARE YOUR EARS TODAY?

The word "hear" is used seven times in our Bible reading today. Whenever the Word of God is being read, do we really listen? How we respond may be the test of whether we have really heard. True hearing inspires faith that moves a person to action. Why then are we so sleepy at the reading of the Word of God?

Maybe we could answer that better if we first asked, "What is this in my hand?" The very Word of God. Isn't it precious? How do we hold and handle it?

Mr. Jacob Ojwang Donji was struggling to pay a 600,000 Ksh. loan that he owed several people. One day he decided to escape his problem by stealing from Securercor, a company he worked for as a driver. He snatched 56 million from the vehicle and disappeared. The police ransacked his house, posted his picture, notified every Kenyan border to watch for him, and gave every bank the I.D. numbers of the stolen cash. What does Jacob Donji hold in his hands? He cannot even spend one of those bills or the C.I.D. will trace him. Do you think he is enjoying his life?

What we hold in our hands is worth much more than 56 million! The Word is like seed with life in it, a wealth untold. It is the single most powerful element ever to be had. Yet why do we get sleepy or gaze out the windows even as we hold it in our hands? How we hear the reading of the Word reflects the true condition of our hearts today. Only after our hearts are prepared by earnest prayer can we truly hear and be moved to believing.

Let us remove the spiritual earwax, so that we may bring forth fruit to maturity.

Mark Kuepfer, Kisumu, Kenya

Listen + Accept + Obey = Glory to Jesus = Increased Hearing

May 21

Bible Reading: Job 12:7-25

One Year Bible Reading Plan: John 8:1-20, 1 Chronicles 35

Thou art worthy, O Lord, to receive glory and honour and power: for thou hast created all things, and for thy pleasure they are and were created.

- REVELATION 4:11

OUR GREAT GOD

It is awesome to ponder the greatness of our God. All of creation is a testimony to the omnipotence and omniscience of our Almighty Lord. As creatures of His, it is our duty to serve Him. It is also a privilege.

God has created an overwhelming array of creatures that inhabit the earth. From the smallest mycoplasma, four millionths of an inch long, to the largest African elephant, weighing in at eight tons and standing thirteen feet tall at the shoulder, the creatures of the earth are living proof of a master designer. From the brotulid, a fish that swims twenty-four thousand feet below the surface of the ocean, to the yak, roaming the Tibetan plateaus at twenty thousand feet above sea level, living creatures dwell in all types of habitats.

The cheetah can run sixty miles per hour. The swift can fly at least seventy miles per hour. A whale, one hundred feet long and weighing one hundred fifty tons, can swim up to thirty-five miles per hour.

We can't begin to fathom the thoughts of God. His ways are infinitely higher than our finite minds can grasp. Since He is the Creator of all things, He has the right to allow things to occur as it pleases Him.

He also has the right to establish absolute laws of right and wrong. When we break those laws, only repentance and the atoning blood of Jesus can reconcile us to God.

Are you serving your Creator? He has a purpose for your life. Lift His name in praise! Tell others how they can live for God. He alone is worthy of your worship, adoration, and allegiance.

Andrew Zimmerman, Foxworth, MS

There is much I do not know about God,
but what I do know has changed my life.

Bible Reading: Ecclesiastes 11

One Year Bible Reading Plan: John 8:21-36, 1 Chronicles 6, 7

And if the tree fall toward the south, or toward the north, in the place where the tree falleth, there it shall be.

- ECCLESIASTES 11:3

NOW IS THE TIME

One day, years ago, as we were riding along, we passed a cemetery. The woman we were riding with asked us to excuse her while she prayed to help her mother out of purgatory.

In early American history, we read of a people who believed that when their dead warriors were scalped they couldn't go to the happy hunting grounds. Many warriors would risk their own lives to keep the enemy from scalping their dead friends.

We know that both of these are false beliefs. The Scripture teaches that we cannot change the destiny of the deceased after they have passed on. What is our reaction to this? Both of these groups faithfully support their deceptive teachings. Are we as diligent in supporting the biblical teachings? Are we witnessing to the lost, admonishing each other, and teaching our children? It is urgent that we do what we can now. There is no more opportunity to influence someone's destiny after his life has fled. Now is the time to teach our children. Now is the time to call our friends and neighbors to the Lord.

May the Lord give us grace to be faithful, for we have something to share that is of great value.

Alvin J. Coblentz, Free Union, VA

Let us rise up and build.

May 23

Bible Reading: 2 Timothy 3:10-17; 4:1-8

One Year Bible Reading Plan: John 8:37-59, 1 Chronicles 8-10

Till I come, give attendance to reading, to exhortation, to doctrine.
- 1 TIMOTHY 4:13

READ THE ITINERARY

We rose early one morning to take our daughter to the airport. I had carefully checked the itinerary the evening before. Yes, the flight left at 6:30 a.m. The itinerary I checked was one I had gotten earlier for my parents, and I thought the schedule was the same for our daughter who was going to the same destination. Before we left, I called the airline's automated service to make certain the scheduling remained the same. I put in the flight number and something didn't make sense. I then checked my daughter's itinerary more carefully and discovered her flight left at 12:20 a.m. It was already 2:30 a.m.!

Reality hit us forcefully. We hadn't read the itinerary carefully enough. The plane wasn't coming back. It was gone.

All of us will someday take another flight. If we miss that flight, there will be no second chance. God left us an itinerary with detailed instructions on how to be ready for this flight.

Many today are rejecting God's itinerary for their own itinerary. Rationalism and intellectualism have replaced God's Word in many circles. Materialism that seeks the latest, the best, and the most up-to-date, has become more important than keeping our Christian life up-to-date. Others drown in the murky waters of worldly philosophy where holiness and purity are considered outdated. They seek fulfillment in fleeting sensual pleasures.

When we come to the judgment bar, God will judge us by His itinerary, not ours. There will be no opportunity to request another itinerary, for there is no other.

Are you reading God's itinerary? It's a matter of life or death.

Jonathan Kropf, Halsey, OR

The Bible does not need to be rewritten, but reread.

May 24

Bible Reading: Mark 8:34-38, Matthew 10:22-42

One Year Bible Reading Plan: John 9:1-23, 1 Chronicles 11–13

For what shall it profit a man, if he shall gain the whole world, and lose his own soul?

- MARK 8:36

SPIRITUAL HEALTH CARE

Can you tell me the worth of our world? If you would attempt to calculate the value of our universe, how much do you think it would be worth? A hurricane once tore apart just a little of our world. It happened in Florida. The storm damaged millions and possibly billions of dollars' worth of property. I read just this evening of a fiddle, made in 1720, worth at least a million dollars. At a show recently, late 1800's pennies, worth thousands of dollars, were on exhibit.

Anna Olander wrote in 1904, "If I gained the world but lost the Savior, were my life worth living for a day? Could my yearning heart find rest and comfort in the things that soon must pass away?"

We cannot compare the universe to our soul. Our soul is worth far more than this world or even a thousand worlds. As we muse on the span of eternity, we should tremble before the Creator of our soul. There is nothing worth more in the life of a living soul, than to accept the Savior as Lord.

Many people today are selling out cheap. There are people exchanging their souls for pleasure, jobs, hobbies, and dishonesty. It is shocking to hold so light a view of what Jesus said is worth so much. If we could visit hell for just a moment and get a glimpse of heaven in contrast, we would suddenly better understand the value of our soul.

If we would care for our soul, we must take up the cross and stay beneath its beam. We must be content to let the world go by, while we glory only in the cross of Jesus.

Harold R. Troyer, Belleville, PA

Care for thy soul, for in it lies thy future.

May 25

Bible Reading: Ezekiel 33:1-16

One Year Bible Reading Plan: John 9:24-41, 1 Chronicles 14-16

So thou, O son of man, I have set thee a watchman unto the house of Israel; therefore thou shalt hear the word at my mouth, and warn them from me.
- EZEKIEL 33:7

ARE YOU WATCHING OR SLEEPING?

The Lord instructed Ezekiel that the children of Israel should appoint a watchman. The watchman would be responsible to warn the people when danger approached. If the watchman saw the enemy coming and did not blow the trumpet, he was responsible if someone was killed. If the watchman saw the danger coming and blew the trumpet, but the people did not listen, then the watchman was not responsible.

God sent Ezekiel to be a watchman for Israel's spiritual well-being. Today God chooses ministers to be watchmen for Him. They teach us in the ways of righteousness and holiness. They warn us of the enemy of our soul who is seeking to devour us. "Obey them that have the rule over you, and submit yourselves: for they watch for your souls, as they that must give account, that they may do it with joy, and not with grief: for that is unprofitable for you" (Hebrews 13:17).

Everyone should be watchful. The worldly allurements and contaminations continually tempt us. Let us submit ourselves to God. "Resist the devil, and he will flee from you" (James 4:7). Satan tries to make sin look attractive. He wants us to take the second or third look at uncleanness. He is the father of all lies, and he will use untruth to try to get us to sin. Let us try the spirits and see whether they are of God (1 John 4:1). Let us all watch and guard against the enemy of our souls.

Samuel Beachy, Belvidere, TN

And what I say unto you I say unto all, Watch. - Mark 13:37

Bible Reading: 1 Timothy 6:6-19

One Year Bible Reading Plan: John 10:1-21, 1 Chronicles 17–19

For here have we no continuing city, but we seek one to come.
- HEBREWS 13:14

I'M LEAVING SOON

I'm leaving soon. This prospect sheds a different light on my stay here. Everything here is only a temporary arrangement since it will be only a short stay. Though I don't know the definite time of my departure, I know it won't be long because those nearer to their time of leaving tell me their stay was brief. My Master also said it is a short time. Sometimes my thoughts turn to the departure. I think of it more the closer it gets. I'm just a stranger here. Worldlings don't recognize me nor understand my standards of value.

Since I'm leaving soon and must leave all behind, a mansion is not only unnecessary, but also has little attraction. My eyes are set on another mansion just over the hilltop. After all, what is a brick or stone mansion in comparison to a mansion in heaven?

It doesn't matter so much if my car isn't new since it's only a means of transportation while I'm here. It is sort of like a rental. It doesn't matter if my furniture and clothes aren't the finest, as long as they meet my needs. My Master didn't even have a place to lay His head.

Nothing I have really belongs to me. The King I serve only loaned it to me to use during my sojourn here. Why not invest in my brothers' needs on behalf of the eternal kingdom?

Because I serve this King, I claim no allegiance to any earthly kingdom, but view all men as equal with a priceless soul to save. My Master saw them this way. He especially seemed to relate to the poor and lowly. I should live like that too.

I'm leaving soon. You are too. Are we ready?

David Keeney, White Hall, IL

Rather than laying down our souls for money,
we lay down our money for our souls. - Tertullian

May 27

Bible Reading: Isaiah 1:1-18, 2 Timothy 3:1-9

One Year Bible Reading Plan: John 10:22-42, 1 Chronicles 20-22

This know also, that in the last days perilous times shall come.

- 2 TIMOTHY 3:1

ROTTEN TO THE CORE

Our world is rotten to the core. Along the highway, toward the town I was approaching this evening, there were at least five billboards displaying the heart of mankind. "For out of the heart proceed evil thoughts, murders, adulteries, fornications, thefts, false witness, blasphemies" (Matthew 15:19). I'll add immoral billboards to that list.

As I passed the Penn State stadium, I saw many indecently dressed people streaming toward the doors. The world is avalanching toward hell, subtly dragging many with it.

The reason for moral decline in our world is the nature of man. Without moral compass, man tends to become extremely corrupt in nature, to the point of taking pleasure in his unrighteous state. Another reason for moral decline in our world is the gravitational effect sin has on us. The influence of others has destroyed many innocent souls. Still another reason for moral decline in our world is that the church is also sorely lacking in moral discipline. The church too often is fighting to keep her head out of the water when she should be a lighthouse along the shore. Jesus said the church is the light of the world.

Spiritual cleansing comes only through Jesus Christ. "Come now, and let us reason together, saith the Lord: though your sins be as scarlet, they shall be as white as snow" (Isaiah 1:18).

Harold R. Troyer, Belleville, PA

Keep yourself from worldly thought, and you will keep yourself from worldliness.

May 28

Bible Reading: 2 Corinthians 5

One Year Bible Reading Plan: John 11:1-16, 1 Chronicles 23–25

Therefore if any man be in Christ, he is a new creature: old things are passed away; behold, all things are become new.

- 2 CORINTHIANS 5:17

WE WILL MIGRATE

Butterflies are beautiful insects. But this insect was not always beautiful. Before it went through metamorphosis, it was only a caterpillar and a pest to humans. Changes start to take place when metamorphosis begins. The caterpillar spins a cocoon around itself, and its transformation begins. The useless caterpillar develops into a beautiful, useful butterfly. Besides being attractive, butterflies pollinate flowers.

Before we were converted, we were like the caterpillar. We were a hindrance to the work of God. When we gave our heart to God, He transformed us and created a new heart within us. We can now be useful creatures for Him. We can spread God's Word to others and be an encouragement to those we meet.

When an enemy attacks, some butterflies put off a sour odor to protect themselves. We also have an enemy of our soul who is seeking to devour us. We can overcome him by the blood of the Lamb. Christ gives us grace and strength to live a victorious Christian life.

Butterflies are known to migrate. They are fragile creatures and need each other's help to survive in life. As Christians we need each other. We all become discouraged at times and need some encouragement from each other. We will also migrate someday. With God's help, we can migrate to our heavenly home. "Whosoever will, let him take of the water of life freely" (Revelation 22:17).

Samuel Beachy, Belvidere, TN

Are you Satan's caterpillar or God's butterfly?

May 29

Bible Reading: 2 Corinthians 6:14-18; 7:1-12

One Year Bible Reading Plan: John 11:17-46, 1 Chronicles 26, 27

Now then we are ambassadors for Christ, as though God did beseech you by us: we pray you in Christ's stead, be ye reconciled to God.
- 2 CORINTHIANS 5:20

AMBASSADORS FOR CHRIST

Someone asked one of our ambassadors, "What does being an ambassador consist of?"

He replied, "First, let us take a look inside the embassy. Inside the embassy, we have a picture of George Washington and a picture of Abraham Lincoln. The American flag hangs on the wall. Inside the embassy, we practice all the laws of our land. When our country practiced prohibition, we did the same in the embassy."

As ambassadors from a heavenly country, we practice the laws of heaven. Christ taught us to pray, "Thy will be done in earth, as it is in heaven" (Matthew 6:10). The church is a heavenly embassy. When we are yoked with the world in its earthly pursuits and pleasures, we betray our duty as ambassadors for Christ.

We are not here to see who can make the most money, hit the ball the farthest, or rack up the highest score. We are here to beseech the world to be reconciled to Christ.

Our Bible reading reminds us not to be unequally yoked with the world, but to come out of the world, and be separate.

In 2 Corinthians 7:11 Paul explains how the church members cleared themselves. They showed fear, carefulness, and zeal. He goes on to explain that he did not write to them because of the one who had done wrong or because of the one who suffered wrongly. He wrote to help them see his care for them.

Today, let us clear ourselves and recognize how the ones God has placed over us care for our souls. May the church truly live by the laws of heaven.

Melvin L. Yoder, Gambier, OH

Can the world see that we are ambassadors from a heavenly country, or are we ashamed to let them know?

May 30

Bible Reading: Psalm 121, 123

One Year Bible Reading Plan: John 11:47-57, 1 Chronicles 28, 29

Behold, the LORD's hand is not shortened, that it cannot save; neither his ear heavy, that it cannot hear.

- ISAIAH 59:1

UNDER GOD'S WATCHFUL EYE

Sometimes we hear people say, "I need a vacation," or, "She is not here because she went on vacation." This summer the children are out of school because they are on vacation.

If God would go on vacation, who would be there for us? Who would be there to dry the tears of grief from our eyes? When we cry, who would hear us? Who would hear us when we pray? Who would answer us when we call? Who would be there to pick us up when we fall?

Praise God for the Scripture that says that the Lord never sleeps. Imagine God taking a nap. In just that one moment Satan would wreak havoc in the church and the world. Oh, how I thank my God for His never-ending love, His watchful eyes, His listening ears, and His outstretched arms!

He said, "Call unto me, and I will answer thee," (Jeremiah 33:3a), not only at a certain hour, but any time of the day. He said that "having loved his own which were in the world, he loved them unto the end" (John 13:1).

His hand is not shortened to pull me out of the miry clay and that horrible pit. By His strength He put me on the rock. He also put a new song in my heart.

What an awesome God we have! We can go to sleep knowing that we are under His protecting eyes.

Mark G. Meighn, Belize City, Belize

Our God is never on vacation.

May 31

Bible Reading: Romans 6:1-13, Colossians 3:1-17

One Year Bible Reading Plan: John 12:1-19, 2 Chronicles 13

Likewise reckon ye also yourselves to be dead indeed unto sin, but alive unto God through Jesus Christ our Lord.

- ROMANS 6:11

A NEW CREATURE

Recently I saw a dead dog lying by the road, probably hit by a car. If I would have stopped and given it a kick it likely would not have moved. It was dead to the world around it. But if there had been life in the dog, it probably would have snarled or at least whimpered at me.

How is it with us as born again Christians? We have died with Christ to self, sin, and the world. When someone gives us a kick–scorns us, or mocks our faith or modest dress–are we really dead? Do we lie in a pitiful heap, dead to the world? Or do we snarl and bite? Perhaps we only whimper? Do we make some weak defense or an excuse? If sin or the desires of this world attempt to arouse us, we must be completely dead with Christ. We dare not lift our heads weakly and gaze longingly at the passions which have aroused us.

If we are truly crucified with Christ, then we are also risen with Him. We are no longer a dead dog. We are a new creature, alive through Jesus Christ. Through the Holy Spirit, He will give us power to remain dead to sin and the desires this world offers us. He will also give us grace to answer men who ask the reason of the hope that dwells within us.

Let us earnestly seek the face of the Lord that we may honestly say with Paul, "I die daily."

Edward Martin, Alta Vista, IA

Wise men are not always silent, but know when to be.

Bible Reading: 2 Timothy 3

One Year Bible Reading Plan: John 12:20-50, 2 Chronicles 4-6

But be ye doers of the word, and not hearers only, deceiving your own selves.
- JAMES 1:22

FOLLOW THE INSTRUCTIONS

Purchases often come with instructions that explain how to install, assemble, or operate the object. The instructions help us get the best use out of the purchased product. In eager anticipation of using the new item, it is easy to disregard the instructions and proceed in our own way.

If we don't pay attention to the instructions, it is possible that we miss an important part in the use of the new product. If we end up with difficulty and frustration, we need to carefully follow the supplied instructions. They can usually help us solve the problem.

Meditating on this thought, I wondered if we are guilty of doing this in our spiritual lives. We also have a Book of instructions to guide us through life. It is the Bible. If we carefully follow the guidelines in this Book, we can proceed through life with fewer problems than if we only follow our own selfish inclinations. Although we cannot expect to have a life of ease with no problems, it is for our benefit to be well acquainted with the Bible. If we thoroughly read the manual we receive with a purchased item, we will have a better idea where to look if we have problems or questions about the product. This principle also applies to our spiritual lives. If we are familiar with the "Manual of Life," we will also know where to look for help and encouragement in times of need.

The Bible will definitely help us through life here on this earth, but ultimately it will guide us into knowledge and faith in Jesus Christ. When we have attained this, we will also have hope and a promise to be able to enter into eternity with God and our Savior Jesus Christ.

Darrell Frey, Drayton, ON

If all else fails—read the instructions!

June 2

Bible Reading: 1 Corinthians 11:1-16, Ephesians 5:22-33
One Year Bible Reading Plan: John 13:1-17, 2 Chronicles 7-9

For this cause ought the woman to have power on her head because of the angels.

- 1 CORINTHIANS 11:10

CHRISTIAN WOMEN'S HEADSHIP COVERING

Christian women have, for centuries, practiced the symbolic covering of their heads. But gradually the practice has been lost by all but a few churches. Some years ago I traveled in Europe and visited different churches in Romania, Ukraine, and Poland. In the churches we visited, nearly all the women wore a covering, regardless of what church they belonged to. Although practice has changed in our country, the scriptural significance remains, and the blessings of wearing the covering are abundant.

The woman's covering, symbolizing God's order of headship, is not only a suggestion, but a command of authority. As this order of authority is exercised in a God-fearing way, it produces harmony, blessing, and peace. It is not, as some say, just a Mennonite belief. It is the Word of God. "The things that I write unto you are the commandments of the Lord" (1 Corinthians 14:37). Some may say this command was given only to the Corinthians, but Paul says in 1 Corinthians 1:2 that he is not only writing to the Corinthians but to all that in every place call upon the name of the Lord, Jesus Christ.

There is special protection available to women who willingly wear this sign of authority on their head. No woman is safe in today's sinful society apart from her submission to God's order of headship and her visible evidence of being subject to that order.

This is a call for Christian women everywhere to return to this biblical practice. And may those who already practice it be strengthened in their convictions and be able to teach it to the next generation.

Eli A. Yoder, Stuarts Draft, VA

Where the need is greatest, let us be found gladly obeying the Master's command.

June 3

Bible Reading: Jeremiah 17:1-10

One Year Bible Reading Plan: John 13:18-38, 2 Chronicles 10–12

And be found in him, not having mine own righteousness, which is of the law, but that which is through the faith of Christ, the righteousness which is of God by faith.

- PHILIPPIANS 3:9

AND BE FOUND IN HIM

I was a twelve-year-old boy at my older sister's wedding. I wanted to be somebody, so I asked my brother to buy a pack of cigarettes. I thought no one would find out, but I forgot to take them out of my pocket Monday morning. Of course, Monday was wash day, and Mother always checked our pockets. I didn't hear anything for about a week and was beginning to think that I slipped through.

One evening our family was sitting on the back porch and Dad asked me to run out and shut off the gas engine that we used to pump water. I ran out to the barn and back quite fast. When I came back to the porch Dad asked, "Allan, where did you get those cigarettes?" I was so taken aback in being asked in such a way that I could not think of an alibi. So I told my father where I got them. I will never forget that moment as long as my mind is clear. I was found out, but not as I wanted to be.

My mother used to say, "Would you want to be doing what you are doing when Jesus returns?" How will it be when we stand before God and are found out? If we still have our own righteousness, it will be as filthy rags. The righteousness we want to be found in is of God by faith. I cannot think of a worse experience than to stand before God and be found out like I was before my father. I was speechless! How much more so on the Judgment Day if I am not found in Him?

Allan A. Miller, Sarcoxie, MO

How will I be found on the Judgment Day?

June 4

Bible Reading: Genesis 18

One Year Bible Reading Plan: John 14, 2 Chronicles 13-16

For I know him, that he will command his children and his household after him, and they shall keep the way of the Lord, to do justice and judgment.
- GENESIS 18:19

FOR I KNOW HIM

Abraham. The very mention of his name reminds us of a man of faithfulness. His very character speaks of nobility and integrity. The first eight verses of our Bible reading show us he was a man given to hospitality. James 2:23 speaks of him as "the friend of God." There are some characteristics of the life of Abraham that are so desperately needed today.

Abraham made it his responsibility to promote godly living. He taught his family to "keep the way of the Lord, to do justice and judgment," that is, to be serious and devout in their worship of God and be honest in all their dealings. I see a man who prayed with his family and taught them as a man of knowledge, careful in his instructions and authority.

Abraham was also considering his posterity. He was not only concerned for those in his immediate household, but also for those who would come after him "to keep the way of the Lord." He realized that he would not always be here.

That is what God is looking for in our time—men who walk like Abraham, who are willing to rise to the challenge and be faithful in word and deed. He needs men who are willing to shoulder responsibility and put their hand to the plow. God can be depended upon, and He is looking for those who are also dependable, reliable, and stable.

Can God say of us that we are commanding our children and our household after us, to keep the way of the Lord? May that be our goal!

Robert Burkholder, Brooksville, KY

Rise up, O men of God.

June 5

Bible Reading: John 15:1-16

One Year Bible Reading Plan: John 15, 2 Chronicles 17-19

Abide in me, and I in you. As the branch cannot bear fruit of itself, except it abide in the vine; no more can ye, except ye abide in me.
- JOHN 15:4

ABIDING IN THE VINE

When I was young, my father grafted buds into trees. I enjoyed watching him make the careful cut on the little tree. Then he would carefully open the bark and place the fragile little bud inside and gently close up and wrap it with just the little bud peeping out. After years of abiding together, the bud would be firmly connected.

To abide in the Lord is to continue loving and serving Him and obeying His word on a daily basis. He abides in us by letting His word be in our hearts and minds. "If ye abide in me, and my words abide in you" (John 15:7a). "This is the covenant that I will make with them after those days, saith the Lord, I will put my laws into their hearts, and in their minds will I write them" (Hebrews 10:16).

Our key verse states that a branch cannot bear fruit unless it is connected to the vine. It also gives us a clear description of our condition if we are not grafted to Him.

Branches that bear fruit are purged to make them bear more fruit. Purging is to cut off unwanted or unneeded parts. Maybe we have notions or passions that need to be cut off so we can bear more fruit. The Lord may cut off the notion of self-dependence and show us that He wants all our cares by bringing us to total helplessness. "Casting all your care upon him; for he careth for you" (1 Peter 5:7).

May we abide in the Vine, allow ourselves to be purged, and bear much fruit.

Johnny Miller, Loudonville, OH

Abide in me and I in you.

June 6

Bible Reading: Luke 18:9-14, Philippians 2:1-11

One Year Bible Reading Plan: John 16:1-15, 2 Chronicles 20-22

Humble yourselves therefore under the mighty hand of God,
that he may exalt you in due time.

- 1 PETER 5:6

HUMILITY

In 1 Peter 5:5 we are told that we should be clothed with humility. It could mean our clothes, but it probably means the attitude people see in our daily walk of life. It may be good to ask ourselves the following questions: What is my response to authority at home, in the church, or in society? Do I openly accuse and discredit the church when its stand or decision differs from my opinion? How do I respond when church leaders or other brethren share a concern with me? When divisions arise in my congregation, do I quietly and earnestly work for peace even when the situation appears to be mishandled or misunderstood? In everyday situations among my brethren or associates, am I polite and courteous or am I self-centered? Am I quick to offer my opinion and advice? Am I considerate of others' schedule and habits? Am I hospitable when I am unprepared? What is my response to commendation or criticism? Am I willing to risk my own reputation and appear foolish for the benefit of another?

Pride is displeasing to the Lord and is reckoned among the abominations of the wicked. It is directly opposite of humility. In this life, though we desire this virtue, though we pursue it, though we pray for it, we will always face conflict with self. It is ingrained within us to serve self. This self needs to be crucified.

Let us pray earnestly for a meek and humble attitude.

Eli A. Yoder, Stuarts Draft, VA

Humility is the first quality of a truly great man.

June 7

Bible Reading: Exodus 14:9-31

One Year Bible Reading Plan: John 16:16-33, 2 Chronicles 23-25

Fear thou not; for I am with thee: be not dismayed; for I am thy God: I will strengthen thee; yea, I will help thee; yea, I will uphold thee with the right hand of my righteousness.

- ISAIAH 41:10

OUR RED SEA

When the children of Israel left Egypt, they soon came to the Red Sea. They were afraid, and things looked pretty helpless. This great body of water was before them, which was impossible to cross, and the Egyptians were behind them. They started to complain and blame Moses for leading them out into the wilderness to die. They were wishing to be back in Egypt again, serving the Egyptians.

What did Moses do? Was he also discouraged? No! He knew God would make a way of escape. With all the miracles God had done when He led them out of Egypt, Moses knew God would make a way. He told the people to stand still and see the salvation of the Lord. God did make a way of escape. He parted the waters, and all the people crossed on dry land. The Egyptians thought they could also cross through the great path but were drowned in the sea. The children of Israel did not have to worry about the Egyptians anymore.

Do we ever come to a Red Sea where it looks like we can't go forward anymore and the enemy is right behind us? Do we also get scared? Let us stand still, and we will see the salvation of the Lord. Just as God didn't let the Israelites down, He will not let us down. He will not destroy the enemy so we will never be tempted again, but He will always make a path through our Red Sea if we come to Him.

Daniel Miller, Dunnegan, MO

The prayer of a righteous man availeth much.

June 8

Bible Reading: Psalm 96

One Year Bible Reading Plan: John 17, 2 Chronicles 26-28

O sing unto the LORD a new song: sing unto the LORD, all the earth.

- PSALM 96:1

SING UNTO THE LORD

Numerous times in the Scriptures we are told to sing unto the Lord, especially in the Psalms and Isaiah. Singing today has shifted from good wholesome heart-expression in song to being entertained by fancy recordings.

What is sweeter music than to hear the tender voice of song from the lips of a mother in the home as she busies herself with household duties? This singing is the expression of an inner peace and contentment that prevails in her atmosphere. She is at peace with her loving husband and the children are peaceful because of controlled and loving discipline. Hence there is praise flowing from her lips to the heavenly Father.

Today many are losing their song because their minds are filled with other things. Business, debts, cares, riches, responsibilities, lusts, and other things are tying the tongue so that it will not express praise to God in song.

Some may try to muffle that inner turmoil with the blare and blast of the "box." It may even be good, sound music, but where is the heart that is filled with praise to God in song?

Songs are not only expressions of our praise to God, but they are also a means of teaching and admonishing one another. "Teaching and admonishing one another in psalms and hymns and spiritual songs, singing with grace in your hearts to the Lord" (Colossians 3:16). Certainly listening to singing is honorable, but it is good spiritual exercise to engage ourselves in songs of praise to God.

If you have lost your song, seek to be restored to that inner peace and tranquility of heart that will inspire you to a new song of praise to God. Many will see it and fear the Lord.

James Yoder, Lewisburg, PA

Sing the songs of Zion in the land of the free!

June 9

Bible Reading: Psalm 92, Revelation 22:14

One Year Bible Reading Plan: John 18:1-23, 2 Chronicles 29-31

But I am like a green olive tree in the house of God: I trust in the mercy of God for ever and ever.

- PSALM 52:8

A TREE FOR GOD

All trees have roots. If you want to completely get rid of a bad tree, you must dig it up by the roots or it may grow back. John the Baptist said, in Luke 3, that the bad trees will be destroyed by cutting the root. This is complete destruction.

God wants His people to be like good trees, bringing forth fruit for Him. What are some trees that we should be like?

In Psalm 52, after talking of evil, the writer says, "I am like a green olive tree in the house of God." To be like an olive tree speaks of beauty. An olive tree grows slowly but grows to an old age. Its fruit is for food, oil, and healing. It is easily transplanted.

Hosea 14 speaks of the fir tree or cypress; a tree of beauty—tall, evergreen, a tree for God.

In Psalm 92:12, the righteous are identified as the palm tree. Here in Belize we often see these trees used to line the driveway to a house. The palm tree is a stately tree of beauty, with leaves bursting forth from the top in praise to its Maker. According to the encyclopedia, the palm tree has at least 360 different uses. Ropes, timber, bags, baskets, and fruit are all products that can come from the palm tree.

What kind of tree am I? Do I stand straight and tall for God? Do I have fruit flowing from my life? Do I have beauty that shines from my inner being, giving praise to God?

I am blessed by three more things in Psalm 92:13-15. Those planted in God's house will flourish. They bring fruit in old age. They show that the Lord is upright, a witness to others that He is my rock.

Be a tree for God, fruitful in His kingdom. Only then will we have the right to the Tree of Life in heaven.

David Good, Punta Gorda, Belize

Be a tree for God's glory.

June 10

Bible Reading: Deuteronomy 5:29-33; 6

One Year Bible Reading Plan: John 18:24-40, 2 Chronicles 32, 33

Choose you this day whom ye will serve . . . but as for me and my house, we will serve the Lord.

- JOSHUA 24:15

HOME OF THE BLESSED

An artist sought to paint the most beautiful picture in the world. He asked a minister, "What is the most beautiful thing in the world?"

"Faith," answered the minister. "You can feel it in every church and find it at every altar."

The artist searched further and found a young bride. Upon asking her the same question, she replied, "Love. Love turns poverty into riches, sweetens tears, and makes much of little. Without it there is no beauty."

The artist made the same inquiry of a soldier who answered, "Peace is the most beautiful thing in the world. War is the ugliest. Wherever you find peace you will find beauty."

Here I have faith, love, and peace. The artist thought. *How can I paint them?* Entering his house, he found faith in the eyes of his children and love in the eyes of his wife. In his home was the peace and love that faith builds. So he painted the most beautiful thing in the world and called it "Home."

Home is where each cheerfully lives for the others and all live for Christ. The husband is the divinely ordained head of the home. If he fails in leading the family in Bible reading and prayer, he is failing his wife and children.

Every home needs the Way, the Truth, and the Life. Without the Way there is no going, without the Truth there is no knowing, and without the Life there is no living.

Eli A. Yoder, Stuarts Draft, VA

A house is built by human hands, but a home is built by human hearts.

June 11

Bible Reading: Philippians 2:1-18

One Year Bible Reading Plan: John 19:1-22, 2 Chronicles 34–36

The sons of God, without rebuke, in the midst of a crooked and perverse nation, among whom ye shine as lights in the world.

- PHILIPPIANS 2:15

GLOW WORMS

I walked out into the early morning darkness. It was warm and the earth was moist. Then I saw them–soft little glowing lights in the otherwise dark earth. I did not know what they were, but my heart warmed to them. I turned my flashlight on but could see nothing. I scooped up some dirt and held it up for closer inspection. Then I saw the small grub wriggling in the loose dirt. As I put it down and went on my way, I saw many more.

My mind went to this verse: "For the eyes of the Lord run to and fro throughout the whole earth to shew himself strong in the behalf of them whose heart is perfect toward him" (2 Chronicles 16:9).

What does God see when He looks down on this dark, sin-cursed earth? Does He see lots of soft glowing lights that warm His heart, or are those lights too rare? I may not be a light that the entire world can see, but I can be a small glow worm for God in my place in life. If I shine in my place, you shine in your place, and many millions of others shine who have the glow that radiates from the love of God within, we can make a difference.

Someday when we are all gathered together and we burst forth into that glorious light of the Son of God, we can together glow in the presence of the Sun of righteousness for all eternity. What glorious beauty!

Come; let us stand united in this effort of being glow worms for God.

Wilmer S. Beachy, Liberty KY

Youth and beauty fade; integrity endures forever.

June 12

Bible Reading: Luke 21:34-38, Matthew 24:36-51

One Year Bible Reading Plan: John 19:23-42, Ezra 1, 2

Lord, Lord, open to us.

- MATTHEW 25:11

REMAINING WATCHFUL

Rather than being terrified by what is happening in our world, we should confidently await Christ's return to bring justice and restoration to His people. Christ is coming again, and we need to watch and be spiritually fit. We must work faithfully at the tasks God has given us. Don't let your mind and spirit be dulled by careless living. Don't let the problems of life weigh you down. Be ready to move at God's command.

The time of Christ's return is God the Father's secret to be revealed when He wills. No one can predict by Scripture or science the exact day of Jesus' return. We need preparation, not calculation. We spend months planning for a wedding, the birth of a baby, or the purchase of a home. Do we place the same importance on preparing for Christ's return? His return is the most important event in our lives. We dare not postpone preparing for it because we don't know when it will occur.

Christ's second coming will be swift and sudden. There will be no opportunity for last-minute repentance or bargaining. The choice we have already made will determine our eternal destiny. Jesus asks us to spend the waiting time taking care of His people and doing His work here on earth, both within the church and outside it. This is the best way to prepare for Christ's return.

Marvin C. Hochstetler, Nappanee, IN

We need not fear the future as long as we hold the hand of Him who knows the future.

June 13

Bible Reading: Jonah 4

One Year Bible Reading Plan: John 20, Ezra 3–5

For the wrath of man worketh not the righteousness of God.

- JAMES 1:20

GOD'S PERFECTING WORK IN US

Jonah had just experienced a miraculous demonstration of God's mercy through deliverance from the belly of the fish. Yet he was very angry to see mercy extended to the entire city of Nineveh. How ungrateful! Did Jonah not have a valid reason to be angry? The Ninevites were not God's chosen people as the Jews were. They did not deserve such mercy after all their wickedness. This made Jonah look like a fool. After he had prophesied imminent destruction, it wasn't going to happen at all!

A self-focused person will:

Become angry (verse 1) when things don't go his way. When things don't turn out like he thinks they should, he lashes out in frustration. If it is God's work, we are His servants. We will do what's right according to His bidding and leave the outcome with Him.

Blame God (verse 2) for not holding up His end of the deal. Jonah points an accusing finger at God for his anger. If we are God's servants, we will rejoice to see His work prosper, even if we are made to look like a fool in the process.

Become depressed and discouraged (verse 3) even to the point of wishing to die, feeling totally worthless. When we fight against God, we always lose. True worth and joy in life is found in submission and service to God.

Be extremely moody (verses 6-8), angry when things go against him, and ecstatic when things go well. True peace and stability is found in tuning in, by faith, to God's eternal purposes rather than focusing on the adverse effects of the present.

That little worm or that vehement east wind was custom prepared and lovingly sent our way for an eternal purpose. Will we lash out at it in defiance? Or will we pause to see the God behind the scenes, perfecting His eternal work?

Nathan Kreider, Squaw Valley, CA

Self creates the darkest eclipse of God's truth shining into our hearts.

June 14

Bible Reading: Revelation 3

One Year Bible Reading Plan: John 21, Ezra 68

Wherefore he saith, Awake thou that sleepest, and arise from the dead, and Christ shall give thee light.

- EPHESIANS 5:14

DROWSY CHRISTIANS

One day as I was driving home from Harrisonburg, I was becoming a bit drowsy. Then all of a sudden there was a stopped car in front of me. A car ahead wanted to make a left turn. I suppose my eyes closed for just a little bit, but a little bit was too long. I stepped on the brakes and turned to avoid hitting the car. But I was too close to stop so suddenly, and I hit the car.

Isn't that the way it is in our Christian walk of life? Sometimes we get drowsy and the first thing we know, we do something we know we shouldn't have done. Or maybe we neglect to do something we know we should have done. We only did it because we were spiritually drowsy. If we keep on being sleepy, we are bound to have some more accidents. When we do have a spiritual accident and do something wrong, we should wake up, make our wrongs right, and Jesus will forgive us. I had the pickup taken to a garage to have it repaired. Now it looks as good as new. I was glad nobody was hurt. Isn't it wonderful that when we have a spiritual accident, we can also have our soul repaired and restored?

I like the words in Romans 5:1, "Therefore being justified by faith, we have peace with God through our Lord Jesus Christ." Being justified is so wonderful. If we make our wrongs right and ask Jesus to forgive us and live for Him, it will be just as if we had not sinned. What a wonderful promise for a sinner who has decided to follow Jesus.

Eli A. Yoder, Stuarts Draft, VA

The Devil is never too busy to rock the cradle of a sleeping saint.

Bible Reading: Psalm 1

One Year Bible Reading Plan: Acts 1, Ezra 9, 10

For the Lord knoweth the way of the righteous:
but the way of the ungodly shall perish.

- PSALM 1:6

THE WAY SHALL PERISH

"Dad, are you sure this is the right road?" I was having my misgivings as soon as the narrow road had a grassy middle. Then we entered a woods. The ladies with us were sure we would get stuck in the muddy spot ahead, but we pulled through. When we got to the other side of the woods, the path was gone and we had no more direction. We found ourselves in a hay field.

We were in northeast Kansas, the boyhood home of my father. Fortunately for us, a farmer was there bringing up large bales of hay.

"Where is Glenlock?" I asked him.

"Oh, you are half a mile too far east." The farmer had a quizzical look on his face as we turned around, and then he noticed the plates on our van. We could easily retrace our way, and soon found old familiar landmarks of Glenlock because we had someone to give us directions.

This reminded me of the way of the ungodly which perishes. It comes to naught and disappears so that they have no more direction. They flounder in uncertainties, following the crowd to an aimless nowhere. They lose all sense of direction, become lost, and spiral downward.

They need someone to point them back to the right way. Can we fulfill that calling to be guiding lights for the lost, helping someone find direction and life? The world needs it.

Wilmer S. Beachy, Liberty, KY

He who takes the wrong direction has a long road ahead.

June 16

Bible Reading: Proverbs 1:10-33

One Year Bible Reading Plan: Acts 2:1-13, Nehemiah 1-3

To day if ye will hear his voice, harden not your hearts, as in the provocation, in the day of temptation in the wilderness.

- HEBREWS 3:7,8

TODAY IS OUR OPPORTUNITY

Jim was a lad who had the opportunity to attend a mission Sunday school in a nearby village. He did not have Christian parents, but through these Bible classes he learned about the creation, Noah and the flood, Joseph and his forgiveness, Daniel in the lion's den, and Christ's birth, death for the sins of man, and the resurrection. He enjoyed these teachings and looked forward to being picked up Sunday mornings for church.

He was blessed with many wonderful times of Bible study, but as he reached his teen years he began to close doors to these spiritual opportunities.

In my early years of marriage I met up with Jim where I worked. I did not know the young man, but had several opportunities to discuss spiritual things with him. He had an increasingly mocking attitude towards the Bible and Christianity.

When I told my wife about him, she recognized him as the same boy from Sunday school. How our hearts went out to him with a desire to help. We often prayed for Jim.

Our ways parted, and we heard nothing about Jim for some time. Then one day the sad news came. Jim had died in a drunken state. How sad! Our hearts ached. Jim had no more opportunity to get right with God.

If you hear God's voice today, don't harden your heart. Now is your opportunity to be right with God!

David E. Huber, Vanessa, ON

Only one life 'twill soon be past, only what's done for Christ will last.

June 17

Bible Reading: Luke 12:22-31

One Year Bible Reading Plan: Acts 2:14-47, Nehemiah 4–6

And having food and raiment let us be therewith content.
- 1 TIMOTHY 6:8

GOD PROVIDES

A person must wonder sometimes if the words of Jesus in Luke 12:22 are realistic. After all, shouldn't we be concerned about tomorrow? Suppose we get laid off from our job. What if we get sick? What if we have a large financial loss, like a fire or an accident? Isn't the fear of not having enough food to eat or enough clothes to wear one of the greatest fears a person can have? There are no words in any language that can cause more anxiety than the question, "What if?"

As we think or say these words, we begin to imagine one bad possibility, then another, and pretty soon both bad possibilities together. We seem to forget that our needs have always been supplied in the past and that we have enough for today. Look at our key verse. We are to be content if we have food and clothes. Why are we fretting or uneasy that our well may run dry tomorrow? While it is wise to plan for the future, we must also say, "If the Lord will" (James 4:15). Even though our well is full today, the imagined thirst for tomorrow is one thirst that is unquenchable. Jesus taught that worrying about the future is in vain. We shouldn't be worried by what might happen tomorrow. The imaginary need of tomorrow is one need that God cannot meet.

As Christian people, let us commit everything into God's hands and not worry about tomorrow. Our heavenly Father knows that we have need of these things. If we first seek the kingdom of God, all these things will be given to us. "I have been young, and now am old; yet have I not seen the righteous forsaken, nor his seed begging bread" (Psalm 37:25).

Daniel Miller, Dunnegan, MO

Worry is interest paid on trouble before it is due.

June 18

Bible Reading: Matthew 25:31-46

One Year Bible Reading Plan: Acts 3, Nehemiah 7, 8

My little children, let us not love in word, neither in tongue;
but in deed and in truth.

- 1 JOHN 3:18

HAVE YOU ANSWERED THE CALL?

The call comes every day and in many different ways. It might be a desperate plea from a person in distress. A plane or ship is going down and radios an SOS to anyone who can hear. A house is on fire, or an ill person's life is in mortal danger, and a concerned loved one quickly dials 911. Police rush to the scene of a potential suicide where a stricken mother reports that her son is about to use his gun on himself.

Our local and national governments care about the lives of their civilians. There are many different government agencies such as police, firefighters, or coast guard that are set aside for the preservation of human life. There are obviously many people that care about the lives of others–people who are willing to lay their lives on the line. Do we Christians have such a care for others?

Imagine with me that a desperate person dials 911 but receives no answer or is told to wait while the operator finishes his dinner. Imagine the consternation, the public outcry. Yet this very thing happens in America every day. Not with our government, but with our churches.

One of the primary reasons Christians have been placed on this earth is to help others. In Matthew 5 Jesus went so far as to say that whether or not we help the needy can determine the destiny of our eternal souls. Tragedy is all around us, yet so often we turn a deaf ear. All because the situation is too messy or it requires too much of our precious time. There is so much being left undone in a world where so much could be done for Christ. The call comes every day. If you listen closely, you can hear it. Heed it today!

Craig Eicher, Butler, IN

If God is love, what does that make His children?

Bible Reading: Acts 9:32-43

One Year Bible Reading Plan: Acts 4:1-22, Nehemiah 9–11

Naked, and ye clothed me. I was sick, and ye visited me: I was in prison, and ye came unto me.

- MATTHEW 25:36

WOMEN OF BLESSING

When we follow the Bible teaching that men should lead out, it may seem that our women do not have enough to do. Perhaps we are tempted to dwell on denied privileges. We might think that men are more privileged or that their place is more important. Some women have decided not to stay within the parameters that God has placed for them, thinking that many of their capabilities and talents will lie dormant or be lost.

Dorcas stands out in her resolve that her placement in life, by an all-knowing God, was by design and would not lessen her usefulness. She discovered that her life was enhanced. Instead of succumbing to defiance, faultfinding, and idleness, Dorcas busied herself with good works and alms deeds. The widows were blessed, the cause of Christ was furthered, and God was glorified.

Women like Dorcas fill a needful place in the church. The service they perform is done best from within their capacity as godly women, adorning themselves with good works (1 Timothy 2:10). They teach the younger women to be keepers at home, to love their husbands, etc. They help the widows and the fatherless. They minister to the needy and serve those who minister in the Gospel. Their children are blessed with the positive influence of a godly mother. When women serve in this way, they can maintain their feminine distinction and graceful charm. Society is then blessed with their lives. On the other hand, when we interfere with God's role for men and women, we lose His blessing and guidance.

Roger Rangai, Lott, TX

If there were more mothers like Mary, there would be more men with the spirit of Christ.

June 20

Bible Reading: James 1

One Year Bible Reading Plan: Acts 4:23-37, Nehemiah 12, 13

But the fruit of the Spirit is love, joy, peace, longsuffering, gentleness, goodness, faith, meekness, temperance: against such there is no law.
- GALATIANS 5:22-23

THE GOD OF ALL COMFORT

Someone was once talking to an intelligent agnostic, and wished to influence him to become a Christian. After listening politely for awhile, the agnostic said, "Well, if you Christians want to make us agnostics inclined to look into your religion, you must try to be more comfortable in the possession of it yourselves. The Christians I meet seem to be the most uncomfortable people anywhere around. They seem to carry their religion as a man carries a headache. He does not want to get rid of his head, but at the same time, it is very uncomfortable to have it. And I, for one, do not care to have that kind of religion."

Is that the way we appear to the unbelievers who are watching us? Are we living our Christian life like it is a burden?

A religion whose fruits of the Spirit are love, joy, and peace should have the opposite effect and develop a comfortable, joyful Christian. It should be a life that the non-Christian can see is worth living. The fruit of the Spirit should drive out the fruits of doubt, fear, unrest, conflict, and discomfort of every kind. We can trust our earthly friends and be comfortable in their companionship. Then why can we not trust our heavenly Father and be comfortable and happy in His companionship and service? Jesus said, "My yoke is easy, and my burden is light" (Matthew 11:30).

Daniel Miller, Dunnegan, MO

May the God of comfort be our companion.

June 21

Bible Reading: 2 Thessalonians 2

One Year Bible Reading Plan: Acts 5:1-16, Esther 1–3

Now our Lord Jesus Christ himself, and God, even our Father, which . . .
hath given us everlasting consolation . . .

- 2 THESSALONIANS 2:16

BEWARE—DANGER IS NEAR

I am glad for the everlasting consolation of God. Without that
consolation, I would be shaken in mind (verse 2) or troubled by the
mystery of iniquity (verse 7). How would it be possible to withstand
such a foe?

This foe has a wide array of tools to work in us the works of darkness.
Our Bible reading displays some of his tools and labels: man of sin,
son of perdition, he opposes God, exalts himself, with all power and
signs and lying wonders, deceivableness of unrighteousness.

A neighbor asked me one spring to look at his maple tree. It was a
straight, tall, young tree but no leaves were appearing. "What could be
wrong?" he asked. There was no sign of damaged bark or cold injury.
I was baffled. He trimmed the tree and fed it with enriched mulch. The
tree sent out a few bunches of leaves, but I could see it was dying.

In late September the neighbor again stopped me on the road. He
asked me what the large wasps were and what they were doing to his
tree. We had the answer to the dying tree puzzle. They were pigeon
horntails. These wasp-like insects were drilling into the base of the
maple and laying eggs with their tools of trade, a special ovipositor
(egg-laying organ). The larvae had turned around inside under the
bark and were killing the tree. The insects even inject fungi spores to
decay the wood so it will be softer for the larvae.

Satan also has his tools of trade. He can inject the seeds of
bitterness, hatred, moral impurity, rebellion, or other sins into us. In
verse 15 it says, "Brethren, stand fast."

Were it not for the consolation of God, many of those seeds would
sprout and the mystery of iniquity would take a heavy toll on us.

James M. Beachy, Sugarcreek, OH

The consolation of God is not a mystery.

June 22

Bible Reading: Ephesians 4:11-32

One Year Bible Reading Plan: Acts 5:17-42, Esther 46

Wherefore, my beloved brethren, let every man be swift to hear, slow to speak, slow to wrath.

- JAMES 1:19

A HARMLESS WEAKNESS?

Do we look at bad temper as a harmless weakness? Perhaps we say, "My mom or dad was that way too."

The Bible condemns anger as one of the most destructive elements of human nature. Some people quickly lose their temper and say and do things that are not fitting for Christians. The account of the prodigal son shows a good example of this. The prodigal son's brother was angry, jealous, self-righteous, and proud. Such attitudes have no place in the kingdom of heaven. It would make it a miserable place for others. We all have a temper, but with a renewed spirit, we need to keep it under control.

When Moses came down from the mountain and saw the people worshipping the golden calf in Exodus 32:19, his anger waxed hot. When Jesus saw the moneychangers in the temple, He made a scourge of small cords, drove out the animals, and overthrew the money tables. Anger at sin may sometimes be right. People get angry in order to set wrong things right. In Ephesians 4:26 right after it says, "Be ye angry," it says, "sin not." We need to remember, when we get angry at sin, not to do more harm than the sin itself.

Some may try to justify anger by saying, "Temper doesn't last long." A tornado doesn't last long either, but it can do a lot of damage. Let us keep our temper under control so we can be a light to the world.

Eli A. Yoder, Stuarts Draft, VA

Action powered by anger can cause terrible destruction.

June 23

Bible Reading: Matthew 6:5-15, John 4

One Year Bible Reading Plan: Acts 6,

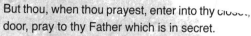

But thou, when thou prayest, enter into thy closet,
door, pray to thy Father which is in secret.
- MATTHEW 6:6

GOOD CONNECTIONS WITH GOD

"Hello . . . wondering . . . bring . . . yesterday . . . when . . . come . . ."
It is hard to understand a message on a cell phone when you only hear a word here and there with pauses in between. You say, "I don't understand," and the caller tries again with the same results. Unless something changes, you might as well hang up.

Perhaps you are the one on the cell phone. The road dips down between two wooded hills and you start losing your connection in the middle of an important conversation.

I was reminded of these poor connections when I saw construction starting on a new tower locally. Without towers and wires, telephones cannot work. Think of all the time and money spent to put wire in the ground and to build towers to make telephones work properly.

Another communication line is available. If we are sincere, this line is not choppy like a bad cell phone connection. We don't have to worry about losing connection when we go through a valley. We will not get a busy signal when we want to talk with God. The line is called prayer. We can pray to God anytime. He is always there to hear and answer us.

Matthew 7:7 says, "Ask, and it shall be given you; seek, and ye shall find; knock and it shall be opened unto you." There are no wires needed and no cell phone towers to make the connection with God. If we yield our lives to Him for His service, the connection is made.

Titus D. Coblentz, Cincinnati, IA

Prayer is the Christian's vital breath—our connection with God.

Reading: Psalm 31:1-14; 73:23-26

Year Bible Reading Plan: Acts 7:1-19, Job 13

Trust in the Lord with all thine heart; and lean not unto thine own understanding. In all thy ways acknowledge him, and he shall direct thy paths.
- PROVERBS 3:5-6

IS OUR GUIDE TRUSTWORTHY?

Many serious mountain climbers dream of climbing to the top of Mt. Everest, the highest peak on earth. In May, 2004, a sixty-nine-year-old American doctor was getting ready to attempt the climb. He would be the oldest American to accomplish the feat. He had hired a guide from another country who claimed to have climbed to the peak several years before (a claim he later denied). The doctor had to depend on a trustworthy guide, and this man seemed to be a good choice.

The climb proved to be a struggle for the elderly doctor, and he was soon having doubts about his young guide who often left him behind in their climbs. After a long, hard climb, they finally reached the "top of the world."

The doctor was very weak from altitude sickness. They soon began their descent again, but he was getting weaker fast, and darkness was coming. The guide, fearing they would both perish if he stayed to help, left the faltering man on the icy mountain.

Late that night the guide reached a camp where he gladly accepted a tent. He made no mention of the elderly doctor he had left on the icy peak. The doctor died there during the night.

Isn't that the way Satan works? He gladly helps us achieve worldly honor and fame, but when we need help, he has nothing to offer. He leaves us in despair.

As we climb the mountains of life, let us choose the Lord for our Guide. We can trust Him to safely guide us to the end.

Michael Hershberger, Millersburg, OH

For this God is our God for ever and ever: he will be our guide even unto death. - Psalm 48:14

Bible Reading: Romans 12

One Year Bible Reading Plan: Acts 7:20-43, Job 4–6

Looking diligently lest any man fail of the grace of God; lest any root of bitterness springing up trouble you, and thereby many be defiled.
- HEBREWS 12:15

WEEDS IN THE CHURCH

As I was pulling weeds out of the flowerpots where I work, I thought of similarities between the flowerpots and the church. Quite a few pots had dandelions in them, sometimes two or three. Often the roots went straight down to the bottom of the pot, but they were usually not hard to pull out either. They had a straight root, without many roots branching out.

The other day I came to a weed that was almost impossible to pull out. I believe it was a ragweed. Not only did it have deep roots, but the roots were all over the pot. To get it out, some of the flower plants came out too.

Sometimes there are small problems in the church. When the problems are properly taken care of in time, it is often not hard to get that weed out of the flowerpot (church). However, sometimes the trouble may not be noticed, or maybe the problems are just neglected for awhile. Then they may become like the ragweed and spread throughout the church. If we properly deal with church weeds at this stage, the whole church will be affected. Some of the flowers (members) of the church may even be damaged or pulled up with the weeds.

Let us be careful that we are not like the ragweed in the church, nor even like the dandelion. Let us be like the flower.

Eli A. Yoder, Stuarts Draft, VA

Church members are either caterpillars or pillars. The pillars hold up the church, the caterpillars just crawl in and out.

June 26

Bible Reading: Luke 10:25-37

One Year Bible Reading Plan: Acts 7:44-60, Job 7-9

And he said, He that showed mercy on him. Then said Jesus unto him,
Go, and do thou likewise.

- LUKE 10:37

THE GOOD SAMARITAN

A lawyer came to Jesus hoping to trap Him. Lawyers in Jesus' day
studied the law and kept it to the letter, seldom showing compassion or
mercy for those who were hurting. This lawyer came with a legitimate
question. "What must I do to have eternal life?"

Jesus prompted the lawyer to answer his own question. Love the
Lord with all your . . .

• heart. The heart is the central organ of our being. It pumps 70
times a minute. With each beat, we should love and serve our Lord.

• soul. God breathed into Adam and he became a living soul. With
each breath we breathe, we must love and serve our God.

• strength. We must be willing to use the talents God has given us
to God's glory.

• mind. Let our brain, which gives our body signals, be controlled
by the Spirit.

• and thy neighbor as thyself.

"Who is my neighbor?"

The priest and the Levite were more interested in themselves
than in taking care of the beaten man. The Samaritan showed love,
compassion, and mercy. He bound up the man's wounds, brought him
to the inn, and even paid the bill.

The lawyer was humbled. It was not a Jew helping a Jew, but a
Samaritan helping a Jew who had been ignored by his fellow Jews.
The Samaritan had love for the man who hated him. We imagine that
by the time Jesus was done, the lawyer's head was bowed and his
shoulders slumped. Jesus told him, "Go, and do thou likewise."

Jesus' answer reaches down to us today. We need to help people
in whatever way we can.

Jason Schlabach, Sugarcreek, OH

Love thy neighbor as thyself.

June 27

Bible Reading: Psalm 34

One Year Bible Reading Plan: Acts 8:1-25, Job 10-12

And let us not be weary in well doing: for in due season we shall reap, if we faint not.

- GALATIANS 6:9

DOES GOD GET TIRED?

I am tired of people asking me for money. Last week the mason who fixed the drain in the shower wanted his pay before he earned it. The day before yesterday, the neighbor lady sent her son to borrow 100 lempiras to buy medicine. Today my friend Gregorio wanted to borrow money to pay his water bill. I wouldn't be surprised if someone would come tomorrow for help to buy some sugar for his coffee.

It is not that I don't like to help people. I like when my neighbor tells me, "God will repay you" after I have supplied his need. (If you decipher that, it means that my neighbor isn't planning to repay me.) I am thoroughly enjoying the rich rewards of a bountiful God. Why should I be frustrated when my neighbors ask for help?

What if God would get tired of my requests? I ask Him every day for health and happiness, courage and compassion, food and friends. I plead with Him to protect my children, encourage my brethren, and save my ungodly neighbors. I beg Him to bless His church and send more missionaries to His harvest fields. Don't you think He must be overwhelmed?

I praise God for His patience and love. I thank Him for never being too busy to listen to my petitions. I pray, "Lord forgive me for my resentment and selfishness. Help me to love my neighbor as myself."

Joel Showalter, Choluteca, Honduras

Ask and ye shall receive.

June 28

Bible Reading: Psalm 46; 47:1-2

One Year Bible Reading Plan: Acts 8:26-40, Job 13-15

God is our refuge and strength, a very present help in trouble.

- PSALM 46:1

A HELP IN TROUBLE

On November 15, 2004, we were involved in a serious accident. Eight adults and seven children were traveling back to Masaya, Nicaragua from Costa Rica after attending an ordination there. Sadly, the four-year-old son of Myron Diller died at the scene from head injuries. My wife had both legs broken, and one of mine was broken, too. Brother Myron was seriously injured. But what I want to write about is the help God gave us at that time.

I was sitting on the blacktop, not able to stand, nor able to help free my wife from the wreckage. My mind went to God and to my Savior, Jesus. I prayed to Him Whom I knew could help more than I could. The peace and consolation that came to my heart was beyond comprehension. God indeed was my refuge. He was the place that provided protection and the place from whence I received strength at that time, as well as many times since. He gave me the strength to sing several songs as my wife was moaning and subconsciously saying she was going to die.

What joy in my heart to know our sins were under the blood of Jesus! If we were to leave this life, we had the assurance of being at peace with God. We can truly say, "God is our refuge and strength, a very present help in trouble."

Allan A. Miller, Sarcoxie, MO

You can better appreciate the worth of an anchor when you are in a storm.

June 29

Bible Reading: Psalm 119:98-128

One Year Bible Reading Plan: Acts 9:1-22, Job 16-18

Thou through thy commandments hast made me wiser than mine enemies: for they are ever with me.

- PSALM 119:98

AM I THINKING RIGHT?

"I'm not sure how to feel about that."

"It's hard to know what I should do."

"I wish I knew."

"If only God would audibly tell me what I should do!"

Probably all of us have made such comments as the pressures, problems, and questions of life have rained upon us. At times we aren't sure just what to do or how to think about matters.

Life can seem complex and situations challenging. We are bombarded with secular wisdom, desires of our flesh, and the powers of Satan. Then we may wish for a personal interview with God to find answers to everything. We long to know exactly how things are and how they should be.

Can we know what the truth is? Is there something that holds all the answers? How can we know that the way we think is right?

Christians are the most privileged people on earth in that they serve the Creator, God, and His Son, Jesus Christ. God has left His Word with us as a manual for all of our questions. When we base all our beliefs on God's Word, we can be confident that we are on the right road.

Instead of, "I'm not sure how to feel about that," we can say, "The Bible will tell me how to feel (or think) about that." "I wish I knew" is replaced with, "God knows, and if I need to know, He will show me." When life becomes challenging, let's ask, "What does the Bible say?"

The Bible contains solutions for every problem ever encountered by mankind. Its message is so simple—its solutions so effective. A God of love would never leave His children without answers. Nor would He tell them everything, for human flesh couldn't bear it.

Marcus Troyer, Belle Center, OH

Earnestly and regularly search the Scriptures.

June 30

Bible Reading: Luke 15:11-32

One Year Bible Reading Plan: Acts 9:23-43, Job 19, 20

I say unto you, that likewise joy shall be in heaven over one sinner that repenteth, more than over ninety and nine just persons, which need no repentance.
- LUKE 15:7

THE DESERT AWAKENS

We have not had a drop of rain for two months (as of this writing). The night-time temperatures were below freezing during the second week of May, rising to the eighties during the day. And they should drop below freezing again by the end of August. Those are the extremes we deal with here in the Arizona mountains. It's no wonder the ground is bare, brown, and rocky.

Then comes a sprinkling of rain that's not even a measurable amount, and it's immediately soaked up by the cracked, thirsty ground. Yet it is the start of a miracle. Soon tiny plants poke through the hard ground, and within weeks, the desert is in full bloom. Hundreds, thousands, and then millions of bright wildflowers cover the landscape, bringing bees and butterflies. Around our property alone, I count over a hundred varieties of wildflowers: wild lilies, sunflowers, four-o-clocks, cliff rose, and more, in every color imaginable. The dry desert awakens in awesome beauty.

God can do the same thing in our lives. Nothing compares to the beauty of a sin-trapped soul released from bondage. There is a pouring out of the Spirit and new growth that is a blessing to others. But many remain in the dry, parched ground, deceived by Satan into believing that is where they are doomed to stay.

Have you accepted Christ as your personal Savior? "Behold, now is the accepted time: behold, now is the day of salvation" (2 Corinthians 6:2). Do you have hidden sin in your life? "If we confess our sins, he is faithful and just to forgive us our sins, and to cleanse us from all unrighteousness" (1 John 1:9). Do you struggle with an area of your life? "Confess your faults one to another" (James 5:16). Do you know a brother or sister who needs encouragement? Perhaps you can help bring that refreshing rain into their life.

Joseph Jones, Ash Fork, AZ

Consider the flowers—the real beauty comes only when they open.

Bible Reading: 1 Thessalonians 5:1-23

One Year Bible Reading Plan: Acts 10:1-23, Job 21, 22

Take ye heed, watch and pray: for ye know not when the time is.
- MARK 13:33

BE YE ALSO READY!

After a heart-searching sermon, the preacher gave an invitation for anyone to come forward for spiritual help. Among the number that responded was a young man named Daniel. I had the opportunity to counsel with Daniel. The Holy Spirit had convicted him of his need. I still remember those tear-filled eyes as he brought to light his besetting sins. He believed the Word of God, "if any man sin, we have an advocate with the Father, Jesus Christ the righteous" (1 John 2:1). What a comfort he experienced that day by recommitting his life to the One who had originally called him by His grace. There again he pledged faithfulness to the God of his salvation. After a time of praying together, his smile returned and his tears dried.

A few months later Dan was among several young men who donated their time and physical labor at a mission in Honduras. After a period of toil, the group decided to go to the water for a swim. They all enjoyed the splashing waves, the refreshment from the heat, and of course, the excitement.

Then suddenly Dan was in serious anguish and desperately called for help. His fellow swimmers quickly swam over to the area preparing for the rescue when he would surface. But to their dismay, only a hand and an arm became visible for an instant. After that tragic moment, no one ever saw Dan again, not even a shred of his clothes. A sea creature was to blame for that shocking and dreadful loss.

What if you had been so suddenly called to answer the summons of your Creator? Would you be ready to meet the Lord at such an unexpected moment? Would I? We have enough warnings in Scripture to ponder the fact that we will not continue here very long.

Brother Dan left a good testimony before leaving this world. Will we?

Willis Halteman, Carlisle, PA

Let us live each day as though it was our last day on earth.

July 2

Bible Reading: Matthew 7:21-29; 25:1-13

One Year Bible Reading Plan: Acts 10:24-48, Job 23-25

When once the master of the house is risen up, and hath shut to the door, and ye begin to stand without, and to knock at the door, saying, Lord, Lord, open unto us; and he shall answer and say unto you, I know you not whence you are.

- LUKE 13:25

LORD, LORD

Just recently a mother died, leaving her family behind. The mother was lying in the hospital and very weak—too weak to hold her little one-year-old child. The child was not allowed in the room with the dying mother. As someone held the child outside the mother's hospital room, he put his hands on the door crying, "Mommy, Mommy." Through the window, mother and child could see each other, but could not touch. How sad. The little child's heart was aching to be with his mommy. The mother's heart was aching to hold her child.

One day the Lord will come and there will be a great multitude crying, "Lord, Lord, open to us!" But the door will be shut, and those on the outside will never be able to enter. Today we have the opportunity to know the Lord and to help others know Him as well. Are we doing our part?

Although the mother had a yearning to hold her little one, the Lord has a greater yearning to hold His children. The Lord does not want any one of us to perish (2 Peter 3:9).

We should not be like the five foolish virgins saying, "Lord, Lord, open to us." We don't want to be too late when the Bridegroom comes.

Menno H. Eicher, Miami, OK

---

*The only sure test of true religion is the doing
of the known will of God.*

July 3

Bible Reading: Galatians 1

One Year Bible Reading Plan: Acts 11, Job 26-28

For do I now persuade men, or God? or do I seek to please men?
for if I yet pleased men, I should not be the servant of Christ.
- GALATIANS 1:10

THE SCARY MOMENT

While cleaning up around the farm on a busy summer day, we were burning trash a good distance from the barn. Suddenly the wind picked up, and in just a matter of minutes, my son shouted, "Fire!" pointing towards the old barn. Yes, way up on the roof, the old wooden shingles had caught fire. It was burning at five different spots already. It was so clear that none could be mistaken. Very quickly we all ran for the barn. With great effort we managed to save the barn from destruction.

Here we were giving all our strength to save an earthly possession. What portion has God given of His riches to save you and me from eternal fire? He gave all that He had. He made the biggest sacrifice ever to save His church from destruction.

Jesus says, "Follow me." What does He require of us? What am I doing for the lost and dying world? There are false teachings, and many are falling away from the truth. Let's take a good look at ourselves. Are we offering something that stands true and firm, unchangeable as the Scriptures? Our lives must line up with all Scripture. Are you on fire for the truth? Or is the church only on fire the day the church house burns?

Will there be blood on our hands when we see the Lord Jesus standing at the right hand of the Father? Happy and joyful we will be when we hear Him say, "Thou good and faithful servant, enter into my everlasting joy." Are you ready for Him today? If not, getting ready is the most important thing you can do today.

Ben Penner, Polonia, Manitoba

You're born into the world; let not the world be born into you.

July 4

Bible Reading: John 8:12-38

One Year Bible Reading Plan: Acts 12, Job 29, 30

If the Son therefore shall make you free, ye shall be free indeed.

- JOHN 8:36

INDEPENDENCE DAY

The United States, like many other countries, celebrates a day of independence. This is normally a day of rejoicing and celebration because of freedom from some controlling kingdom. Usually there was a price to pay for this freedom. July 4th is the day the United States of America commemorates its independence.

We too, as God's children, rejoice that we are liberated from the kingdom of Satan and sin. We were under the control of the wicked one and slaves of the kingdom of darkness. We were strangers from the covenant of promise, without God, and headed for eternal destruction.

Our Father in heaven sent His only Son into this wicked world to give His life to bring us liberty and peace from our enemy and his controlling kingdom. Jesus Christ paid the blood-price to set us free.

We have great reason to rejoice in thankfulness for the wonderful freedom we experience in the glorious liberty our Lord has wrought for us. We do not have only one day of the year to commemorate our freedom. We should remember it daily. We do not put on the show of the world. We do stand prepared to herald forth the glory of our God and Father. We lift up the banner of His Word in testimony of life and in spoken word whenever and wherever we have opportunity.

James Yoder, Lewisburg, PA

Lift up the banner of the Word for our heavenly country.

July 5

Bible Reading: Psalm 63, Isaiah 32:15-20

One Year Bible Reading Plan: Acts 13:1-24, Job 31, 32

And the work of righteousness shall be peace; and the effect of righteousness quietness and assurance for ever.

- ISAIAH 32:17

THE WARM SUN OF SUMMER

Summer–the warmest season of the year. The beautiful spring flowers are wilted. The lush green yards and pastures are turning brown. The crisp spring air has been replaced by hazy, muggy air. Would we really need summer? Wouldn't it be nice to have spring six months of the year and then fall and winter?

When the beauty, vigor, strength, and crispness of youthful lives are changed into more sore, forgetful, middle-aged lives, do we also wonder why?

If spring planting went well, the summer sun will now mature our ears of corn, watermelons, and pumpkins. It is now too late to replant. If in our vigorous spring of youth, we properly established Christian homes . . .

• If we watered our young growing children with regular church attendance–spring rains . . .

• If we fed them daily with family devotions . . .

• If we trained them with the rod of correction . . .

• If we shone on them the warm spring sunshine of love . . .

. . . they are now ready for the warm summer sun of middle-aged parents to mature them into sturdy and fruitful Christians.

Job rose up early every morning to sacrifice for his family. Fathers, we should follow the example of Job and rise up early on every warm summer day (and all other days) and pray for our growing families. On a quiet summer morning we can experience the work of peace, the effect of quietness, and assurance forever.

James M. Beachy, Sugarcreek, OH

God's mercies are new every morning. We need to be up and awake to receive them.

July 6

Let no man despise thy youth; but be thou an example of the believers, in word, in conversation, in charity, in spirit, in faith, in purity.

- 1 TIMOTHY 4:12

CHRISTIAN READING

What kind of reading do we enjoy? Do we enjoy the romantic books, or books which demonstrate shooting, bloodshed, and murder? Do we like to look at the sports section in the newspaper to see who won the last softball, football, or basketball game? We should put nothing into our minds which is condemned in God's Word.

There are churches today who are getting so involved in sports that they are dying spiritually. When sports are more important to us than studying God's Word, they become an idol to us. "Thou shalt have no other gods before me" (Exodus 20:3). "But ye are a chosen generation, a royal priesthood, an holy nation, a peculiar people; that ye should shew forth the praises of him who hath called you out of darkness into his marvelous light" (1 Peter 2:9).

With what are we filling our minds? Do the things we sing, speak, and read benefit our Christian life, or are we building on the sands of worldliness and materialism? Are we building on Jesus Christ who died for us and rose again that we might have life in Him? Jesus is now interceding for us. He wants to help each one of us to live a victorious Christian life. Let us faithfully serve and praise God in every aspect of our life.

Samuel Beachy, Belvidere, TN

What you read is what you are.

Bible Reading: Psalm 18:1-26

One Year Bible Reading Plan: Acts 14, Job 35–37

When I cry unto thee, then shall mine enemies turn back: this I know; for God is for me.

- PSALM 56:9

IF GOD BE FOR US . . .

What accolades of worship David uses to describe God! His love seems unbounded as he seeks to describe the One he loves. He employs no less than ten different ways to name the great One he worships.

David describes God as solid, safe, and strong. He delivers, protects, and guards. In God, David found his refuge.

What prompted this outburst of lavish praise? It seems David felt overwhelmed by his enemies. Death stared him in the face. Fear followed him. Distress brought him to the brink of despair. What could he do? He did what saints know how to do when facing distress and despair: He called upon the Lord and cried unto his God. Does that seem too simple and trifling? The results were anything but simple and trifling.

The verses that follow are divinely impressive. All heaven's forces were marshaled against the enemies of David and of God. Even the resources of the earth turned against them.

We should be humbled to realize that this God is all for us. That statement could be taken two ways. All of God's power is available to us, or He is dedicated to the cause of our salvation. God doesn't promise and not deliver. He doesn't invite us to call upon Him and then sit back and grin. The humble petition that goes from us to Him is never put on back-order, even if it sometimes seems like it to us.

Why does God bother? Why does He respond to us with such force against the enemy? Verse 19 simply and yet profoundly says, "He delivered me, because he delighted in me."

Our part is to live upright, holy lives and to call upon God for our help. He commands the defenses of heaven and earth to bring us through to victory. Praise His Holy Name!

Delmar R. Eby, London, KY

We need to love and live as though it all depended on us, then pray and trust as though it all depended on God.

Bible Reading: Psalm 18:24-50

One Year Bible Reading Plan: Acts 15:1-21, Job 38, 39

Thou shalt guide me with thy counsel, and afterward receive me to glory.

- PSALM 73:24

. . . WHO CAN BE AGAINST US?

What does God do for us that immobilize the forces that oppose us? Yesterday we saw Him marshaling the forces of heaven against the enemy. Today, let's see how God makes our lives impenetrable to the enemy's attacks.

Satan asked God, "Dost Job fear God for nought?" The answer to that was "No." However, Job's fear was not based on material blessing, as Satan assumed, but on the recompense of a good conscience and God's benediction on Him. This settled peace keeps the enemy from gaining ground in our lives.

Verses 25 and 26 concisely portray another reason the enemy will fail in the life of a righteous person. God makes payment in kind to all men. While there is a threefold statement concerning the righteous, the single one against the wicked is very effective and almost frightening. Do you want God to show Himself froward toward you? No! But when God rewards the upright, pure, and merciful in kind, what a vision we have of God to spur us on. We become impervious to Satan's efforts against us.

How wonderful is natural light on our path, especially when the lights have been turned off in a cavern! God provides the light of truth for His people. Their feet become like hinds' feet, as they traverse life's rocks. Meanwhile the wicked stumble in the darkness. The same Rock that is our defense becomes the undoing of the wicked.

We see in verse 18 that God sets the wicked in slippery places, even while He enlarges our steps. In gentleness He guides with His right hand, while He is being froward with the froward.

Finally, the wicked have nowhere to turn for help. When they cry for help, any answer they get is vain and useless. In verses 46 and 47 lies the reason no man can be against us.

Delmar R. Eby, London, KY

Jesus said, "Be of good cheer; I have overcome the world"
(John 16:33).

July 9

Bible Reading: Philippians 3

One Year Bible Reading Plan: Acts 15:22-41, Job 40–42

I press toward the mark for the prize of the high calling of God in Christ Jesus.
- PHILIPPIANS 3:14

DON'T GIVE UP

As far as I could see in front of me, there were taillights. As far as I could see behind me, there were headlights. It was the time of the morning that we often refer to as rush hour, and the stretch of road that I was on was noted to have a lot of traffic that time of the morning.

I didn't think anything of it until two police cars drove up from the back in the opposite lane. It was about a twenty mile stretch of two-lane road, so I figured there was an accident ahead, especially since it was a little slippery that morning.

As time went on, I noticed people were getting tired of waiting and were turning around and going back where they came from. Some were taking side roads, looking for another way to get to where they were going. When I got to where I could see the lights of the police cars, there were still people in front of me turning around and going the other way. At last, when I was within a half mile of the accident, I could still see people half way between the accident and myself, turning around and going back.

It was at this point that the thought hit me. Christians who become discouraged and turn around or seek some other way to their destiny (heaven) are like these people who had spent close to an hour to get to where they were, only to become discouraged or impatient in the final stretch.

Less than ten minutes after I had seen the last car turn around, I was past the accident scene and traffic moved at near normal speed again. This also reminded me that the prize is not promised in the beginning, neither in the middle, but to those who endure to the end.

Joe Miller, Hartville, OH

I am pressing on the upward way.

July 10

Bible Reading: Romans 6:12-23

One Year Bible Reading Plan: Acts 16:1-15, Psalms 1-3

For the weapons of our warfare are not carnal, but mighty through God to the pulling down of strong holds.

- 2 CORINTHIANS 10:4

VICTORY IN JESUS

What can be more irritating than that dreaded buzzing while trying to relax? Such was my experience some time ago when my dreamy thoughts at first were interrupted by a tickling sensation on my nose. Brushing it aside, I resumed my slumber. But by the second or third touchdown on my face, I knew that this was more than just a passing problem. My swatting became more frequent and frantic. I was obsessed with a strong urge to lash out at the troublesome fly, chase it down, and kill it. Instead, I clung for awhile to a faint hope that soon this would pass and my sleep could resume. But only after dealing a death blow to the unfortunate fly could I rest undisturbed.

Found all over the world, the housefly is a pest and a carrier of germs and diseases. Most of our homes have fly swatters hanging in strategic places within easy reach. Still they invade at will, from the mansion on the hillside to the hut in the slums.

But there is a much greater threat that exists in this world. Think about it. The small fly may be a global irritation, but the universal curse of mankind is sin. Why do people put up with the effects of pride, hate, love of money, and immoral living when all sin will bring is eternal damnation? God has provided a permanent solution through His beloved Son. Tragically, many people have developed callousness toward certain sins. Their conscience is stilled and seared.

So the struggle against sin must continue. We have the weapon of the Word to fight against and overcome those sins that beset us. Otherwise our lives will end in misery and failure. But to the faithful, Jesus Christ has promised an eternal rest which will forever free us from the cause and consequence of sin.

Raymond Fisher, Nakuru, Kenya

Christians fight not for victory, but in victory.

July 11

Bible Reading: Proverbs 6:1-25

One Year Bible Reading Plan: Acts 16:16-40, Psalms 4–6

These six things doth the Lord hate: yea, seven are an abomination unto him.
- PROVERBS 6:16

ABOMINATIONS

In today's Bible reading we read of seven things the Lord hates. The Bible even calls these things an abomination to God. If we are doing something that is an abomination to God, we need to repent. We should never think that the seventh one is worse than the first six, because they are all wrong, and sin is sin. Let's look more closely at this list.

1. A proud look. Expressions can be deceiving, but a proud look is usually not hard to recognize. God always recognizes it and hates it. It is an abomination to Him.

2. A lying tongue. Anything that is not true is a lie.

3. Hands that shed innocent blood. When we read this, we tend to think of war; but Jesus teaches us that one who hates his brother is a murderer.

4. A heart that deviseth wicked imaginations. We know the heart is deceitful above all things and desperately wicked. We also know God can change the heart if we yield to His perfect will.

5. Feet that be swift in running to mischief. Do we have control of where our feet take us, or do we yield to Satan by going where we should not?

6. A false witness that speaketh lies. To knowingly say something untrue about others is an abomination to the Lord.

7. He that soweth discord among brethren. This is a bad attitude problem, and we need to remember and personally apply and live according to the golden rule.

Emanuel Erb, Conneautville, PA

The future that we study and plan for begins today.

July 12

Bible Reading: Matthew 6:19-34

One Year Bible Reading Plan: Acts 17:1-15, Psalms 7-9

For where your treasure is, there will your heart be also.

- MATTHEW 6:21

INTEREST IN HEAVENLY THINGS

The Bible explains that instead of laying up treasure on this earth, we should lay up treasure in heaven. Moths and rust will devastate treasure that is laid up on earth, and thieves will break in and steal it. The energy we spend to lay up riches for future enjoyment is vain and will someday come to nothing. Too many modern Christians are worldly-minded in their outlook on life. It is sad to see how the materialistic view found in modern Christianity is robbing the church of her heavenly vision. They can only see as far as the elements of time permit. Obviously Abraham had a different outlook when he looked for the city whose builder and maker is God (Hebrews 11:10).

True Christians are interested in their heavenly welfare. We naturally center our attention and energies on our own interests in life. Since the utmost interest of every child of God should be spiritual things, our attention should center on those things. Could it be that our lack of interest in spiritual things is the reason there is not more revival in our churches? It would be wise for every Christian to stop and consider just where his treasures and interests are. May God help us!

Simon Peter Asafo, Accra, Ghana

Put your treasure in heavenly things—your heart will follow.

July 13

Bible Reading: Hebrews 10:19-39

One Year Bible Reading Plan: Acts 17:16-34, Psalms 10–12

And let us consider one another to provoke unto love and to good works.

- HEBREWS 10:24

EXHORT ONE ANOTHER

One of the wonders of Kansas is the wide open sky. Another wonder is the many flocks of geese flying overhead in V-shape formation.

One particular goose in a certain flock intrigued me. While most of the others were flying in a V-shaped formation, he was off to the side approximately one hundred feet, by himself.

I have not studied "goose philosophy." Maybe he had a sound "goose" reason for flying by himself. However, his position brought to my memory many professing saints who seemingly had a problem associating themselves with a local body of believers.

I thought of all the blessings forfeited by not being in a group:

• The stronger, older ones are up front leading the flock. I noticed one particular goose leader was almost twice the size of the one behind it.

• The stronger ones up front break the wind so the younger, weaker ones can more easily keep up.

• The group is encouraged by fellow honkers.

• The group enjoys fellowship when they land to feed and rest.

• There is added protection from many watchers versus one lone goose.

Perhaps the one lone goose can survive. However, when we evaluate all the blessings he forfeited, not only for himself, but also for his mate, family, and ongoing posterity, it compels us to question his philosophy.

The Biblical reason for group fellowship is found in Hebrews 10:25, "Not forsaking the assembling of ourselves together, as the manner of some is: but exhorting [encourage and warn] one another: and so much the more, as ye see the day [the soon return of the Lord] approaching."

Rudy Overholt, Melvern, KS

A Christian without a church is like a bee without a hive.

July 14

Bible Reading: Acts 9:1-22

One Year Bible Reading Plan: Acts 18, Psalms 13-16

And said, Behold, I see the heavens opened, and the Son of man standing on the right hand of God.

- ACTS 7:56

PERFECT VISION

I recently went to the optometrist to have my eyes examined for a new set of contact lenses. Without contact lenses in my eyes and my vision very blurry, the doctor asked me to read some letters on the eye chart. I could not. After the doctor made a few adjustments on his device, I could look through it and easily read the letters.

This made me think of how the Holy Spirit corrects our vision. The Lord Jesus will radically alter our vision—how we view the world around us—when we accept Him into our hearts and become familiar with His teachings. If Jesus is not in our hearts, Satan, the great deceiver, blurs our view of the sins and so-called pleasures of this world. We may see fornication, divorce and remarriage, abortion, homosexuality, and other social ills as being acceptable. We may take pleasure in sports, movies, and worldly music. After the Lord corrects our vision, we see these things for what they really are—sin that is displeasing to the Lord.

In our Bible reading, God radically altered Paul's vision by taking his physical eyesight from him. When God restored Paul's vision, his eyes opened to spiritual truth. He had accepted Jesus and from then on he lived a life of true devotion to God.

May we strive to keep our vision clear by communicating with Jesus, the Great Physician, through prayer and meditating in the Word so we may be pleasing in the sight of the Lord.

Neil Smith, Decker, MI

Fixed **O**n **C**hrist's **U**ndying **S**acrifice

Bible Reading: Matthew 7:12-29

One Year Bible Reading Plan: Acts 19:1-20, Psalms 17, 18

Jesus answered and said unto him, Verily, verily, I say unto thee, Except a man be born again, he cannot see the kingdom of God.
- JOHN 3:3

HOW DID YOU GET THERE?

The story is told of an elderly man who was trying to cross a busy street in New York City. It seemed hopeless. In desperation, he called to a man on the other side, "How did you get over there?"

The reply bounced back, "I was born over here."

Many who are on the broad road to destruction are trying to get over to the narrow way but cannot find a way to get there. In our Scripture reading, Jesus warned of false prophets. These false prophets prescribe many easy solutions. Some even say that you need not get on the narrow way. It is all a matter of having your heart right with God.

There are two ways and two kingdoms. If you are indeed on the narrow way, and in God's kingdom, then you were born there. We cannot get there by changing clothes, acting right, or putting more money in the offering basket. Jesus told Nicodemus, "Except a man be born again, he cannot see the kingdom of God."

For many it seems hopeless. The thought of giving up their will, their sports, the glamour of fashions, and the lure of worldly pleasures is too great a sacrifice. To take up their cross and follow Christ sounds too difficult.

Let us remember, we are on the narrow way by the new birth, not by our own merits. Only by the new birth can we overcome the obstacles Satan wants to place before us. Only by the new birth can we hear God's sayings and do them. Thank God for a new life in Christ.

If you are struggling, remember there is only one hope of getting onto the narrow way. Like the man on the other side of the street, we must be born there.

Melvin L. Yoder, Gambier, OH

If you are on the right side, you were born there by the new birth.

July 16

Bible Reading: Exodus 3:1-15

One Year Bible Reading Plan: Acts 19:21-41, Psalms 19-21

And when the Lord saw that he turned aside to see, God called unto him. . . .

- EXODUS 3:4

ARE YOU KEEPING BUSY?

Have you ever heard that question? We seem to have the idea that it is good to be busy because we know the Devil likes to play in an idle mind and with idle hands. However, I believe we are often too busy to hear whether God has other plans and priorities for us.

In today's Scripture reading, we find Moses busy tending sheep. It was the way he supported his family. However, he took the time to turn aside and check out a curious sight, not knowing that God was trying to get his attention. God had quite a message for him, but Moses took time to hear all that God had to tell him. He did not say, "I've got to be moving along now. It will take me all day to round up the sheep again if I let them wander too far."

After quickly asking God to bless our plans for the day, we then limit communication with God by saying, "I've got to run along now. I'm already late for work." Did God even have a chance to tell us that He had something else to work into our schedule for the day, or something else to consider for the future? We may not even want to give God time to say anything for fear that He does indeed have something else in mind for which we really don't have time.

Slow down. Take off your shoes, not only because you are stepping on holy ground, but because God may have a lot to say and you need to settle in to hear it out to the end.

Lamar Hochstetler, Madison, VA

On the Day of Judgment, God will not have time to listen to the excuses of those who do not have time to listen to Him now.

July 17

Bible Reading: Luke 4:13-32

One Year Bible Reading Plan: Acts 20:1-16, Psalms 22–24

And all bare him witness, and wondered at the gracious words which proceeded out of his mouth.

- LUKE 4:22

JESUS WAS DIFFERENT

When Jesus preached His first message in Nazareth, His hometown, the audience wondered at the gracious words which proceeded from His mouth. In the city of Capernaum, the people were astonished at His doctrine, for His words were with power. After Jesus preached His sermon on the mount, the people were also astonished at His doctrine, for He taught them as one having authority. His manner of teaching was different from the lifeless teaching of the scribes. The officers who were sent to arrest Jesus testified of Him that, "Never man spake like this man" (John 7:46). These men were saying that, of all the speeches they had heard, they had never heard a man speak like Jesus. Wherever Jesus went and whenever He spoke, it was in the power of the Spirit (Luke 4:14). Jesus was different from other men.

We believe it was evident to all men that Jesus was the Son of God. Already at twelve years of age, the doctors of the law were astonished at His understanding and answers (Luke 2:47). Jesus stood out in His understanding of Scripture, His manner of teaching, His ability to perceive people's thoughts, and to perform countless miracles.

The followers of Jesus were also different from other men. The Jewish leaders took knowledge of Peter and John that they had been with Jesus. When the Jewish elders falsely accused Stephen, his face shone like an angel. They were not able to resist the wisdom and the spirit by which he spoke because of his close companionship with Jesus (Acts 6:10-15).

As followers of Jesus today, others should see in us that we have been with Jesus. Do we take enough time and effort to sit at His feet and hear His words?

Raymond Martin, Lewistown, PA

So let our lives and lips express the Holy Gospel we profess.

July 18

Bible Reading: Galatians 6

One Year Bible Reading Plan: Acts 20:17-38, Psalms 25-27

Let him that stole steal no more: but rather let him labour, working with his hands the thing which is good, that he may have to give to him that needeth.

- EPHESIANS 4:28

CHANNELS ONLY

Tears dripped into my food, but I didn't mind. I had prayed, and somehow I knew God would answer. As I looked at the meal before me, I thought of the love of others who gave to me and wondered how I could eat.

I thought of all the people around our world that are hungry, cold, naked, without shelter, and lonely. I understand a few of these, although not to the extreme that some may. I pray for them and wish I could do more.

We know that if we are willing to help others, God will richly bless us. Let us give willingly from the heart so that the cold may be clothed, the hungry may be fed, those without shelter can have shelter, and the lonely might have a friend. Ideally, the best friend would be Jesus.

First, we should care for our immediate members, and when they have sufficient, reach out to others. I hope we give that God might be glorified and not to exalt ourselves. After all, when we have given as much as we can spare, we are but unprofitable servants having done our duty.

Sometimes giving takes a crucifying of our plans and dreams in behalf of providing for others. "Give until it hurts," someone has said. "Then give until it quits hurting."

May we give of our time, money, talents, and our very being to God in behalf of all those in need. God's divine favor will rest upon those who give in Jesus' name.

Harold R. Troyer, Belleville, PA

It is possible to give without loving,
but it is impossible to love without giving. - Braunstein

July 19

Bible Reading: Psalm 90

One Year Bible Reading Plan: Acts 21:1-14, Psalms 28–30

Remember now thy Creator in the days of thy youth, while the evil days come not, nor the years draw nigh, when thou shalt say, I have no pleasure in them.
- ECCLESIASTES 12:1

TEACH US TO NUMBER OUR DAYS

A story was once told of a man who told God, "Lord, give me a warning before I die. Then I want to get right with You."

Life continued for this man, and as usual, life brought constant change. Some changes were drastic; some were subtle. Knee joints and finger knuckles began to feel stiff in damp weather. His hips ached at the end of a strenuous day at work. One day, while visiting the optometrist's office, the doctor prescribed a set of bifocal glasses to improve his reading ability. Several years later, the dentist examined his mouth and suggested removing the remaining decaying teeth and fit a new set of dentures.

As the aging process continued, the man experienced occasional blackouts. A concerned friend advised him to see a heart specialist. "Your heart is poor. You will need bypass surgery," was the doctor's solemn conclusion. After his surgery, a cane remained his constant aid. His repeated, "Huh?" finally convinced the family that he did need hearing aids.

A slip and a fall on the icy sidewalk confined him to bed. He was dependent on others to bring him his meals. Arthritis in his hands meant someone needed to feed him. Little by little, life ebbed away.

One night life fled from this man. His soul was not prepared to meet God. Standing before God, he said, "Lord, you didn't tell me I'm going to die."

God said, "Friend, I have been giving you warnings throughout your life and you gave no heed: your aching joints, failing eyes and ears, the poor heart condition, confinement to bed, and helpless hands. Did these not remind you that you would die?"

David J. Stoltzfus, Clymer, PA

Today is the first day of the rest of your life.

July 20

Blessed are they that keep his testimonies,
and that seek him with the whole heart.

- PSALM 119:2

THE BIBLE FIRST

When Matthias Baldwin, an engineer, picked up the morning paper to read it, his little son climbed on his knee and said, "The Bible first, Daddy, the Bible first." The busy father didn't pay much attention to his little son. He thought he didn't have time to read the Bible and pray every morning. But he always did take time to read the morning paper.

Sometime later, the little boy passed away. The childish voice was silent and there was no one to climb up on Father's knee. But God kept the boy's words ringing through the lonely father's heart. Repeatedly, he seemed to hear those piercing words, "The Bible first, Daddy, the Bible first." The heartbroken father could stand it no longer. There in the silent chamber, where the body of his little son lay, Matthias Baldwin fell on his knees and gave his heart to the Lord. The words of his little son became his motto for life. He put the Bible first in his heart, in his home, and in his business. God wonderfully blessed him, and he found great joy in using his money for the Lord's work. When he died, there were five churches he had started in needy districts.

Are we more interested in reading the daily paper than we are reading the Bible? If we spend more time in reading the daily paper than we do in reading the Bible, we are carnally minded. "For to be carnally minded is death; but to be spiritually minded is life and peace. . . . So then they that are in the flesh cannot please God" (Rom. 8:6, 8).

Eli A. Yoder, Stuarts Draft, VA

Sampling the Word of God only occasionally will never give you a real taste of it.

Bible Reading: Philippians 4:4-23

One Year Bible Reading Plan: Acts 22, Psalms 34, 35

And the peace of God, which passeth all understanding,
shall keep your hearts and minds through Christ Jesus.
- PHILIPPIANS 4:7

PERFECT PEACE

My car spun across the interstate and flipped over and over, front to back, seven and a half times. The car was completely out of my control. As I felt the car crushing in on me, the only thought that went through my mind was, *Well, Lord, I'm coming home.* There was no fear; there was only a feeling of complete and total peace—the kind of peace that only God can give. What a wonderful feeling it is to know the peace of God!

The same peace the martyrs experienced in centuries past is still available today. We can have peace in the midst of turmoil, pain, and even death. "Peace I leave with you, my peace I give unto you: not as the world giveth, give I unto you. Let not your heart be troubled, neither let it be afraid" (John 14:27).

We don't need to experience a life-threatening situation to know the peace of God. It is always available to those who call on the name of the Lord and are willing to rest in Him. Yet how often do we continue to cling to our troubles, hurts, and disappointments? All we need to do is to let go and let God take control.

It is only as we take our focus off of ourselves and set our hearts and minds on Christ that we can truly enjoy the promise of Isaiah 26:3, "Thou wilt keep him in perfect peace, whose mind is stayed on thee: because he trusteth in thee."

Joseph Jones, Ash Fork, AZ

To know the peace of God, we must know the God of peace.

July 22

And he said unto me, My grace is sufficient for thee:
for my strength is made perfect in weakness.

- 2 CORINTHIANS 12:9

SING THE SONG OF THE REDEEMED

I looked again. The trees were too leafy to see almost anything at all. The bird call was so strange that I was determined to see it. There it was again. *Sure not much of a song,* I thought. Just a few notes scrapped together. When I finally saw the bird, I was further chagrined. *Not much for show either.* The Great Crested Flycatcher was neither handsome nor musical. At that moment it "sang" again. The lack of applause and my criticism sure didn't stop it from doing what it was made to do.

Then it hit me. I realized that God had made the bird just the way it was, with just the song it sang. God is pleased that the Flycatcher sings the song He created it to sing, even if it isn't very musical. The bird and its song are special to God because He made it that way. The bird itself could be no happier than if it sang and sang just the song it was made to sing, no matter how tuneless it was by other standards.

He made us the way we are, too. He made us with freckles, bald heads, curly hair, loud voices, or without talents we think we need. He gave your voice the sound it has, even if you think you'd rather have mine. Sometimes we'd all rather just stop singing because we hear a voice that we think sounds better than ours. Sometime in our life we have all tried to sing with someone else's voice. We all know it doesn't work.

Let's learn a lesson from that bird. Ignore the critics; forget how it sounds to others; and sing the song you were made to sing. It will make both you and God smile.

Delbert Yoder, Millersburg, OH

Contentment makes poor men rich.
Discontentment makes rich men poor.

July 23

Bible Reading: Luke 16:19-31, Matthew 24:36-42

One Year Bible Reading Plan: Acts 23:12-35, Psalms 38–40

All scripture is given by inspiration of God, and is profitable for doctrine, for reproof, for correction, for instruction in righteousness: That the man of God may be perfect, thoroughly furnished unto all good works.

- 2 TIMOTHY 3:16-17

THINK!

Years ago an alcohol-related accident claimed a life on the highway near our home. It was a real tragedy. Later a sign was erected at the site with bold letters, "Think!"

This sign served as a grim reminder to everyone who passed. "Here was a scene of tragedy. Do not repeat the mistake that was made here. You are responsible for your own life and the lives of others! Be careful!"

In the Bible we find many spiritual "Think" signs, examples of tragedy resulting from wrong choices. In Luke 16 Jesus gave the account of the rich man who lived sumptuously and selfishly, without compassion for poor Lazarus who was in need. This rich man did think when he found himself in need, when he opened his eyes in hell, but it was too late. How tragic! When we read this account, we find the "Think" sign still there. We are to think!

In the days shortly before the flood, "they were eating and drinking, marrying and giving in marriage, until the day that Noah entered into the ark." They "knew not until the flood came, and took them all away" (Matthew 24:38-39). It was a tragedy that should make us think.

By the words "knew not" we could assume they were unaware of the impending doom. However, the Luther German translation states, *"sie achteten's nicht,"* which translated leaves the impression that they did not give heed to warning or give attention to it. In unbelief, they went their own way.

To think is to understand and respond to God's will for our lives, to be ready and prepared. "Watch therefore: for ye know not what hour your Lord doth come" (Matthew 24:42). Think!

David Bender, Aylmer, ON

Think about the future—it was not raining when Noah built the ark.

July 24

Bible Reading: 1 Kings 11:1-13, 26-40

One Year Bible Reading Plan: Acts 24, Psalms 41-43

Examine yourselves, whether ye be in the faith; prove your own selves.
- 2 CORINTHIANS 13:5

EXAMINE YOURSELF

While I was reading 1 Kings, a short sentence caught my attention. "Solomon sought therefore to kill Jeroboam" (1 Kings 11:40). Why would a man who was blessed with riches, who was known to be the wisest man of his time, and who called the people to be wholly devoted to the Lord, now want to kill Jeroboam?

Something significant had happened. Solomon's heart drifted from God to loving forbidden, foreign women. "And the Lord was angry with Solomon, because his heart was turned from the Lord God of Israel" (1 Kings 11:9).

Solomon's disobedience caused God to raise up adversaries against him. God said He would give ten tribes to Jeroboam. What was Solomon's response? He sought to kill Jeroboam. Solomon's real problem was not Jeroboam, but his own disobedience. His own actions brought on the adversaries. Killing Jeroboam would not have solved the problem.

What can we learn from this account of history? If Solomon would have seen his own fault and repented before the Lord, the Lord probably would not have raised up an adversary against him. Then Solomon would have had no reason to take revenge on Jeroboam.

Solomon's kind of behavior is still alive in the human race. Persons who do not walk obediently and wholeheartedly with God often see their faults in others. We are admonished to examine ourselves. Many church problems could be avoided if members would first examine if they are at fault before blaming others.

Jealousy, bitterness, and anger are some of the heart sins that make people critical and cold toward one another. Careful and prayerful self-examination with continued repentance will help us not to fall into the same trap that Solomon did.

Simon Schrock, Fairfax, VA

Bringing your life in line with God's standards will go a long way in avoiding problems.

July 25

Bible Reading: John 3:1-21

One Year Bible Reading Plan: Acts 25, Psalms 44–46

For the Son of man is come to seek and to save that which was lost.

- LUKE 19:10

GOD'S TIRELESS SEARCH FOR MAN

Nicodemus was hesitant about opening himself to the gift of God, taking the leap of faith that could save him. He had to accept a God who suffers, a God who was crucified. The cross is the most vivid sign of God's love for the world.

God, the faithful One, is ever looking for man, "Thou huntest me as a fierce lion," cries Job from his bed of pain (Job 10:16). God doesn't like to be alone, and has chosen man to help Him. When Adam was trying to hide after he sinned, God cried, "Adam, where are you?" (Genesis 3:9) All humanity can still hear this cry today.

The Spirit continues to call, "Come. And let him that heareth say, Come. And let him that is athirst come. And whosoever will, let him take the water of life freely" (Revelation 22:17). God is ever faithful to us, looking for us because He loves us.

The problem with man is that he hides from God's relentless search. God wants us all to live in heaven someday with Him. God's love for us is a gift that shows we are worthwhile in His eyes. Despite all our sinfulness, He is constant in love and forgiveness. Let us always obey His voice, heed His spirit, and blend with His body (the church). Then we can help God in His relentless search to bring lost souls into His marvelous light.

Samuel Okoth Oliech, Nakuru, Kenya

Have you felt God nudging you lately?

July 26

Bible Reading: Genesis 13:10-13, 19:1-26

One Year Bible Reading Plan: Acts 26, Psalms 47-49

Then Lot chose him all the plain of Jordan; and Lot journeyed east . . .
and pitched his tent toward Sodom.

- GENESIS 13:11-12

THE CONSEQUENCES OF UNWISE CHOICES

Lot chose the well-watered plain of Jordan and pitched his tent toward Sodom. Later he moved into Sodom. "The men of Sodom were wicked and sinners before the Lord exceedingly" (Genesis 13:13). Lot should have considered the effect this wickedness would have on his family before he moved there. It was a disastrous move that resulted in the loss of his family, though Lot himself did not become involved in the wickedness of the city.

Sodom is a type of the world. "The whole world lieth in wickedness" (1 John 5:19). We want to learn from Lot's unwise choice. The decisions we make in choosing a marriage companion, our church affiliation, or our occupation have far-reaching consequences. They will affect our children and succeeding generations in a spiritual way for good or evil.

Which direction are we pitching our tent– toward the world or toward heaven? We pitch our tent toward the world when we love money, when our life consists in the abundance of things we possess, when we accept technology without reservation, when we follow after worldly pleasures and sports, or when we are influenced by worldly fashions and fads.

May we choose, as Abraham, to be strangers and pilgrims on the earth and to command our children after us in the faith once delivered to the apostles and saints.

Lehman Martin, Worthington, IN

Satan is willing to wait on our grandchildren if he can get us to make an unwise choice that leads to their apostasy.

Bible Reading: Genesis 13:14-18, Hebrews 11:8-19

One Year Bible Reading Plan: Acts 27:1-26, Psalms 50–52

Then Abram removed his tent, and came and dwelt in the plain of Mamre, which is in Hebron, and built there an altar unto the Lord.

- GENESIS 13:18

ABRAHAM'S WISE CHOICES

Abraham made wise choices. He obeyed the voice of God. By faith He accepted the call and direction of God. "He staggered not at the promise of God through unbelief; but was strong in faith, giving glory to God" (Romans 4:20). His faith was so outstanding that he is called the father of the faithful. All the faithful are the children of Abraham (Galatians 3:7).

The first call of Abraham was to separate himself and his household from idolatrous relations and practices. Our first call is to repent and believe the Gospel of the Lord Jesus Christ. That call involves separating ourselves from sin and the world, and denying self. At baptism we confess that we are sorry for past sins and are willing to renounce Satan and the world with all works of darkness and our own sinful desires, committing ourselves wholly to Jesus Christ. If we are true to that commitment, we will be strangers and pilgrims in this Satan-dominated world.

God told Abraham to offer Isaac, the son of promise, as a sacrifice to Him. This was a call to a supreme commitment of self-denial and faith. Are we called to any lesser commitment? We are to present our bodies a living sacrifice, holy, acceptable unto God which is our reasonable service. We are not to be conformed to this world (Romans 12:1-2).

May God enable us to realize what true faith costs and, as Abraham, may we find the blessedness that complete obedience brings.

Lehman Martin, Worthington, IN

There is no harmony in the heart without the joyful notes of obedience.

Bible Reading: Matthew 5:43-48, Romans 5:1-12

One Year Bible Reading Plan: Acts 27:2744, Psalms 53-55

But I say unto you, Love your enemies, bless them that curse you, do good to them that hate you, and pray for them which despitefully use you, and persecute you.
- MATTHEW 5:44

LOVE YOUR ENEMIES

It is our duty to love our enemies, no matter how cruel they are to us or how much they hate us. John Staneser was in a Romanian labor camp. Colonel Albon, a cruel man, was very angry when he came into Staneser's prison cell one morning. He said, "I have heard that someone in this cell has dared to preach the Gospel of Jesus Christ!" Glaring about, he roared, "Who is the culprit?" No one answered.

"Well," said Albon harshly, "then all shall be flogged." Soon the cell was filled with cries of pain as the heavy stick fell again and again.

When he came to John Staneser, John said calmly, "My friend, there is a God in heaven to Whom you must someday give account." Everyone knew John would be beaten to death. At that moment, a guard hurried in with an urgent message.

Albon was wanted right away as a group of high ranking generals had just arrived. Eyeing John, Albon snarled, "Don't forget, we'll finish this soon."

The hand of God intervened. The generals had come to arrest Albon. Soon he was back in the cell, but now as a prisoner. The inmates soon took the opportunity for revenge. They leaped on him and would have beaten him to death had not John Staneser thrown himself over Albon to shield him from the fearful blows. The beating stopped as the men realized what John was doing.

What kind of love was this? After all, Albon would only have received his own treatment. But John Staneser possessed the love of God. The wonder of Jesus Christ is that He died for us when we were yet sinners. True love can go no further than that. God sent His Son to die for us while we were yet enemies, traitors, and rebels. That is real love.

Daniel Miller, Dunnegan, MO

It is easy to love our good neighbor, but loving our enemy does not come naturally.

Bible Reading: Daniel 6

One Year Bible Reading Plan: Acts 28:1-15, Psalms 56–58

If ye abide in me, and my words abide in you, ye shall ask what ye will, and it shall be done unto you.

- JOHN 15:7

OPEN WINDOWS

Daniel is one of the outstanding characters in the Bible. Being a Hebrew, he found himself in a foreign empire. He was admired and promoted by King Darius "because an excellent spirit was in him" (Daniel 6:3). Daniel didn't waver from his faith in God, even though he lived among all the wickedness of heathen Babylon. He maintained his integrity.

Daniel's peers did not like him and were successful in making a decree and having it signed by the king. No one was to ask any petition of any god or man save King Darius for thirty days or they would be cast into the den of lions. Daniel didn't waver but kept his faith in God as he had before. His windows were opened toward Jerusalem and he kneeled and prayed, giving thanks to God in heaven.

The open windows toward Jerusalem are a type of open windows to heaven. Daniel had a peace and connection in communing with God, an avenue of fellowship that brought the power of God upon his life. When Daniel was cast into the den of hungry lions, a stone was laid upon the mouth of the den and was sealed by the king's own signet and the signet of his lords. It did not close the windows of heaven. God heard Daniel's prayers!

We need to keep the windows of heaven open. We choose to have that connection of communing with God through Jesus Christ. We can have His blessings and power as we come to Him in full repentance and obedience to His will. But "if I regard iniquity in my heart, the Lord will not hear me" (Psalm 66:18).

The decree that Darius wrote to all people, nations, and languages that dwell on the earth included, "I make a decree, That in every dominion of my kingdom men tremble and fear before the God of Daniel: for he is the living God, and stedfast for ever, and his kingdom that which shall not be destroyed, and his dominion shall be even unto the end" (Daniel 6:26).

Edward Hochstetler, Hicksville, OH

I will remember the works of the Lord.

July 30

Bible Reading: Genesis 1:6-31; 2:1-3

One Year Bible Reading Plan: Acts 28:16-31, Psalms 59-61

And on the seventh day God ended his work which he had made;
and he rested on the seventh day from all his work which he had made.

- GENESIS 2:2

RUSHING HERE AND THERE

In today's fast-paced world, with everything instant, many people with day planners, pagers, and cell phones are pushing themselves to the limit. People with clenched fists run from their job, to school meetings, to an appointment with a client, grabbing something to eat on the run.

Collapsing into bed at night, exhausted, they find themselves still too keyed up to relax and fall asleep. Is it possible that followers of Jesus Christ also approach life too intensely? It seems we often put ourselves under extreme pressure to succeed in everything. When we don't meet our expectations, it is hard to forgive ourselves for failing. Is this the way God wants His people to live?

When we study creation in Genesis 1, we see a simple pattern. First was the work of making the universe—everything from atoms to animals to man. After His work, God was satisfied with what He had made. He saw that it was very good. Then He rested. God rested, not because He was weary, but because He was satisfied with a job well done.

Maybe our hectic schedule and intense lifestyle has robbed us of our peace, joy, and satisfaction in life. If so, let's follow God's pattern of work, satisfaction in a job well done, and then rest. We will be amazed how satisfying life can be.

When we take time for joy and play,
For rest along life's busy way,
And when we pause to kneel and pray,
We are renewed from day to day. - D. Dehean

Daniel Miller, Dunnegan, MO

Beware of the barrenness of a too busy day.

Bible Reading: Matthew 6:1-15

One Year Bible Reading Plan: Romans 1, Psalms 62–64

Our Father which art in heaven, Hallowed be thy name.
- MATTHEW 6:9

OUR FATHER

As we say, "Our Father," we can have the confidence that we are His children. If we are His children in this life, we can be His in eternity. As we are heirs to our natural fathers, so we can be heirs to our heavenly Father.

How do we respond to the words "Our Father" in the Lord's Prayer? Can we say "Our Father" from our heart? Do we consider God, the Father, as we do our earthly father? Growing up, that is usually the case. But as we grow into adulthood, we realize that our earthly fathers are humans. Our heavenly Father is not human. He is an all-wise, all-seeing Father.

Our heavenly Father is a life-giver. Even our next heartbeat depends on His loving care. He helps us through troubles and problems, if we can say from the heart, "Our Father which art in heaven . . ."

A true and loving father is more than a friend. God didn't bring us into this life and then forget about us. He didn't say, "Now you are on your own. Hope you make out all right. See you later." Our Father in heaven is not like that. He is a life-giver, a caretaker, a compassionate, loving, forgiving Father whom we can look up to with confidence and trust. After death, we can be with Him as one family throughout the ages of eternity.

Thank God for this blessed hope.

Levi Miller, Millersburg, OH

The refusal to look up to God and trust Him is the greatest mistake of life.

August 1

Bible Reading: Matthew 27:1-26

One Year Bible Reading Plan: Romans 2, Psalms 65-67

Pilate saith unto them, What shall I do then with Jesus which is called Christ?
- MATTHEW 27:22

WHAT SHALL I DO WITH JESUS?

When Jesus was on trial before Pilate, Pilate gave the people the option of releasing Him. But the people chose Barabbas, a murderer, to be released. Then Pilate asked the people this question, "What shall I do then with Jesus which is called Christ?"

Every person faces the same question Pilate faced. Everyone must choose either to accept or reject Jesus. Pilate tried to take a neutral position when he said, "I am innocent of the blood of this just person." Yet in the end, because he was pressured by the people, he gave consent for Jesus to be crucified.

In our initial experience of accepting Jesus as our Savior, we have started out right. But every day we must ask ourselves these questions. *What am I doing with Jesus? Am I giving Him His rightful place as Lord of my life, or am I dishonoring Him in any area of my life?*

Many people stood around the cross when Jesus was crucified. Some mocked Him (Luke 23:35). Some bewailed and lamented Him (Luke 23:27). Probably some just watched and considered themselves neutral. Where would I have been in that crowd? My relationship with Christ now probably shows where I would have been then. Am I honoring and glorifying Him? Or am I sometimes ashamed to be identified with Him?

"What will you do with Jesus? Neutral you cannot be. Someday your heart will be asking, 'What will He do with me?'" (See *Christian Hymnal* No. 266)

Benuel Glick, New Ringgold, PA

What I do with Jesus now determines what He will do with me later.

August 2

Bible Reading: 1 Corinthians 3

One Year Bible Reading Plan: Romans 3, Psalms 68, 69

The Lord is my rock, and my fortress, and my deliverer; my God, my strength, in whom I will trust.

- PSALM 18:2

SINKING SAND OR SOLID ROCK?

Anyone in the building trade knows a solid foundation is very important when constructing a building. Even the most beautiful structure can eventually crack and crumble if its foundation is faulty.

In Matthew 7:24-27 we have the account of two builders. Perhaps for a time nothing seemed amiss with the house built on the sand. But then along came the stormy tempests and torrents of rain, bringing this vulnerable house to its collapse.

Spiritually, many people are trying to build their lives on shifting, changing sand. Instead of building on the foundation of obedience and commitment to Jesus Christ and His Word, they are building on the sinking sand of an empty profession. Self-effort, self-righteousness, and self-assertiveness are faulty foundations.

False concepts which spring from such sinking sand include:

1. Humanism: Man's feeble attempt to live his life and solve his problems independently of God, and his opposition to God's control in his life. The theory of evolution fits into this scheme.

2. Situational Ethics: Where there are supposedly no fixed moral standards of right and wrong. It just depends on the situation, the culture, and the prevailing opinion.

3. Human Reasoning: In place of simple, believing, trusting faith in God and His Word, blind unbelief is sure to err.

Let's make sure we're building on the solid Rock, the Rock of our Salvation. This Rock of Ages is the only secure cleft in which we can safely hide. May we ever rest on the firm foundation of a living faith in Christ that is demonstrated by loving obedience to His will and a life that reflects His love.

Mark Kropf, Cataldo, ID

On Christ the solid Rock I stand; all other ground is sinking sand.

August 3

Bible Reading: 2 Peter 1

One Year Bible Reading Plan: Romans 4, Psalms 70-72

And let the foundations thereof be strongly laid.
- EZRA 6:3

FOUNDATIONAL STONES

In yesterday's reading we considered some of the sinking sands of man's futile effort to live his life without God. Today let's consider some foundational stones on which the believer can build his life.

1. We must begin with God. "But seek ye first the kingdom of God" (Matthew 6:33). "In all thy ways acknowledge him" (Proverbs 3:6).

2. The Word of God. "For ever, O Lord, thy word is settled in heaven" (Psalm 119:89). "But the word of the Lord endureth for ever" (1 Peter 1:25). Man may disbelieve and disobey the Bible and try to discount or distort it. Yet, through the ages, it remains the unchanging, everlasting Word of our unchanging, everlasting God.

3. The church. "Nevertheless the foundation of God standeth sure" (2 Timothy 2:19). Though the church is under attack, the gates of hell shall not prevail against it. Kingdoms rise and fall, but the church of Jesus Christ stands firm from age to age, as an everlasting pillar and an ark of safety for God's people.

4. The Christian home. A godly home is a safe and secure shelter in a sinful and corrupt society. It is a solid bulwark—a powerful, godly force. It is a stabilizing influence on the nation even though the world may not recognize or acknowledge it. It is a haven of rest and a foretaste of heaven.

5. A living hope. We look for the coming of Christ and anticipate the joy of our eternal home. This blessed hope is through the eye of faith, based on the resurrection of Christ and resting upon the promises of God. "Which hope we have as an anchor of the soul, both sure and stedfast" (Hebrews 6:19). As we build upon these solid platforms with Christ as our sure foundation, we can stand with unshaken assurance and confidence through all the storms of life.

Mark Kropf, Cataldo, ID

Jesus, blessed Rock of Ages, I will hide myself in Thee.

August 4

Bible Reading: 1 Timothy 6

One Year Bible Reading Plan: Romans 5, Psalms 73, 74

A faithful man shall abound with blessings:
but he that maketh haste to be rich shall not be innocent.
- PROVERBS 28:20

BE NOT DECEIVED

When I was a young boy, sixteen years old, I had my tonsils taken out. Dad took me to the doctor's office. The doctor made me lie on my back on a table. He placed a white cloth over my face, put ether on it, and said, "Now, if it gets too strong, just blow it away."

When I smelled a little of it, I blew, but it only became stronger and stronger. I blew harder and harder. The doctor kept saying, "Just blow it away," until at last it seemed the doctor was way up on top of a hill and I was way down in the valley. I could faintly hear him say, "Blow it away." What I didn't realize was that the harder I blew, the harder I drew back the ether. That's what the doctor wanted.

Isn't that the way Satan works in our lives? He tries to make us believe that if we work hard enough and make enough money we will be richly blessed for it. The more I blew, the sleepier I got. In our Christian life, the harder we work to make a lot of money to buy another farm or take that pleasure trip, the sleepier we get and the less time we have to do the Lord's work. It's not wrong to work hard to make a living if we do it to support our family or to help those who are in need. But if we haste to be rich, we won't be innocent.

Eli A. Yoder, Stuarts Draft, VA

*It's not sin to work for one's daily bread,
but it is sin to work only for that.*

August 5

Bible Reading: Matthew 25:14-46

One Year Bible Reading Plan: Romans 6, Psalms 75–77

And whatsoever ye do, do it heartily, as to the Lord, and not unto men.
- COLOSSIANS 3:23

FAITHFUL SERVANTS

The story about the three servants and the talents that were delivered to them seems almost sad or even a bit unfair.

The first servant received five talents. He probably felt he had something to work with, so he really went at it. He did his best and made five more talents.

The second servant received his two talents, and our passage says he did likewise. He must have felt he should also work and make more talents with what he had.

The third servant went and promptly buried his talent in the earth. I don't read that he tried to work or trade with his talent in any way. He was simply convinced that he would not get anywhere with so little. The Bible says, "After a long time the lord of those servants cometh, and reckoneth with them" (Matthew 25:19). It wasn't just a little time. The servant had plenty of time to gain at least one more talent (at least some interest, the lord said).

The Lord still requires of us to use our talent or talents in the best way we can. Maybe we feel like we only have one talent so it really doesn't seem any use trying. God knows our abilities, our gifts, and our talents. He gave them to us, and we are required to use them and exercise them regardless of where we are or what circumstances we are in.

We dare not bury any talents lest we be cast into outer darkness. Let us get busy with the talents we have that we may further God's work.

Sanford Nissley, Catlett, VA

Let us work with our might, or sad will be our plight.

August 6

Bible Reading: Deuteronomy 5:29-33; 6:1-25

One Year Bible Reading Plan: Romans 7, Psalms 78

Study to shew thyself approved unto God, a workman that needeth not to be ashamed, rightly dividing the word of truth.

- 2 TIMOTHY 2:15

UNKNOWN TREASURES

The story is told of a poor older widow who lived alone out in the country. She went to her pastor and told him of her poverty. She told him she would have to find work to do in her old age or come to want. The pastor asked her if she had no friend or member of her family who would give her support. She told of a son who was in service as a missionary in India.

"Does he not write to you?" the minister asked.

"Oh yes, he often writes," she said. "He sends the kindest letters, and he usually encloses some fancy paper with pictures on the corner. I keep them all in my Bible. But I am too proud to tell him how poor I am, and I cannot expect him to send me money."

"Would you mind showing me some of those fancy papers he sends you?" asked the minister.

She went to her Bible and took, from between the pages, some of the strips and showed them to the minister. They were bank checks, each for a fair sum.

"Why, you have all kinds of money," said the minister. "You have a Bible full of treasure, and you didn't know it."

The poor widow rejoiced when she realized how much her son was doing for her.

There are many people today who have a Bible in their home with untold riches between the covers, but they don't know it. The Bible tells us in John 5:39, "Search the scriptures; for in them ye think ye have eternal life: and they are they which testify of me." There is nothing more valuable than eternal life found in Jesus, of Whom the Scriptures tell.

Eli A. Yoder, Stuarts Draft, VA

If a man is not familiar with the Bible, he has missed a great treasure.

August 7

Bible Reading: Psalm 32:1-4, 1 Peter 3:9-22

One Year Bible Reading Plan: Romans 8:1-18, Psalms 79-81

Let your light so shine before men . . .

- MATTHEW 5:16A

IS YOUR LANTERN LIT?

Around the beginning of the twentieth century, when railroading wasn't automated like it is today, a man was killed one night at a railroad crossing. His relatives sued the railroad company, claiming negligence on the part of the watchman.

During the ensuing trial, the watchman on duty at the crossing when the accident happened was called to the witness stand. The prosecuting attorney asked him several questions:

"Were you on duty at the crossing at the time of the accident?"

"Did you have a lantern at the time of the accident?"

"Did you wave your lantern in warning?"

To all of these questions the watchman answered affirmatively. His testimony helped the railroad win the case. Later an officer of the railroad came and talked to the watchman to thank him for giving evidence in favor of the railroad. The officer inquired, "Tell me, Mr. Armstrong, were you nervous during the questioning at the trial?"

The watchman replied, "Yes sir, I feared any moment the attorney would ask if the lantern was lit."

Because the watchman failed to put oil in his lantern, the man who was killed could not see him swing the lantern.

Many today are like the five foolish virgins. They are waving their lanterns, a form of Christianity, but they have no genuine oil to light their lives. Those passing by continue on to their destruction because the warning lanterns are unlit.

Let's always be truthful even though the truth may hurt. We have a forgiving God. Let us cover our sins with the blood of Christ and they will be whiter than snow. Then our lanterns will shine in warning to others.

Daniel Weaver, Holmesville, OH

Don't hide your lantern under a basket of deceit. Let the truth shine.

August 8

Bible Reading: Deuteronomy 34, Acts 7:54-60

One Year Bible Reading Plan: Romans 8:19-39, Psalms 82–84

Precious in the sight of the Lord is the death of his saints.

- PSALM 116:15

GRAVESTONES

This afternoon as I passed a cemetery, I thought of death and its thought-provoking certainty. Just as sure as you were born, you will die, unless Christ returns first. It's not a debatable subject.

I remember when my grandmother passed away and we drove nearly a thousand miles to her funeral. God took her home when it was her time to go, and nothing could change that, outside of a miracle. She was up in age and it's perfectly natural for the aged to pass on to their eternal reward. It's to be expected. But young people can also die.

God doesn't guarantee us life. In Luke 12 a certain rich man said to himself, when he had plenty, "I will pull down my barns and build greater . . . and I will say to my soul, Soul, thou hast much goods laid up for many years; take thine ease, eat, drink, and be merry. But God said unto him, Thou fool, this night thy soul shall be required of thee."

A child under the age of accountability is safe under the blood of Jesus and at death will be ushered into heaven to join the innocent. May we strive to find the simplicity of a child and the peaceful innocence that guarantees entrance into heaven after death.

Harold R. Troyer, Belleville, PA

Death cannot sever what the cross unites.

August 9

Bible Reading: 1 Samuel 15:10-31

One Year Bible Reading Plan: Romans 9, Psalms 85-87

Behold, to obey is better than sacrifice, and to hearken than the fat of rams.
- 1 SAMUEL 15:22

REBELLION IS AS THE SIN OF WITCHCRAFT

We were gathered for our weekly Bible study in the detention center in our local town. This facility is provided for juvenile delinquents who are charged with misdemeanors or felonies.

Their charges vary from serious crimes to violating probation or running away. They can be held here for only a week or up to several months until further decisions are made.

Many of the detainees are from broken homes with little parental direction and so resort to drugs and alcohol. They find their associates among the street folks. Their religion varies from nominal Christian churches to Islam and Satanism. Some are fairly acquainted with the Scriptures, professing conversion at one time, while others have hardly seen a Bible, much less know what's in it.

On this particular occasion a seventeen-year-old, the son of a Presbyterian minister, professed to be a follower of Satanism. We asked him what attracted him to Satanism.

His answer was, "Satanism is rebellion, and I am rebellious. In Satanism, you can be rebellious without feeling guilty."

How many are pursuing the paths of rebellion, desiring to get away from guilt, and end up in the downward course portrayed in Romans 1:21-28? Their foolish hearts are darkened. They change the truth of God into a lie. God gives them up to a reprobate mind, and eventually they go to their eternal destiny in the lake of fire. They don't deliberately choose that destiny, but the choices they are making now, in the day of grace, are leading them there.

Willis H. Martin, Wellsboro, PA

Rebellion is the broad road to destruction.
Obedience is the narrow road to life everlasting.

August 10

Bible Reading: Hebrews 2

One Year Bible Reading Plan: Romans 10, Psalms 88, 89

Looking unto Jesus the author and finisher of our faith.
- HEBREWS 12:2

KEEP YOUR EYES ON JESUS

A missionary lady in the heart of Africa had to cross a river one day. The bridge had been washed away except for two poles which still spanned the river high above the rushing waters. The lady said, "I cannot possibly cross on those poles."

Her guide said, "I will help you get across, but you must trust yourself completely to my help." They started to cross with the guide walking backwards holding the hands of the fearful missionary. All went well until, nearing the center of the rickety supports, the lady looked down at the rushing waters and immediately became giddy. In desperation she cried, "I cannot go another step!"

Gripping her firmly, the guide replied, "Look at me. Only if you look at my face can I save you." She didn't take her eyes from his face until at last they safely reached the other side.

This is the only way we can safely reach our heavenly destination. We must keep our eyes on our guide, Jesus. If we take our eyes off Jesus and look around at the wickedness, immorality, and wars, we will also become giddy in our Christian life. Sometimes the road seems rocky and unsafe to travel, and we almost despair. We, too, must look at the face of Jesus for help to keep going. We dare not have our focus on the things of this world.

Daniel Miller, Dunnegan, MO

When the downward look makes you dizzy, try the upward one.

August 11

Bible Reading: Psalm 19:7-14; 119:161-168

One Year Bible Reading Plan: Romans 11:1-21, Psalms 90-92

And now, brethren, I commend you to God, and to the word of his grace, which is able to build you up, and to give you an inheritance among all them which are sanctified.

- ACTS 20:32

THE VALUE OF THE TREASURE

God has a treasure for us. It has great value for those who search for it with all their hearts. Here in America it is quite plentiful, yet so many neglect it. In some parts of the world there are people who would gladly sacrifice time and earthly goods to be able to own a copy of this treasure, or even part of it.

Is the eternal Word of God precious to me? It shows me that I need Jesus, the Living Word. He is our only hope. The key verse tells of the value this treasure has for believers both now and in the life to come.

It seems we are not able to grasp the full value of this treasure that God has given us. Let us take a few moments to consider some of the facts about it:

When it is received with meekness, and engrafted, it is able to save our souls (James 1:21).

This law of liberty brings blessings to those who continue in it (James 1:25).

It is alive, powerful, and sharp enough to be used by the Lord when doing heart surgery (Hebrews 4:12).

It was written for our learning, that we may have comfort and hope (Romans 15:4).

It is complete; it is sure; it is right; it is pure; it is true and righteous altogether. It is more to be desired than much fine gold and sweeter than honey (Psalm 19:7-10).

O Lord, teach us to live the Bible, and then the world will see that knowing You is the key to abundant life.

Calvin King, Harrison, AR

The Bible—pearl whose great value no mortal can measure.

August 12

Bible Reading: John 3:15-21, Psalm 119:105-112

One Year Bible Reading Plan: Romans 11:22-36, Psalms 93–95

For ye were sometimes darkness, but now are ye light in the Lord:
walk as children of light.
- EPHESIANS 5:8

THY WORD IS A LAMP AND LIGHT

A lumberyard in our area had a series of break-ins one summer.
When fences and security systems didn't solve the problem, they
installed floodlights in the parking lot that lit up the entire property. As
far as I know, that effectively halted the burglaries.

These thieves operated boldly under cover of darkness, but when
the lights shone, they had to avoid the area so the light would not
reveal their evil works. John 3:19-21 tells of those evildoers who avoid
God's Word in fear. It will force them to acknowledge their evil works
and make them feel ashamed and condemned. By loving darkness
(an evil lifestyle) more than light (grace and truth) they completely
disregard verses 15 to 18 which explain God's purpose in sending His
Son to earth–not to condemn but to save. Denying truth just to avoid
feelings of guilt will not remove the penalty for sin.

Satan operates within a heart full of darkness and remains
concealed there through one's indifference and ignorance of God's
Word (Ephesians 4:18). Satan can be recognized, identified, and
exposed through knowledge of sin, and repentance of sin defeats him.
Darkness is merely the absence of light. A room will remain dark until
light is brought in, then darkness must depart. Darkness has no power
over light and cannot resist its force. This illustrates God's almighty
power over Satan. When someone receives the true Light into his
heart, Satan must flee. We know this experience as conversion. Sin
is the fruit of Satan's influence on our carnal flesh, but crucifying and
denying that flesh by walking the path lighted by the lamp of His Word
produces the fruit of the Spirit. God's Word can make our personal
light shine brightly.

Melvin Schwartz, New Haven, IN

A sunbeam looking for darkness will never find it.

August 13

Bible Reading: Isaiah 55

One Year Bible Reading Plan: Romans 12, Psalms 96-98

But as for me, my prayer is unto thee, O Lord, in an acceptable time:
O God, in the multitude of thy mercy hear me, in the truth of thy salvation.
- PSALM 69:13

MISSED OPPORTUNITY

Otieno longed to go to Mombasa, that great city in the coastal region of Kenya. He listened to different stories about the city. He heard of the great ocean that goes on a journey in the morning and returns in the evening and of Fort Jesus built by the Portuguese in the 15th century.

When one of Otieno's clan members died in Mombasa, his body was brought home for burial. The family of the man who died decided not to travel back to Mombasa right away, leaving room for others to travel to the city. Otieno requested a ride, which he was granted.

He was informed that the bus was to leave immediately after burial. He went to his home to prepare for the journey. Not knowing the exact time they were to leave, he was not in a hurry. He packed into his briefcase all the necessities for the journey. Finally he came to the place where the funeral was, only to find out he was two hours late. The bus had already left. He was very disappointed. He had missed the best opportunity he had. What could he do? He did not have any money to catch another bus. He went back home disappointed, knowing that he would not make it to Mombasa.

As Otieno told me the story, I was reminded of Jesus' second coming to take the saints with Him to the heavenly Jerusalem. Only those who are ready will accompany Him. The unprepared will perish.

Erick Ouma Ogwe, Kasongo, Kenya

The greatest business of life is to prepare for the next one.

August 14

Bible Reading: Psalm 23, 2 Corinthians 5:1-10

One Year Bible Reading Plan: Romans 13, Psalms 99-102

And as it is appointed unto men once to die, but after this the judgment.
- HEBREWS 9:27

NOW OR NEVER

A brother in the church called me late one night and asked if I would go along to the hospital to pray for a dying man. The wife of the dying man wanted someone to come in and "bless" her husband. This was a first-time experience for me. I was glad the brother who asked me to go along was more experienced.

After we shared the Gospel and challenged the dying man to give his heart to Jesus, we prayed. The prayer was not a "blessing" like the wife was possibly expecting. We sat there in the hospital with the dying man and some of his family and friends for several hours.

It is sad to see people face death without having lived their lives for God. Yes, God is willing and anxious to save anyone who comes to Him, even on their deathbed. Many people ignore God through life, yet in death they want the blessing of God. God has given us all we need to know and do if we want God's blessing in death. The blessing of others when we are near death will in no way take the place of giving our lives to Jesus. Are we being careful to follow Christ the whole way every day, or are we willing to live in the gray areas hoping the grace of God and the "blessing" of others will carry us through?

It is not worth being a miser with ourselves. Give it all to Jesus now and have His blessing both now and in eternity.

Tim Burkholder, Burns Lake, BC

As the tree falleth so shall it lie.

August 15

Bible Reading: Romans 14:13-23; 15:1-14

One Year Bible Reading Plan: Romans 14, Psalms 103, 104

And through thy knowledge shall the weak brother perish, for whom Christ died? But when ye sin so against the brethren, and wound their weak conscience, ye sin against Christ.

- 1 CORINTHIANS 8:11-12

ARE YOU LISTENING?

It had been a hot, muggy day in late summer. It seemed no matter what a person did, the sweat rolled. It had been especially warm for several of the neighborhood boys who had spent the day making hay. They were now taking advantage of the cool waters of a nearby pond, obviously having an enjoyable time.

After a little while they began leaving the cool depths of the pond. Suddenly somebody asked, "Where's Fred (not his real name)?" He was nowhere to be seen! They quickly searched the nearby woods while somebody ran for help. Still no Fred! Frantically the boys jumped back into the water and began searching. Soon professionals were on the scene and took charge of the search. After some time they found Fred's body. His life here on earth was ended.

A sober group left the pond that evening. Many questions raced through their minds. What had gone wrong? Most of the boys were excellent swimmers, and Fred had been among the best. Had Fred called for help and the other boys had not heard? We will never know.

Are we listening for those calls of help? Do we have a close enough relationship with our fellow brethren that we sense when they have a need? God forbid that we should ignore those pleas for help. We do well to encourage, not only the weaker brother, but also the one who seems to have everything going for him. Perhaps right at this moment he is facing a struggle. God alone can see the heart. If we allow Him to direct us, He will help us fill the need in our brother's life.

Philip Cross, Leitchfield, KY

Bear ye one another's burdens, and so fulfill the law of Christ.
- Galatians 6:2

August 16

Bible Reading: Joshua 2

One Year Bible Reading Plan: Romans 15:1-21, Psalms 105, 106

And she sent them away, and they departed: and she bound the scarlet line in the window.

- JOSHUA 2:21

WHERE IS YOUR SCARLET LINE?

Somewhere in the midst of this mass of anxious, fearful people of Jericho, a harlot named Rahab gave refuge to Joshua's two spies. Rahab and the spies made an agreement. She let the men out her window, down the scarlet line, and then tied the line in her window. This line typifies the blood of Jesus. As it was an escape from Jericho, so the blood of Jesus is the escape from the traps of Satan.

Rahab did not wait to tie the scarlet line in the window. It meant life to her. To delay was negligence. Do not neglect to apply the blood of Jesus today. The same line that brought deliverance for the spies was also instrumental for Rahab's deliverance. The blood of Jesus now avails for Jews and Gentiles alike.

The scarlet line demonstrated Rahab's faith in Israel's God. It served as a confirmation of her commitment in keeping her part of the promise and that she was anticipating the spies' commitment of deliverance. The blood of Jesus bears testimony to God of our commitment to Him and our anticipation of Christ's appearing.

The scarlet line hanging in Rahab's window became a source of identification. It identified her and all her house with God's people. The blood of Jesus identifies those of like precious faith with God and His kingdom.

As the enemy advanced toward Jericho, Rahab remained behind the scarlet line. There she was safe. With the blood of Jesus between us and the enemy, we are safe.

When the Lord returns, will He find the scarlet line hanging in the window of your heart?

David J. Stoltzfus, Clymer, PA

Faith ascends but doubt descends.

August 17

Bible Reading: Genesis 5:18-27, Hebrews 11:1-6
One Year Bible Reading Plan: Romans 15:22-33, Psalms 107, 108

And Enoch walked with God.
- GENESIS 5:24

THE BELIEVER'S WALK

The genealogy in Genesis 5 mentions that Enoch walked with God. It is written of the others that they lived, but it says of Enoch that he walked with God. Enoch's walk so pleased God that God translated him and he "was not." He did not die nor was he buried. Hebrews 11:5 says, "By faith Enoch was translated that he should not see death."

"Walk" in Scripture means "a decidedly willful choice in pursuit of a particular course in life." Not only did Enoch live a righteous life, but he also lived by faith.

This faith is still available for believers today to help them in their walk of righteousness. Our walk must be in a new life because we are under grace (Romans 6:14). "For we walk by faith, not by sight" (2 Corinthians 5:7). We believe in God even though we do not see Him.

Believers walk in the Spirit and by that power refuse to fulfill the lust of the flesh (Galatians 5:16). They walk in consistency, making them worthy of the holy life to which they are called. They walk in love, as Christ also has loved them. They walk cautiously and circumspectly, considering all pros and cons of the choices they make (Ephesians 4:1; 5:2, 15). Believers walk in the light as He is in the light and have fellowship one with another (1 John 1:7). Why all the disunity?

How did Christ walk? "I am meek and lowly in heart" (Matthew 11:29). This is the high calling of believers. It is a course we should not reject nor be ashamed of.

Wilmer S. Beachy, Liberty, KY

No man, having put his hand to the plough, and looking back, is fit for the kingdom of God. - Luke 9:62

August 18

Bible Reading: Colossians 3

One Year Bible Reading Plan: Romans 16, Psalms 109–111

And I saw three unclean spirits like frogs come out of the mouth of the dragon, and out of the mouth of the beast, and out of the mouth of the false prophet.
- REVELATION 16:13

THE DEADLIEST VENOM

We might think the deadliest venom is found in some big snake. But it actually comes from a little frog. This frog is the little Koki frog found in the country of Colombia. The Koki frog's venom is produced in the form of a skin secretion. About one hundred-thousandth of a gram of the frog's venom is enough to kill a full-grown man, if it enters into his bloodstream. Most people are afraid of snakes, never even thinking about a frog.

Like the Koki frog's venom, the smallest of sins can, and almost always will, lead to bigger sins. Too often such sins as a little "white" lie, not being quite honest, or cheating your neighbor a bit are considered only small sins. Ever since the fall of mankind in the Garden of Eden, human nature has been such that it is easy to allow sin to rule our lives. Sin causes us to want to live our own way rather than God's way. Sin cuts us off from God.

When we do fall into sin, we always need to ask God to forgive us, as all sins need to be acknowledged before Him. This will lead the way to true repentance. Jesus died for all mankind. Now the benefits of that death–salvation and restored fellowship with God–are available to all who respond in faith.

"For by grace are ye saved through faith; and that not of yourselves: it is the gift of God: not of works, lest any man should boast" (Ephesians 2:8-9).

Andrew Miller, Apple Creek, OH

Wrong is wrong, no matter who does it or who says it.

August 19

Bible Reading: Hebrews 10:19-39

One Year Bible Reading Plan: 1 Corinthians 1, Psalms 112-115

In your patience possess ye your souls.

- LUKE 21:19

A LESSON ON PATIENCE

One beautiful spring day we planned to make hay, but there was something to accomplish that day that was of more eternal value.

During our busy spring schedule of planting and haymaking, I checked on a hayfield between chores one evening and found it was already dry enough to bale. It was a day earlier than I had expected. The dew was already setting, so we had to leave it overnight. The next morning at family devotions, I specifically asked the Lord to help us get the hay baled and stored. I took pride in getting up good quality hay, and this was already past the peak.

That morning after breakfast something else needed immediate attention, and it seemed we made no progress all day. That evening as the sun was setting, we were finally ready to start raking and baling, but the dew was already setting.

When I realized how the Lord answered my selfish prayer, my heart throbbed. We did not need the hay as badly as I needed a good heart-searching lesson on patiently waiting on the Lord. I needed a thorough lesson on self-denial, patience, trusting in the Lord, and setting my affections on heavenly values.

As the Scripture reading states, "For ye have need of patience, that, after ye have done the will of God, ye might receive the promise."

May our goal be to seek first the kingdom of God and His righteousness, and then He will supply all our needs, both spiritual and physical. God knows what is best for us. "And we know that all things work together for good to them that love God, to them who are the called according to his purpose" (Romans 8:28).

Enos R. Martin, Harrodsburg, KY

We can have victory in patience when self is crucified.

August 20

Bible Reading: Matthew 18:21-35

One Year Bible Reading Plan: 1 Corinthians 2, Psalms 116-118

And be ye kind one to another, tenderhearted, forgiving one another,
even as God for Christ's sake hath forgiven you.

- EPHESIANS 4:32

FORGIVE US OUR DEBTS . . .

. . . as we forgive our debtors. Someone took note of this request
in the Lord's Prayer and called it the most dangerous prayer. May I
suggest that we consider this plea in a positive manner?

A forgiving heart is the fertile environment in which blossoms the
gentle fruit of mercy unhindered by ill will, animosity, arrogance, or the
least thought of self-importance. A noted author has this to say about
forgiveness, "Please understand. Relationships don't thrive because
the guilty are punished, but because the innocent are merciful."

All of us have a compelling reason to forgive: it is in our best interest.
When we are wronged, we have three options. We can respond
with anger, revenge, or forgiveness. The first two, as we know by
experience, are self-destructive, which leaves only forgiveness.

Lest we hesitate at the brink of forgiveness, let us consider this.
"There is something akin to the divine when man chooses to forgive.
Forgiveness is a gift; it is mercy. It is a gift that I have received and
also given away. In both cases it has been altogether satisfying" (from
Why Forgive? by Johann Christoph Arnold).

Nowhere else is this experience more important than in the marriage
relationship. There was a husband who betrayed the trust of his wife.
His wife found out and was devastated. In an effort to find healing for
their hurt, they went on a trip together. On the tenth evening of the trip,
the husband found a note on his pillow. This is what it said: "I'd rather
do nothing with you, than something without you. I love you. I forgive
you. Let's move on."

Why forgive? We have absolutely nothing to lose and everything to
gain.

Jerry Yoder, Auburn, KY

You are richer today if you have given or forgiven.

August 21

Bible Reading: Jude

One Year Bible Reading Plan: 1 Corinthians 3, Psalm 119:1-48

Knowing therefore the terror of the Lord, we persuade men; but we are made manifest unto God; and I trust also are made manifest in your consciences.
- 2 CORINTHIANS 5:11

ARE WE CONCERNED?

Recently an officer of the law stopped me for driving without my seatbelt fastened. I recognized the officer as one with whom I had spoken on the subject before, and I expected to get a fine.

I am not opposed to wearing seatbelts and actually believe they are a good safety precaution. However, what I believe about them has not overridden my forgetfulness at times. In our discussion that morning, I assured the officer that my not wearing the seatbelt was not rebellion but forgetfulness. To my gratefulness, he only gave me a verbal warning.

In our discussion, the officer said to me, "Tim, I stopped you because I'm concerned for your safety." I know it is their job to enforce the law, but somehow I got the feeling he was not just doing his job but was actually concerned about my safety on the icy roads we had at the time.

If we see someone in a dangerous position who is not aware of the danger, we try desperately to warn him. This is a challenge to me spiritually. Am I willing to stop people on the expressway of life and show them honest concern for their souls? Am I willing to make others late for their appointments? Am I willing to risk causing others to think I am a fanatic? Am I willing to take time to warn others of the impending danger? We cannot compare spiritual warnings to physical warnings. The danger of eternal damnation is real and near for many around us. Let's persuade men. Let's step up and out for God.

Tim Burkholder, Burns Lake, BC

Don't leave for tomorrow what can be done today.

August 22

Bible Reading: Psalm 17

One Year Bible Reading Plan: 1 Corinthians 4, Psalm 119:49-104

Thou hast proved mine heart; thou hast visited me in the night; thou hast tried me, and shalt find nothing; I am purposed that my mouth shall not transgress.
- PSALM 17:3

INTEGRITY

Recently I have been newly impressed at the integrity of King David. In verse two of our Bible reading, his sentence or verdict is coming from the presence of God, who is a righteous Judge. Then in verse three in his prayer of integrity, he states that God will find no wickedness in his heart because he purposed not to transgress with his mouth. In the context of this verse, he is crying and pleading for God's attention in verse one because his prayer is sincere and without pretense.

David has the testimony from God that he was a man after God's own heart (Acts 13:22). We see clear evidence of David's devotion and love toward God in how he was moved to take action when he heard how Goliath defied the armies of the living God. David knew that the strength and the weapons of Goliath were useless in standing against the living God. In the integrity of his heart, he knew the Lord did not depend on human strength to fight against the giant, but the battle was the Lord's.

In our dispensation, our warfare is not physical but spiritual. We are in a spiritual warfare against the wiles of the Devil. We cannot gain the victory by our own human strength any better than Goliath did by his strength and weapons.

We need to surrender our will to God daily, having our life hid in Christ by the shed blood on the cross. We need to set our affection on things above where Christ sits on the right hand of God. Then we can have the lively hope with King David, "I will behold thy face in righteousness: I shall be satisfied, when I awake, with thy likeness."

Enos R. Martin, Harrodsburg, KY

A man of integrity is a man after God's own heart.

August 23

Bible Reading: Luke 15:1-10

One Year Bible Reading Plan: 1 Corinthans 5, Psalm 119:105-176

My sheep wandered through all the mountains, and upon every high hill . . . and none did search or seek after them.

- EZEKIEL 34:6

LOST CHILDREN

While we were serving at a mission in Ghana, West Africa, I was called over to another compound one evening after dark. Since my oldest son was outside with me, I took him along but left my younger son at home. To get to the other compound, we had to go through an outdoor repair shop, a deserted lot, past a small drinking spot where liquor was sold, and past a painting shop where people often loitered around.

I did what I was called to do and was visiting briefly when someone opened the gate of the compound and toddled in. It was my two-year-old son! You can imagine how shocked I was. Many things went through my mind. How did he know where I was going? Living on the edge of a slum, he could have roamed around in the dark and gotten lost. On my way back, a drunk confronted me and asked, "Why do you let your children go out after dark like this?"

If you have small children, you can feel the horror that we felt as we imagined what could have happened to our dear little one. Why did the Lord allow this to happen? I think it was for me to feel His protecting power, but most of all, it was to show me how He feels for His dear lost ones wandering in the slums of sin.

Elvin Fox, Shiloh, OH

And other sheep I have, which are not of this fold:
them also I must bring. - John 10:16

August 24

Bible Reading: John 1:1-12

One Year Bible Reading Plan: 1 Corinthans 6, Psalms 120–123

But the path of the just is as the shining light,
that shineth more and more unto the perfect day.

- PROVERBS 4:18

A SHINING LIGHT

We miss many opportunities to share a word for the Lord by waiting for some spectacular moment. We want to be like Nathan, the prophet, and say, "Thou art the man," or like John the Baptist, who said, "She is not thy wife." Jesus called John the Baptist one who gave a true testimony and was "a burning and shining light."

It should be our goal to be a burning and shining light, but let's take a look at Isaiah 42:3: "The smoking flax shall he not quench." This speaks of a motive and desire that the Lord can work with. It is a fire doing its best to burn. It is a spark the Lord can fan into a burning and shining light.

When the Lord asked Ananias to go and lay hands on Paul, Ananias went. This account is the first time Ananias is mentioned in the Bible, and he is only referred to once after this. Wasn't he serving the Lord effectively before this incident? Of course he was, or the Lord would not have used him in this account. Ananias was obedient. He was concerned about his safety, but he went willingly after the Lord assured him that all was well. The Lord used him to help Paul, and then He used Paul's gifts to fill a larger calling.

The Lord doesn't always give us a noted position, but He always gives us a place to fill. He asks us to have a willing heart and mind that says, "Lord, what wilt thou have me to do?" (Acts 9:6). The Lord can fan that spark into a burning and a shining light.

Elvin Fox, Shiloh, OH

A little candle doing its best is better than no light at all.

August 25

Bible Reading: 1 Peter 4

One Year Bible Reading Plan: 1 Corinthians 7:1-24, Psalms 124-127

Grudge not one against another, brethren, lest ye be condemned: behold, the judge standeth before the door.

- JAMES 5:9

ME CARRYING A GRUDGE?

The great Methodist pastor, Charles Allen, wrote that when he was in the fourth grade, the superintendent of the school mistreated him. There was no doubt about it. The man committed a deliberate wrong because he had fallen out with Charles' father. The Allen family moved from that town and years passed. One day during Charles' first pastorate, he heard that his old antagonist was seeking a job with the schools in the area. Charles knew that as soon as he told his friends on the school board about the man, they would not hire him.

"I went out to get into my car to go see some of the board members, and suddenly I realized what I was doing. Here I was out trying to represent Him who was nailed to the cross, and me carrying a grudge! That realization was a humiliating experience. I went back into my house, knelt by my bedside, and said, 'Lord, if you will forgive me of this, I will never be guilty of it anymore.' That experience and that promise are among the best things that ever happened in my life."

We know a family who has had many struggles. There were problems between husband and wife. The oldest child, a daughter, left home at sixteen years old. She never came home, unless she was sure that her father was not there. Over the years all the children left home and moved from their community.

The parents were only middle-aged when the mother passed away suddenly. All the children were gone, and the husband was away on business. The neighbors found her and reported the death. There was no chance for any reconciliation, no goodbyes, no hugs, no making plans, and no time to voice regrets.

Friends, if you have any differences, anything that needs to be confessed, anything that needs to be brought in order, or any grudges to take care of, don't wait. Tomorrow may be too late.

Melvin L. Yoder, Gambier, OH

No grudge is worth harboring.

August 26

Bible Reading: Ephesians 4

One Year Bible Reading Plan: 1 Corinthians 7:25-40, Psalms 128-131

But if ye bite and devour one another, take heed that ye be not consumed one of another.

- GALATIANS 5:15

FIGHT THE GOOD FIGHT

I heard an account of a man who had two roosters to enter into a rooster fight. He was busy with his work that day, so he worked until it was time to go. He quickly put the two roosters into the trunk of his car and left for his destination, two hours away. When he got there and opened his trunk, to his dismay, he found lots of feathers and blood and two dead roosters. His comment struck me. "Oh, I forgot to tell them that they are on the same team."

Let us all understand that we are on the same team. It is Satan who is causing all the conflict, not the brother or sister with whom you have a problem. Next time you have a conflict with someone, remember, you are both on the same team.

Don't make feathers fly or use the tools Satan may offer–hate, envy, strife. Don't try to ruin their reputation by telling everyone else about the incident. Let us not bite and devour one another but team up against Satan and not let him weaken us by picking each other's feathers out. Do not let him get between us so we can stand together and fight off all the fiery darts of Satan.

Editor's note: We don't condone rooster fighting, but we appreciate the lesson taught in this illustration.

Mel Wenger, Denver, PA

Let us overlook molehills and move mountains.

August 27

Bible Reading: 2 Corinthians 3

One Year Bible Reading Plan: 1 Corinthians 8, Psalms 132-135

Let us hear the conclusion of the whole matter: Fear God, and keep his commandments: for this is the whole duty of man.
- ECCLESIASTES 12:13

TRUE COMMITMENT

From the very beginning of our Christian walk, we should remember who we are. We are unworthy of the name Christian, except for what Christ has done for us. God cleansed us from all our impurities. Now He wants to see our wholehearted surrender and voluntary commitment in return. This makes it impossible for us to be secret Christians under the banner of Christ, but puts in us a strong desire to do God's will.

We must believe with certainty that it is both pleasing to God and good for us to sacrifice ourselves. In true sacrifice we will use our strength, time, and resources to glorify God and to lead other people to Christ. Let us remember that those of the world seldom read the Bible. They read us. The godly man is the ungodly man's Bible. Our lives should always show a true commitment. Our hearts should be in tune with the holy Word of God to reflect the true image of our Master, Jesus Christ. Without this complete and voluntary submission of our hearts and minds to God's will, He cannot work in us to make us perfect.

The devil is waging a fierce and continuous war against our souls. Commitment will put us in the active zone. Although this total commitment may sometimes go against our human nature, God takes great pleasure in it.

Our best example is God's Son. Tired, weary, hungry, and tortured, He never faltered in His resolve. He committed His entire life to the bitter end to do His Father's will (John 4:34).

Let us follow His example.

Samuel Okoth Oliech, Nakuru, Kenya

Until you are sacrificial, you are artificial.

August 28

Bible Reading: Psalm 77

One Year Bible Reading Plan: 1 Corinthians 9, Psalms 136-138

And let us not be weary in well doing: for in due season we shall reap, if we faint not.

- GALATIANS 6:9

NEVER GIVE UP

Our family recently took a trip to western Canada. It all went well as we had hoped until we were nearing the end of our two-week trip and discovered we had lost an undeveloped roll of film.

This caused some anxiety that morning, and I soon was on the phone making some calls in search of the lost film. After an unsuccessful search, we gave up on the idea of ever seeing that film again. We asked our friends to take some pictures for us to help fill in the gap in our photo album.

About three or four months after our trip, we got a package in the mail from British Columbia with our developed pictures. Who would have guessed this could happen? We had stopped along the road to take a picture of scenery and somehow this film had dropped out of the car. About one month later, a man picked it up and took it home. After awhile he developed it and took it in to the RCMP (Royal Canadian Mounted Police) who took a license plate number off a picture of my friend's truck. The RCMP mailed the pictures to my friend who mailed them to us.

Whether you are a parent, a teacher, a preacher, or you feel like a nobody, please don't give up. God is working behind the scenes! Sometimes you may feel awful, like the writer of Psalm 77, but don't give up! God is preparing you for something.

It is difficult, but let us try to focus on what God has done in the past (v. 10-20) and remember that, after the storm, the sun will shine.

Richard Martin, Bancroft, ON

You're never a loser until you give up.

August 29

And the elements shall melt with fervent heat, the earth also and the works that are therein shall be burned up.

- 2 PETER 3:10

WHAT MANNER OF STONES

Today's Scripture reading shows us that the magnificence of the temple was still an impressive attraction in that era. The disciples brought this to Jesus' attention but did not get the response they were expecting. Jesus did not show more interest in this magnificent building because He knew that it had served its purpose. Soon after His resurrection, the Holy Spirit would come to live in the hearts of man rather than in a man-made structure. He told them that the thing that was glorious in their minds would one day be a pile of rubble. Jesus went on to inform the disciples about the trials future Christians would experience.

Today there are many impressive accomplishments when measured by the standards of man, but even the most complex projects are foolishness in comparison to the wisdom of God. As Christians, we may also be awed by the magnificence of these engineering marvels, but we should consider that all earthly things are subject to destruction. They will be destroyed either at the end of time, by natural disaster, or by the hands of men. The attacks on the twin towers of New York City showed how quickly this can occur.

What can we learn from this? Is it a reminder to keep us from spending excessive time, effort, and money for our homes, farms, or businesses? Are we attached to the things of this world? Are we keeping our foundation and focus on Jesus so that when the carnal things are "thrown down," we still have something to stand on?

Perhaps the next time you gaze in wonder at some man-made object, it can serve as a reminder of how quickly something can be destroyed. Then it should also remind us of what things are really important.

Darrell Frey, Drayton, ON

Hold lightly to things of earth, but cling tightly to heavenly things.

August 30

Bible Reading: Hebrews 12:1-14, Psalm 51:8

One Year Bible Reading Plan: 1 Corinthians 10:14-33, Psalms 141–143

He shall feed his flock like a shepherd: he shall gather the lambs with his arm, and carry them in his bosom, and shall gently lead those that are with young.
- ISAIAH 40:11

THE SHEPHERD'S CHASTENING

The story is told of a shepherd who was caring for his sheep. Beside him lay a lamb with a broken leg. A passerby stopped to chat with the shepherd.

"What happened to that poor lamb's leg?" asked the visitor.

"I broke it," replied the shepherd.

"Why were you so cruel to your lamb?" he asked.

The shepherd answered, "My lamb had a bad habit of wandering away from the rest of the flock. It would not listen to me when I called the sheep. As a last resort, I broke his leg. Every day I carry it to and from the pasture. When the lamb's leg heals, he will be an obedient lamb. When his leg was broken, his stubborn will was also broken. This lamb will be more useful to me when he obeys my voice."

As we go through life, the Lord may need to chasten us. None of us enjoy being chastened by the Lord, but it can produce precious fruit in our lives. God wants to mold us to His honor and glory. How useful would we be to the Lord if He would not chasten us? Some things in life we may not understand, but usually something good can come out of our unpleasant situations.

A young ox was yoked to a master ox. If he balked at the yoke, he would only hurt himself. This young ox discovered that the more he matched his step with the master ox, the more pleasant his work would be. The closer we walk with God, the easier the road will become.

Samuel Beachy, Belvidere, TN

Though chastening is unpleasant, it can bring forth precious fruit.

August 31

Bible Reading: Isaiah 59

One Year Bible Reading Plan: 1 Corinthians 11:1-16, Psalms 144, 145

Thou art of purer eyes than to behold evil, and canst not look on iniquity.
- HABAKKUK 1:13

MAN'S LARGEST WALL

Let me tell you about the second largest wall ever built by man. You have probably already heard of the Great Wall of China. The amazing facts of its size and the terrific amount of labor involved in building it are almost unimaginable. Stretching nearly 4,000 miles, the wall was built to keep out invaders from the North. This wall is about thirty feet tall and around twenty feet thick.

But did you notice that this is the world's second largest wall? Can you believe there is a larger wall? Yes, it is true; there is a larger wall.

Most history books do not tell the facts behind this sad story. The largest wall ever built by man was built long before the Great Wall of China. Actually, we must go back in time to where we can envision a perfect world newly created by God. In His instructions to Adam and Eve, God inserted only one prohibition. "Do not eat of the tree of the knowledge of good and evil." Sadly, Adam and Eve disobeyed and ate of that very tree. At that moment of disobedience, a terrible wall was erected that towered all the way to heaven. Sin built this wall.

Where once there had been perfect communication and unity between God and man, there is now a sin-blemished creation. To Satan's delight, the largest man-made wall on earth was built firmly in place. But even as a thick curtain of gloom seemed to be settling down around this wall, a bright flicker of hope could be seen gleaming from the loving heart of God–a promise of a coming Savior (Genesis 3:15).

Joshua Yoder, Clarkson, KY

No small sin is small because all sin opposes God.

September 1

And Jesus said unto him, No man, having put his hand to the plough, and looking back, is fit for the kingdom of God.

- LUKE 9:62

COMMITMENT

Recently our family took a tour of Mammoth Cave. Before starting, the park ranger cautioned us that the tour was somewhat strenuous, and that there were some tight places we needed to go through. He cleared himself by advising that anyone with physical limitations or fear of tight places should reconsider.

Buses transported us to the entrance of the cave. There he repeated his caution, telling us that once we started there could be no turning back. Then we proceeded. We didn't wonder about his comments very long after entering. It was passable, but for some people it could have been distressing or strenuous.

With the park ranger leading the way, we committed ourselves to this two-mile underground trek. There was no turning back. We trusted ourselves to the leadership of this young stranger.

His park service uniform and his authoritative manner reassured us. We proceeded and were not disappointed. We saw the cave and came out at another entrance successfully.

God calls us to that kind of commitment and even much deeper. Our commitment affects our eternal destiny. Christ is our Guide. We make the choice. But choice without commitment gets us nowhere. Naomi called Ruth to consider the cost before committing herself to God's people. But if we would be successful in the Christian life, we must be committed. We must see it as a one-way street we choose that is the only way to victory.

Some people enter the Christian life or marriage with an "I'll try it" mentality. This is not God's way. Commitment is a giving up and a giving over of self to One who knows the way ahead better than we do. Commitment is the only safe way to success.

Delmar R. Eby, London, KY

Commit yourself to God, for He has already committed Himself to you.

September 2

Bible Reading: Joshua 6:1-20

One Year Bible Reading Plan: 1 Corinthians 12:1-19, Psalms 148-150

And he said, Nay; but as captain of the host of the Lord am I now come. And Joshua fell on his face to the earth, and did worship, and said unto him, What saith my lord unto his servant?

- JOSHUA 5:14

THE ILLUSION OF CONTROL

Probably, for most of us, our daily life is fairly predictable. We plan our schedule and usually can accomplish what we planned. We then tend to feel proud and credit our good management when everything turns out as we planned. But it is all an illusion. Consider the big picture. Our life is a mere vapor, a little mass of protoplasm, on a little dirt ball called earth, in a sea of stars called the Milky Way, which in turn is a speck in billions of galaxies. But we still hang tightly onto our steering wheel and smugly feel that we are in control.

Suddenly we are faced with something which is totally out of our control. Something can happen which is out of our hands. God is calling us to a moment of personal surrender, not so we lose, but so we can win.

Consider Joshua, a powerful leader facing a challenge far greater than his resources to overcome. How did he overcome this challenge? By surrendering to the will of the Lord!

God brings us face-to-face with things far greater than ourselves to bring us face-to-face with Him. If we fall face down before Him in total submission, surrendering all control, we will become more effective than before. Get out of the way and let God's power take over!

We seem to think we are in control of our own little universe. We try to get things done by controlling our life. But if we release that control into the hands of the Lord, He will show us answers and approaches we could never think of. All we're really giving up is an illusion of control.

Lester K. Burkholder, Fredericksburg, PA

If one allows God to guide, He will provide.

September 3

Bible Reading: Exodus 10:21-29, Matthew 6:19-23

One Year Bible Reading Plan: 1 Corinthians 12:20-31, Proverbs 1, 2

And the light shineth in darkness; and the darkness comprehended it not.
- JOHN 1:5

HOW DARK IS THAT DARKNESS?

The early morning was so dark when I started out with my first load for the day, that even with my headlights on high beam, it seemed as if they didn't want to pierce the darkness. I was reminded of the plague of darkness God sent on Egypt. Even when it was this dark, it was hard for me to imagine darkness so thick that you could feel it.

We also read of another darkness in the Bible. That is the darkness that dwells inside of us if we do not follow God's teaching. In Matthew 6:22-23 we read that our eyes are what let the light into our body. They not only let the light (sunshine) in, they also let good or bad things into our mind and heart. If we train our eyes to seek only that which is good, then our body (or heart) will be full of light. But if we let our eyes feast on evil things, like adultery, envy, hate, and murder, then our body (or heart) will be full of darkness. That darkness will be darker than the darkness I experienced in the early hours of the morning.

Our verse also indicates that the light (Jesus Christ) shone in the darkness (the world) and the world did not realize it. Why? I believe that, because of the simplicity of the light, it blinded them, and they could not see it because they had their eyes on other things. Our eyes are a vital part of our body. They take a picture of what we see and store it in our minds. Let us be careful where we are looking so the light of Jesus can shine into our hearts.

Joe Miller, Hartville, OH

More is caught than taught.

September 4

Bible Reading: 1 Corinthians 8

One Year Bible Reading Plan: 1 Corinthians 13, Proverbs 3, 4

Then said Jesus, Father, forgive them; for they know not what they do. And they parted his raiment, and cast lots.

- LUKE 23:34

NOTHING SHALL OFFEND THEM

Have you ever let someone in your life offend you? Have you ever licked those wounds you thought were so deep or nursed your self-pity to keep it hurting? Possibly it was something that was said in a casual conversation, a little humor at your expense, or an exhortation of a brother. As brothers and sisters in the Lord, we relate closely and believe in watching out for the good of each other's souls. There are many practical ways this is shown, and at times we are tempted to take offense at what someone has done or said.

If you ever feel tempted to be offended by another, remember to consider the damage done to yourself. "A brother offended is harder to be won than a strong city: and their contentions are like the bars of a castle" (Proverbs 18:19). If we allow self the luxury of being offended, self will be a strong city and the bars of a castle against our soul's salvation.

There is a law that the Psalmist speaks about which we do well to remember. "Great peace have they which love thy law: and nothing shall offend them" (Psalm 119:165). Yes, you read that right, "and nothing shall offend them." If we have peace that comes from being immersed in the Word of God, we cannot be offended. If we spend the time with the Lord that we should, and if we allow His Word and Spirit to permeate our lives, it will be impossible for us to be offended, no matter what is done to us or said about us. God's Word is powerful and can help us have a relationship with Him that will cause us never to be offended. Then we can encourage those who fall into the trap of being offended.

Tim Burkholder, Burns Lake, BC

First keep the peace within yourself,
then you can also bring peace to others. - Kempis

September 5

Bible Reading: Acts 2:22-36

One Year Bible Reading Plan: 1 Corinthians 14:1-20, Proverbs 5, 6

Hope deferred maketh the heart sick; but when the desire cometh,
it is a tree of life.
- PROVERBS 13:12

DISCOURAGED?

Have you ever been discouraged? I have. In fact, I was discouraged just this week. I didn't even realize what it was until it was too late. Satan likes discouragement.

I heard a story of a man who dreamed he talked with Satan. Satan took him to his storehouse of weapons to guide him on a tour. First were big tanks and large artillery. Next were small guns and swords. He had many types of machinery and weapons for every situation. They were all used on people of every kind. As they were leaving the storehouse, the man being guided by Satan noticed a small, short-handled bat standing in the corner. Out of curiosity, the man asked Satan what the bat was used for.

"Ah," said Satan, "that's my most effective weapon. I call it the club of discouragement."

Satan understands the effectiveness of discouragement. He uses it to disarm Christians. As the Christian loses heart, he also loses the power essential for victory, resulting in spiritual failure. Then Satan will tell him that he is not a Christian.

God hates discouragement and has provided a remedy for it. I found the remedy. It's the Bible! After I studied the second chapter in Acts, I felt like a new man—a man with a goal, a vision, and a new heart. Praise God for His Word which can be used effectively against the club of discouragement.

Harold R. Troyer, Belleville, PA

Think less of the power of things over you and more of the power of Christ within you.

September 6

Bible Reading: Proverbs 22:1-6; 4:1-27

One Year Bible Reading Plan: 1 Corinthians 14:21-40, Proverbs 7, 8

A good name is rather to be chosen than great riches, and loving favour rather than silver and gold.

- PROVERBS 22:1

A GOOD NAME

There was a rough boy who attended a Sunday School class and caused many problems. Finally, after consulting with the teachers, the superintendent led him to the door one Sunday with this curt dismissal. "There is the street; go, and never come back to this Sunday School." He never came back, but they heard from him again. He began a career of crime and bloodshed that perhaps has never been equaled in modern times.

The Chicago police force appointed a group of officers and ordered them to bring him in dead or alive. One evening as he approached the door of a theater, a volley of shots rang out. John Dillinger would commit no more crimes.

One newspaper showed an unusual picture. Only the feet of the dead desperado showed. The editorial comment was heart-searching. "Who knows where these feet might have gone if someone would have led them aright?"

How many feet are turned away today because we do not have time to share with the wayward? How many perhaps are turned away when they see inconsistencies among us? Does our name and reputation raise doubts and questions, or does it draw people to the church and to God?

When he is just a child, we must start to train him, so that his feet may go aright. He must be shown the value of having a good name which is more to be desired than silver or gold.

The song writer says, "At the crossing of the Jordan, the king and the beggar will stand side by side." When we approach the Jordan for that final crossing, silver and gold will be of little comfort. Wealth and worldly fame will only be a grief to us.

Let us strive for a godly name that will help to lead others in the right way and bring glory to God.

Melvin L. Yoder, Gambier, OH

God's salvation takes into account the lost, the last, and the least.

September 7

Bible Reading: Isaiah 6

One Year Bible Reading Plan: 1 Corinthians 15:1-32, Proverbs 9, 10

I will sing of the mercies of the Lord for ever: with my mouth will I make known thy faithfulness to all generations.

- PSALM 89: 1

THE VOICE OF THE LORD

The Lord told Jonah to go to Nineveh and cry against it. I don't know if Jonah didn't see God as an all-seeing, all-wise God, or why he tried to escape God by fleeing to Tarshish. God dealt severely with Jonah for not obeying His command. Only after Jonah endured the chastening of the Lord, was he ready to do God's bidding and preach to Nineveh. Jonah showed an unwillingness to do his part in spreading God's word.

The word of the Lord came to Elijah in a cave and spoke to him in a still small voice telling him to go to Damascus and anoint Hazael king over Syria. God also called Samuel, and Samuel said, "Speak, for thy servant heareth." These men were called to do God's bidding.

Where do we find ourselves? God may not call us audibly, but as God's children, there are plenty of opportunities to do God's will. We need to show compassion on those who are still in sin and darkness. If God speaks to us, we want to respond in a positive way. We want to do God's bidding and not follow Jonah's example. When the Lord speaks, we want to be listening, whether He speaks through His Word, His Spirit, or even in an audible voice. The Lord has work for us to do.

Amos Garber, Rosebush, MI

Lord, give us a vision of work to be done. Renew our lost vision of souls to be won.

September 8

For God so loved the world, that he gave his only begotten Son, that whosoever believeth in him should not perish, but have everlasting life.

- JOHN 3:16

WHAT WILL YOU DO WITH THE SON?

A rich man in England had a collection of expensive paintings. The man had only one son and loved him dearly. The world was at war, and the son was called to go fight in the war.

A few months passed, and the father missed his son very much. One day word came to the father, "Your son was killed in battle." The father was distraught. His only son was gone.

Several months later a young man, a fellow soldier of the son, came to the father's house and offered the father a painting of his son. The painting was crude, but it soon became the man's favorite.

Time moved on, and the man grew old and died. A day was set to sell the estate at auction. People came from all over the world to buy these rare paintings.

The first painting to be sold was the painting of the man's son. "Who'll give me $1,000 to start?" Nobody bid. "Who'll give me $100?" No bid. The auctioneer backed down to $50, then $20, then $10, and finally down to $5. The crowd was getting impatient, but the auctioneer was determined to sell this painting first. Finally, from way back in the corner, a man bid $5. He was a poor man, a neighbor of the man that had the gallery. When the impatient crowd urged the auctioneer to move on, he said, "I have sold the painting to the man way back in the corner, and the auction is over. The man's will states that whoever buys the painting of the son gets the entire estate." The poor man became the richest man in the room in a matter of minutes simply because he did not reject the son.

What are you doing with God's only Son? Are you rejecting Him like most of the people in the world? Or are you serving Him and dedicating your life to Him? You, too, can go from the rags of sin to the riches of Christ.

Jason Schlabach, Sugarcreek, OH

Today is the day of salvation.

September 9

Bible Reading: Matthew 3

One Year Bible Reading Plan: 1 Corinthians 16, Proverbs 13, 14

Bring forth therefore fruits meet for repentance.
- MATTHEW 3:8

QUIBBLING

What is quibbling? It is seeking to avoid an issue with a critical attitude or to be evasive of a duty. This attitude can be found anywhere humans abide.

In school the teacher may announce a certain duty to be done. Immediately someone groans or raises his hand.

"Yes?" responds the teacher.

"We haven't done it this way before," replies the pupil. Groaners, complainers—quibblers, to be exact!

In a home setting as well as in schools, this can become a dilemma if not addressed in the early stages. A whining child does not grow up to be an appreciative adult. It is our duty as parents to stop this hurtful quibbling and guide our children towards cheerful and quiet obedience. True, legitimate questions are always in order. The difference can be seen by the manner used in asking. An honest question deserves an honest answer, but woe to those children who have never learned to yield and submit to a higher authority.

The reason there is so much envy and strife in churches today is because there are quibblers. Quibbling against the ministry and against anything that speaks of authority is just natural for someone who has never learned that it is wrong to quibble.

When David was confronted with his sin, he immediately admitted that he had sinned against the Lord. King Saul, in effect, did the same. What was the difference? David blamed no one else for his sin, but Saul blamed others and quibbled. If we would refuse to groan, complain, and quibble, what a lovely picture of fellowship God would see!

Wayne E. Miller, Rushsylvania, OH

God's truths and godly thoughts balance our emotions and bring forth godly actions.

September 10

Bible Reading: Luke 10:25-37

One Year Bible Reading Plan: 2 Corinthians 1, Proverbs 15, 16

And he said, He that shewed mercy on him. Then said Jesus unto him,
Go, and do thou likewise.

- LUKE 10:37

THE IMPORTANT MAN

There is a story about a man walking past a construction site one
day. He saw the workmen pushing and straining their utmost to raise a
heavy wall while their supervisor was running back and forth, shouting
orders.

The passerby stopped, joined the workmen, and with his help the
wall was set in place. Afterwards the supervisor offered his profound
thanks to the man for his help.

"But you," asked the passerby, "why weren't you helping?"

"Me?" the supervisor asked in astonishment, "Me? Why, I'm the
project manager."

The passerby reached into his pocket, pulled out his card, and
showed it to the supervisor. He was the owner of the company.

As we go through life, we meet people with background, training,
personality, and taste that are vastly different than what we are used
to. When we are tempted not to share a word of encouragement or
offer a service or a smile to someone because they do not meet our
standard of acceptability or normality, let's remember that there is not
a single person who is beneath the dignity of Christ. Jesus specializes
in changing odd, different, or rejected people into righteous people. If
we refuse to share encouragement because the person does not fit
our mold, we are very much like the supervisor whose face turned red
in shame that one above him would do what he thought was beneath
him.

Thank God that we still have the opportunity today to repent of our
selfish motives and to reach out to those around us in kindness and
in love.

Josh Eicher, Rosebush, MI

A student is not above his teacher, nor a servant above his master.

September 11

Bible Reading: Mark 13:24-37, Romans 13:11-14

One Year Bible Reading Plan: 2 Corinthians 2, Proverbs 17, 18

Take ye heed, watch and pray: for ye know not when the time is.
- MARK 13:33

WHAT TIME IS IT?

The phrase "What time is it?" is heard wherever people are. We are inclined to want to know what time it is. Unless we carry a time piece, we depend on others who know by some reliable source.

Edward Gibbon said in his *Decline and Fall of the Roman Empire* that the fall of Rome was marked by five attributes. The first was a mounting love of show and luxury (affluence). Second was an ever-widening gap between the very rich and the very poor. The third was an over-indulgence in the arts such as literature and exotic music. Fourth was an obsession with sex. The fifth was an ever-increasing desire to live off the state.

This all sounds similar to society around us today. We have come a long way since AD 1453, but we are back in Rome. We are exposed to forms of manipulation which the world has never known before, such as psychological techniques, the techniques associated with biological sciences, and the new ways in which the media are influencing behavior.

How shall we find our way through all this and come out saved when the stars begin to fall from heaven? We must be familiar with God's written Word. We must walk by faith and not by sight. We must receive our influence from a scriptural fellowship that at times reins in our emotions and says "This is the way; walk ye in it." We cannot be unduly familiar with the news media of our time and not be shortchanged from that which liveth and abides forever. The message comes to us, "Awake thou that sleepest . . . and Christ shall give thee light" (Ephesians 5: 14).

Isaac K. Sensenig, Ephrata, PA

Counting time is not as important as making time count.

September 12

Bible Reading: Psalm 100; 126

One Year Bible Reading Plan: 2 Corinthians 3, Proverbs 19, 20

Speaking to yourselves in psalms and hymns and spiritual songs,
singing and making melody in your heart to the Lord.
- EPHESIANS 5:19

THE VALUE OF SINGING

Do you enjoy singing? I personally enjoy singing. Singing is a vital part of the Christian life. It can help you find victory in your Christian life. God loves it when people get together and sing from the heart.

There are several purposes for singing: to honor and glorify God, to draw people closer together and closer to God, to inspire and convict, and to bring joy and healing to the hurting.

Sometimes when I am having my devotions, I go through a song book and sing verses here and there. When I am tired and discouraged, it lifts my spirits simply to sing. There is something about singing that gives me a boost in my Christian life. However, unless Jesus Christ is in our hearts and our minds, singing is nothing but an emotional high.

How often do we go out and sing for our neighbors? Is it not a blessed experience to go sing for those who are in need? There is no reason why we should be ashamed to let our songs be heard in public.

Several months ago our youth group had the privilege to give a program at one of the local prisons. I thoroughly enjoyed singing to the inmates.

Singing will not only bless the people you are singing for, but you will also receive a blessing. I am afraid that too often we sing because it is our custom to sing, and we miss a blessing because we fail to sing from the heart.

The world puts a lot of emphasis on music. Let us not get caught up in the world's standard of music. Music is a gift from God. My plea is that God could be honored and glorified through the songs and the music that we Christians use.

Mark Overholt, Whiteville, TN

Emotion without devotion is nothing more than commotion.

September 13

Bible Reading: Proverbs 12:1-23

One Year Bible Reading Plan: 2 Corinthians 4, Proverbs 21, 22

Thou shalt not go up and down as a talebearer among thy people: neither shalt thou stand against the blood of thy neighbour: I am the Lord.

- LEVITICUS 19:16

BAD RUMORS

A famous preacher told of a personal experience. When he attended a church conference, his wife didn't care to go along, so he dropped her off with some friends. Hundreds of people from many locations were at the conference.

During the meeting a friend took the preacher aside and asked, "What's this I hear about you leaving your wife?"

The preacher said, "I don't know what you're talking about."

"Well," said the friend, "there is a rumor going around that you left your wife. I have heard it several times now."

At first the preacher could not imagine how such a rumor would have started. Then he remembered. During an intermission, a crowd had gathered around him, and it seemed everyone was talking at once. Someone asked him if his wife was at the conference. He started to say he left her with friends, but he only said, "I left her," when he was cut off and never finished what he started to say. Someone concluded that he had left his wife for good and quickly changed the subject so he wouldn't have to talk about it. This started gossip, and since he was so well-known, it spread quickly.

The next time he got to the pulpit, he set the matter straight. But that still did not settle the matter. Two years later there were still rumors about him and his wife not getting along.

We may think this is an extreme case that would never happen in our setting. But those seeds are planted in our human nature, and unless we are constantly on guard, they will sprout.

John Eicher, Fredericksburg, OH

Rumor is one thing that gets thicker as you spread it.

September 14

Bible Reading: Genesis 3:12-13, Exodus 4:1-14

One Year Bible Reading Plan: 2 Corinthians 5, Proverbs 23, 24

When I have a convenient season, I will call for thee.

- ACTS 24:25

EXCUSES

"Why did you do that even though you knew you weren't supposed to?"

"Well, Mom," replied the five-year-old boy, "that's just the way it is. We're living in a bad world. The Devil tempted me and I did it."

We wonder how a five-year-old came up with that. The boy's mother had been telling him the story about how Adam and Eve fell (Genesis 2:16-17, 3:1-13). This story has been repeating itself down through the centuries. We hear the excuse "It's not my fault" in many forms, such as, "I could be a good school teacher if my students would just behave." "I could be a good husband and father if it wasn't for my wife and children." "I could be a good minister if my congregation would just do some things differently." "If he would just quit doing that, I could love him." "If he would just admit he was wrong, I could forgive him." "If he would just agree with me, then we could come to an agreement."

Only after we see excuses for what they are, can we see how ridiculous they really are. These excuses began to flow as soon as Adam and Eve fell. It is part of the sinful nature we all have. For many, making an excuse is their alternative for repentance. After all, "It wasn't my fault," we say, "so why should I repent?" Excuses will keep many from heaven. Excuses and Christianity do not mix.

Let's stop making excuses and blaming other people or circumstances for our problems. A wise man said that when everyone else is the problem, it is time to look at ourselves. Jesus was willing to die so that we would not need to make excuses but could be forgiven. Let's accept His forgiveness, because excuses won't work when we stand before God on Judgment Day.

Benjamin Christner, Cochranton, PA

It is impossible to repent while making excuses.

September 15

Bible Reading: 1 Kings 19:1-18

One Year Bible Reading Plan: 2 Corinthians 6, Proverbs 25-27

My brethren, count it all joy when ye fall into divers temptations.
- JAMES 1:2

A ROLLER COASTER RIDE

As we view the life of Elijah, we see he was a man the Lord used mightily in His work. In 1 Kings 18 we read of how the Lord gave him the great victory over the servants of Baal. Oh the great joy, as he triumphed over the kingdom of darkness! Truly the Lord was on his side.

Elijah's joy quickly faded into discouragement as Jezebel, the wicked queen, threatened his life. As he begged the Lord to take his life, we can see his focus was on himself. Would it not have been better for him to ask the Lord what to do instead of asking Him to take his life away?

As Elijah's response to God was controlled by his feelings, so our responses to God are sometimes controlled by our feelings; such feelings hinder us in the service of the Lord and are prone to go up and down according to our circumstances. Just as a roller-coaster takes its passengers on a rolling ride, so our feelings have a tendency to do to us at times. We have no control of where feelings take us when something first happens, but by the grace of God, we can help how long we dwell there if the feelings are not God-honoring.

As Christians we have many things to be thankful for. In times of discouragement, we should count our blessings and sing a song that blesses us. Let us look to the Lord, the giver of true joy, and He will be our stabilizer.

Robert Mast, Melvern, KS

We should forget our troubles and remember our blessings.

September 16

Bible Reading: Philippians 4:4-13; Psalm 107:1-15

One Year Bible Reading Plan: 2 Corinthians 7, Proverbs 28, 29

Not that I speak in respect of want: for I have learned, in whatsoever state I am, therewith to be content.

- PHILIPPIANS 4:11

THE WEALTHY BOY AND THE ORPHAN

Once there was a poor orphan boy whom we will call Johnny. Johnny ran errands for people to earn a little cash, but often he had only dry bread to eat. One day as he sat by the sidewalk in town, a fine carriage stopped just in front of where he was sitting. A finely dressed gentleman and a young boy about the age of Johnny were in the carriage. Johnny looked at his own patched clothes and thought he would like to trade places with the boy in the carriage. He kept thinking about this, then said aloud, "I wish I could trade places with that boy."

The boy in the carriage heard what Johnny said and asked him, "So you would like to trade places with me?"

"I'm sorry," said Johnny. "I didn't mean any harm by what I said."

"That's all right," said the boy in the carriage. "I only want to know if you are really interested in changing places with me."

Johnny hesitated a little then said, "All right, I'll trade places."

When the young boy stepped out of the carriage, Johnny saw that he was lame and used crutches to walk. Johnny thought to himself, *Health is better than a fine carriage.*

The young boy asked Johnny, "Would you still like to change places with me? I would give all that I have to be strong like you."

But Johnny said, "Oh, no, not for the world."

The young crippled boy said, "I would gladly be poor if I could run and play like you can. But since it is God's will that I should be lame, I try to be happy and thankful as I am."

How thankful are we for the blessings we have of God?

Eli A. Yoder, Stuarts Draft, VA

A happy person is not someone in a certain set of circumstances but rather someone with a certain set of attitudes.

September 17

Bible Reading: Ephesians 3

One Year Bible Reading Plan: 2 Corinthians 8, Proverbs 30, 31

From that time Jesus began to preach, and to say, Repent: for the kingdom of heaven is at hand.

- MATTHEW 4:17

SURRENDER

Before I became a Christian, I was working on a road construction project. Close to the area where we were working, there was a police helicopter in the air and police cars on a road nearby. A man had gotten into some trouble the night before and was running from and resisting the authorities. He was now at the end of himself and ready to give up. He came to the realization that there was no hope. It was useless to keep being rebellious. He had to make a choice—would he take his own life or surrender to the authorities?

He decided to surrender to the authorities. The moment he made the choice to surrender, he became nonresistant to the law and to his fellow men.

When I saw this taking place, I didn't know that around a year later, I would be surrendering my life to Jesus Christ. I thank the Lord there were people praying for me.

Life was not going as I wanted. Things were happening that brought me to the end of myself. Then someone told me that God loved me. I remembered back when I was a child going to Sunday school. The Holy Spirit convicted me, and I realized my life was headed in a useless direction. With tears of sorrow, I surrendered my life into the hands of Jesus Christ.

The moment I decided to surrender, I became nonresistant to God's will and to my fellow man and went to war against the flesh. Now I have a living hope. Now I have love, joy, peace, and everlasting life. I am a joyful prisoner of the Lord.

Barry Brown, Melvern, KS

Surrender your heart to the Lord today.

September 18

Bible Reading: Luke 12:22-34

One Year Bible Reading Plan: 2 Corinthians 9, Ecclesiastes 1-3

But seek ye first the kingdom of God, and his righteousness . . .
- MATTHEW 6:33

SEEK FIRST THE KINGDOM OF GOD . . .

This life has so many pursuits. With the younger generation, there are preparations for life in education and vocation and the general youthful activities which keep them occupied.

The more mature who have taken on more serious responsibilities of family, business, and the occupational world can be so overtaken in the affairs of life that there is very little time to seek that which is eternal.

The Bible commands us to work with our hands, to provide for our own, and to be able to help the needy. But we need to remember that these earthly things are temporal. The things that are eternal and lasting need to take priority over the temporal. God gave us not only bodies to be provided for, but also spirits and souls.

The Scriptures command us to remember our Creator and bear the yoke in our youth. This needs to be the first pursuit in the life of humankind. To seek first the kingdom would indicate that the first and most important pursuit of life is to prepare our souls for eternity. The empires men build in their own name and honor are usually short-lived and soon forgotten. What we build that is eternal will last forever.

To seek first the kingdom has its daily application as well. We should dedicate our first waking moments to our heavenly Father. It is good to fall directly on our knees in thankfulness and worship to the One who gives us one more opportunity to be of service to our God and Redeemer. For the needed strength for the day, there also must be a good diet of that heavenly manna, the Word of God. Our service for the day should be such that provides some eternal benefit.

James Yoder, Lewisburg, PA

To seek God first is our first goal.

September 19

Bible Reading: Matthew 19:16-30

One Year Bible Reading Plan: 2 Corinthians 10, Ecclesiastes 4-6

. . . and all these things shall be added unto you.

- MATTHEW 6:33

. . . AND ALL THESE THINGS SHALL BE ADDED

This is a wonderful promise from our Lord, but it is contingent on the command to "seek ye first the kingdom of God."

What does "all these things" include? Jesus talks about the birds of the air and the lilies of the field. Jesus is saying that our heavenly Father will provide food and clothing if we first seek the kingdom of God.

Maybe we have thought something like, *If I seek first the kingdom, I can have that new home, that new piece of machinery, that extra vehicle, that modern appliance, or be able to spend time at some famous resort.* Some of those things may not be wrong to have or to experience, but they do not necessarily come under the promise of things "added" to us.

We have so many things to be thankful for. When we compare ourselves with many throughout the world, we must admit that we are not only rich, but very rich. Paul admonishes Timothy, "Godliness with contentment is great gain. For we brought nothing into this world, and it is certain we can carry nothing out. And having food and raiment let us be therewith content" (1 Timothy 6:6-8).

What do we have that God has not given us? Everything we have God gave us. Even if we worked hard for it, the Lord gave us the strength to do it. That means that we owe all to Him. If our heart is on these earthly treasures, then we have treasure that will be left behind.

Let us strive to lay up treasures in heaven that are lasting, and the Lord will sustain us while we are on our earthly pilgrimage.

James Yoder, Lewisburg, PA

Seek first His kingdom. He meets our needs.

September 20

Bible Reading: John 3:1-21, Hebrews 12:11-17

One Year Bible Reading Plan: 2 Corinthians 11:115, Ecclesiastes 7-9

If we confess our sins, he is faithful and just to forgive us our sins, and to cleanse us from all unrighteousness.

- 1 JOHN 1:9

THE ROOT OF THE PROBLEM

In our bathroom we have a medicine cabinet with sliding doors. Something happened that the one door was hard to open and close. I tried to lubricate the door, but it still would not move easily. I was puzzled and didn't know what to do to make it work like it should.

This medicine cabinet had glass shelves in it. One day I noticed something slipped partly down behind one of the shelves. I got this out and pushed the shelf back in place. Then the sliding door worked perfectly. All that time I had tried other things to make the door work, but I had not gotten to the root of the problem.

Isn't that the way it is in the church sometimes? We may have a problem with a certain person who is not willing to abide by the church rules, or he may have a habit of complaining about and criticizing other people. It seems you cannot do anything to please him. We may work at the problem and get him to make restitution or even to make a confession.

Then we may notice there is more wrong than the outward things we have been seeing. It is a heart condition, and unless there is a change of heart, the outward changes will do little good. It may be that this wayward person has a deep sin in his heart that happened many years ago, but he has never truly made restitution for it. Then finally we get him to see his problem and he is willing to make a complete sacrifice for his wrongs. Then he is able to lead a peaceable life in the church and be at peace with God.

Eli A. Yoder, Stuarts Draft, VA

The minute we begin to unload, the Lord begins to fill in.

September 21

Bible Reading: Matthew 10:16-42

One Year Bible Reading Plan: 2 Corinthians 11:16-33, Ecclesiastes 10-12

And whosoever shall give to drink unto one of these little ones a cup of cold water only in the name of a disciple, verily I say unto you, he shall in no wise lose his reward.

- MATTHEW 10:42

REFRESHING, COOL WATER

If you are looking for a reward, give a cup of cold water. What is a cup of cold water worth? Its worth depends a lot on the need. Perhaps when someone is offered a drink, they hesitate before answering, "Yes, I'll take a drink." In that case, a drink or no drink will not make that much difference. However, to a person stranded in the desert for several days without water, a drink becomes a life or death matter. The one giving the offered drink may get a thank you, but the one giving water to the desperate will get a hero's reward.

Most of us will never be called upon to earn a hero's reward. However, there are many opportunities to offer some humble service to those along our pathway of life. It may be an insignificant deed that no one notices. Our reward may not be apparent or may be deferred until the resurrection of the just, but it will not be lost.

Jesus said at another place, "Inasmuch as ye have done it unto one of the least of these my brethren, ye have done it unto me" (Matthew 25:40). He also said that we should do our alms in secret and He that sees in secret will reward openly. If we do our deeds to be seen of men, then we already have our reward (Matthew 6:1-4).

Have you ever received a note or a call from a caring friend when you were discouraged? Was it not like a drink of fresh, cold water? Whatever opportunity comes our way, let's offer the "cup of cold water."

James Yoder, Lewisburg, PA

A servant's deed meets a heavenly creed.

September 22

Bible Reading: Ecclesiastes 2

One Year Bible Reading Plan: 2 Corinthians 12, Song of Solomon 1-3

But lay up for yourselves treasures in heaven, where neither moth nor rust doth corrupt, and where thieves do not break through nor steal.
- MATTHEW 6:20

TREASURES IN HEAVEN

Our key verse came to my mind as I helped dispose of some of our neighbors' possessions after they had passed away. We found many things they had gathered and stored. It became evident they had quite a knack for seeing a useful purpose in things that most people would have discarded.

Someday, if the Lord tarries, someone will go through my possessions. In our Bible reading, we read of one who gathered a lot and was wise, but when he became old, it did not bring the happiness he thought it would.

In sorting through a person's belongings, it becomes evident what their interests were. Sometimes we hear remarks like, "What did he want with all this junk?" Most importantly, we must consider what Christ will say about the accumulation that we have in our closets and attics. Will He also shake His head and ask, "What did you want with all that garbage? Surely you knew that would not bring any peace and joy in your life."

We can choose to let Jesus confess to God that this child dedicated his life to Him. The things he enjoyed were reading God's word, practicing it, and taking time to see the beauty of nature. When we fill our hearts with what God has done for us and when we consider those around us, we have very little time to think about ourselves.

Allen Byler, Albany, KY

Where your treasure is, there will your heart be also.
- Matthew 6:21

September 23

Bible Reading: Isaiah 2

One Year Bible Reading Plan: 2 Corinthians 13, Song of Solomon 4, 5

Wherefore we receiving a kingdom which cannot be moved, let us have grace, whereby we may serve God acceptably with reverence and godly fear.
- HEBREWS 12:28

GOD IS IN CONTROL

The earthquake and tsunami in Southeast Asia, on December 26, 2004, caused one of the biggest losses of lives from a single natural catastrophe in history since the flood of Noah's day. Nearly 200,000 people died, and thousands more may never be found.

We don't always understand God's workings, but we know He is in control. It is hard to comprehend so many people going into eternity in such a short time. We are confident that all the young children who died went to be with the Lord, but probably thousands died whose souls were not prepared.

We believe this to be a definite sign of the nearness of Christ's coming. "For nation shall rise against nation, and kingdom against kingdom: and there shall be famines, and pestilences, and earthquakes, in divers places" (Matthew 24:7). God has spoken with a loud voice to those who are still alive. According to Isaiah 2 and other Scriptures, things are not going to get better, but rather much worse for those who dwell on the earth.

This world will not only be shaken but will also pass away with a great noise. Praise God, as His children, we are part of a kingdom that cannot be shaken but will stand forever. "Seeing then that all these things shall be dissolved, what manner of persons ought ye to be in all holy conversation and godliness" (2 Peter 3:11). We want to be looking for new heavens and a new earth where righteousness dwells. Trust God—He is in control.

Benuel Glick, Indiana, PA

This world is not my home; I'm just a passing through.

September 24

Bible Reading: Luke 18:18-30

One Year Bible Reading Plan: Galatians 1, Song of Solomon 6-8

For whosoever will save his life shall lose it; but whosoever shall lose his life for my sake and the gospel's, the same shall save it.

- MARK 8:35

A WISE PURSUIT

The young ruler was so close to the kingdom. He had many commendable traits. I'm assuming that he went to synagogue every Saturday, had godly parents, and did everything just right. Jesus said that wasn't good enough. He said, "You lack one thing yet. Sell everything you have and give to the poor."

This rich young ruler was ignorant. Men think themselves innocent because they are ignorant. Had he been acquainted with the nature of the divine law and with the workings of his own heart, and had he been Christ's disciple for awhile, the rich young ruler would have said, "All these things have I broken from my youth up!"

Just "one thing," can that really keep us out of heaven? The Bible says that unless we give Christ our all, unless we completely surrender our lives to Him unconditionally, we will not make it. We either go all the way with Jesus or not at all.

"Some men's sins are open beforehand, going before to judgment; and some men they follow after" (1 Timothy 5:24). If there is one thing in our life that we cannot let go, one thing that we cannot get victory over, one thing that we have not completely given over to Christ, that one thing will follow us to Judgment Day, and it will forever bar us out of heaven.

"But one thing is needful: and Mary hath chosen that good part, which shall not be taken away from her" (Luke 10:42). Let's sit at the feet of Jesus in complete surrender and allow Him to be Lord of our lives!

Lewis Overholt, Scranton, KS

Jesus wants to be Lord of all, or He won't be Lord at all.

September 25

Bible Reading: 1 John 4

One Year Bible Reading Plan: Galatians 2, Isaiah 1–3

Jesus answered and said unto him, If a man love me, he will keep my words: and my Father will love him, and we will come unto him, and make our abode with him.

- JOHN 14:23

LOVE YOUR BROTHER

God teaches us in this passage that we are to love our brother. In verse 11, He says, "Beloved, if God so loved us, we ought also to love one another." Sometimes we have a hard time loving our brothers, sisters, friends, in-laws, or our church families. Many times our in-laws become out-laws, our friends become enemies, and our brothers become adversaries, instead of becoming building blocks in our relationship with God. According to our Bible reading, if a man says he loves God but he hates his brother, he is a liar. If we can't love our brother whom we see, we cannot love God whom we have not seen.

A good friend and I were once going through some hard times in our relationship. He felt I was neglecting him and did not want him around, but I felt I was giving him all I could give him. We talked about it and worked things out.

God had something He wanted me to learn in this. He wanted me to learn that my relationship with Him was not what He wanted it to be. I had bitterness, hate, and anger in my heart toward this brother. I couldn't love God properly if I did not love my brother.

If you get your relationship right with God, He will put love in your heart, and you will not have problems loving others. Yes, we will still be tested, but the grace of God is there to help us, and love will always prevail.

Joseph Shell, Burnsville, VA

Love is like a fabric that never fades when washed in the water of adversity and grief.

273

September 26

Bible Reading: Ephesians 1

One Year Bible Reading Plan: Galatians 3, Isaiah 4–6

In whom also after that ye believed, ye were sealed with that holy Spirit of promise.

- EPHESIANS 1:13

DIVINE TOKENS

After the flood God put a rainbow in the sky and told Noah, "This is the token of the covenant . . . for perpetual generations" (Genesis 9:12). God will not again destroy the entire earth by flood. Today we still see this divine token.

Circumcision was a divine token between God and Abraham's descendants. It showed that they were His chosen people above all nations (Genesis 17:11).

Blood on the doorposts was "a token upon the houses where ye are: and when I see the blood, I will pass over you, and the plague shall not be upon you to destroy you, when I smite the land of Egypt" (Exodus 12:13).

Sacrificing the firstborn of their animals was a token to remind the children of Israel of God's deliverance from Egypt (Exodus 13:15-16).

Aaron's flowering rod was brought before the testimony to keep for a divine token against the rebels. The house of Aaron was God's chosen priesthood (Numbers 17:10).

At Jesus' baptism, a dove descended as a token of who Jesus was (Matthew 3:16).

Today we also have a divine token of being God's chosen possession, as we are sealed with the Holy Spirit of promise. The earnest of the Spirit (guarantee, pledge, or down payment) is our anticipation of full redemption and acquiring complete possession of eternal life to the praise of His glory (Ephesians 1:13-14).

Are you sealed with that divine token, the earnest of the Spirit? If not, there is yet time. The day of God's redeeming grace in still at hand. Do not neglect it.

Wilmer S. Beachy, Liberty, KY

Unless we have within us that which is above us, we soon shall yield to the pressures around us.

September 27

Bible Reading: Acts 18

One Year Bible Reading Plan: Galatians 4, Isaiah 7–9

This fellow persuadeth men to worship God.

- ACTS 18:13

SPEAK! BE NOT AFRAID!

The story is told of a young man who, when he came home from school, took a bath and dressed in his Sunday best. His mother was curious about where he was going. He told her that he was going to go talk to Deke Mullins about the Lord. Deke was an ungodly man for whom the church had been praying for a long time. He was big and mean and always hanging around the saloons. The young man said that there is a time for praying and a time for doing. He invited Deke to church and talked with him about the Lord. To everyone's surprise, Deke came to church and accepted Christ as his Savior.

Paul faced a lot of opposition in Corinth. Corinth was a wicked and immoral city. It was not easy for Paul to preach to them. The Lord reassured Paul by telling him that He would be with him. Paul obeyed, and many people came to know the Lord. The Bible says he "persuaded the Jews and the Greeks" (Acts 18:4).

Finally the Jews took action. They brought him to the judgment seat. Gallio, the deputy, saw that Paul was innocent, so he drove the Jews away. The Greeks then turned against Sosthenes, who probably started the whole thing, and beat him.

What about us? Are we willing to put our fears aside and speak to the people we see around us? Are we praying that God will provide someone else to witness? People are dying every day. We may be the only ones who can show them Jesus.

Derek Overholt, Whiteville, TN

The Christian may be the only Bible the world will ever read.

September 28

Bible Reading: 2 Corinthians 6

One Year Bible Reading Plan: Galatians 5, Isaiah 10–12

But he that is joined unto the Lord is one spirit.

- 1 CORINTHIANS 6:17

BE YE SEPARATE

Before Constantine was Emperor, Christians were persecuted. They were charged with being the most unsocial of all people. Society considered Christians queer, hated them, and counted them enemies of society, because they were simple and modest in dress. They were strictly moral in their conduct and would not go to the games and feasts, but reprimanded the people for their popular forms of amusement.

Then Constantine became Emperor. On the eve of the Battle of Milvan Bridge, just outside of Rome, Constantine saw in the sky, just above the setting of the sun, a vision of the Cross. Above it were the words, "In This Sign Conquer." He decided to fight under the banner of Christ, and he won the battle. After that, Constantine favored Christians in every way. He filled chief offices with them, exempted Christian ministers from taxes and military service, and encouraged and helped build churches.

Constantine brought the church and the state together. He regarded himself as the head of the church. The church immediately became an institution of vast importance in world politics.

We see what happens when the church and state work together. God gets pushed out of worship, and worship turns into simply a meeting. We must continue to practice separation from the world, or we will lose out to the kingdom of this world.

Paul Miller, Melvern, KS

---

*We cannot be separated unto God
when we are living for the world.*

September 29

Bible Reading: 2 Peter 3

One Year Bible Reading Plan: Galatians 6, Isaiah 13-15

Howbeit when he, the Spirit of truth, is come, he will guide you into all truth: for he shall not speak of himself; but whatsoever he shall hear, that shall he speak: and he will show you things to come.
- JOHN 16:13

WHEN THE WORLD'S ON FIRE

In 1961, after Hurricane Hattie, I worked at a sawmill where I was responsible for getting in the logs. There I found out that someone from the relief center was giving food to hurricane victims. I met a Mennonite couple who gave me a copy of the tract, "When the World's on Fire!" After reading that tract several times, something came over me that I cannot explain. It caused me to think deeply. When the world's on fire, how would I be able to escape? Unknowingly then, it was the Spirit of God that came upon my heart. John 16:13 says, "He will guide you into all truth."

Some of us refugees asked the Mennonite couple to hold church services. At that time I was living with a woman I was not married to. The missionary brother pointed out that a Christian does not live that way. On April 27, 1963, we were baptized and married all on the same day. In one sense, it has never been an easy road. Jesus said, "In the world ye shall have tribulation: but be of good cheer; I have overcome the world" (John 16:33).

Once, by accident, I almost shot myself. Later I was nearly hit by a truck. But the darkest days of my life were when I was living a godless life. It is the best and wisest decision to acknowledge and confess Jesus Christ as Savior and by Him confess our sins to God. By the grace of God, I have come a long way and am still in His care. Thank God for Hurricane Hattie and missionaries. If it were not for them, no doubt, I would still be lost today. Let's all sow the good seed for eternity. "For I am not ashamed of the gospel of Christ: for it is the power of God unto salvation to everyone that believeth" (Romans 1:16).

Bob Foreman, Scotland Half Moon, Belize

Stayed upon Jehovah, hearts are fully blest.

September 30

If we confess our sins, he is faithful and just to forgive us our sins, and to cleanse us from all unrighteousness.

- 1 JOHN 1:9

CONFESSION-FOOD FOR THE SOUL

"My son, if sinners entice thee, consent thou not" (Proverbs 1:10).

The plan seemed perfect. No one would need to know who did it. A natural gas line had sprung a leak. A few mischievous heads got together and decided to light the leak that was coming up from a hole in the ground. The deed was done. For a short while the boys enjoyed their prank. Then came step number two—put the fire out. To their dismay, the pressure of the gas would not allow the fire to go out, regardless of what they tried. After awhile they told someone what they had done, and the gas company was called. The gas company had a simple remedy to put out the shooting gas flame, after all of the guilt and distress it had caused the boys.

Perhaps the wiles of Satan have enticed you to try something sinful. The fun only lasted for awhile and then guilt settled in. In vain you have tossed and turned from evening to morning. You have experienced remorse day after day, maybe week after week, month after month, or year after year. Isn't it time to rid yourself of that pain of guilt by confessing it? Make yourself responsible to someone and experience deliverance!

The vanity of sin is so awful, and the answer of a good conscience so desirable and simple, that Jesus says, "Come unto me, all ye that labour and are heavy laden, and I will give you rest. Take my yoke upon you, and learn of me; for I am meek and lowly in heart: and ye shall find rest unto your souls. For my yoke is easy, and my burden is light" (Matthew 11:28-30).

Wayne E. Miller, Rushsylvania, OH

He who delays his repentance pawns his soul to the Devil.

278

October 1

Bible Reading: Isaiah 5:1-12

One Year Bible Reading Plan: Ephesians 2, Isaiah 19-21

My wellbeloved hath a vineyard in a very fruitful hill: and he fenced it, and gathered out the stones thereof, and planted it with the choicest vine, and built a tower in the midst of it, and also made a winepress therein.

- ISAIAH 5:1-2

THE FRUITFUL VINEYARD

Let's take some time to think about these verses. His "wellbeloved" planted a vineyard in a good place, not in a place where you don't expect things to grow. One of the first things he did was to build a good fence so Satan could not hinder his good works. The fence would keep out the bad animals and men. After that he gathered the stones to make sure the vines had room to grow.

Only the best vines were chosen to be planted in this vineyard. He built a tower in the middle of the vineyard where He could see what was going on. He did not wait to build the winepress until he saw it would bear fruit. Expecting nothing less than good fruit in such an ideal place, he made the press ready. But he waited, and it brought forth wild grapes. He had done all he could, but since it bore no fruit, he was ready to leave it to the elements. The briers and thorns would overgrow the place.

Now let's consider what Christ did for us. He left His home in glory, a great sacrifice in itself. But then, to fulfill the plan of salvation, He suffered and died here on earth. He also planted a vineyard and put in it everything that was needed. He made the plan of salvation possible through faith in Him.

Now then, do we bring forth good grapes? Did His sacrifice do us any good?

Moses Kinsinger, Dunnegan, MO

Salvation produces a change within that breaks the chains of sin.

October 2

Bible Reading: Matthew 25:1-30

One Year Bible Reading Plan: Ephesians 3, Isaiah 22, 23

The harvest is past, the summer is ended, and we are not saved.
- JEREMIAH 8:20

GRASPING THE OPPORTUNITY

It happened long ago in Kwoi, Nigeria. Madaki was chief elder of the church and also one of the most prosperous farmers. One Sunday this announcement was made: "Madaki wants all the village women to gather at his house the following Wednesday morning. Pass the word around."

On the appointed morning, 104 women and girls gathered at Madaki's house. Madaki asked the women to walk three and a half miles to his farm and bring his corn crop home. So they gathered up baskets of various sizes and walked to the farm. Some brought back a big load—all they could carry. One actually got such a big load that her strength failed before she got home. Others brought small loads, and some only brought a few ears. When all the loads had been brought in, Madaki called all the women together and told them that each could keep what she had brought in.

There were shouts of joy and thanksgiving, but also deep sighs of regret. "If only I had known, I would have taken a bigger basket," was the complaint of some. There were those who had refused to go saying, "I have enough work of my own." These went to Madaki the next morning, their own work seemed less important now, and begged him to let them go, too, and bring in a load. But he told them quietly, "The time is past. The corn was brought in yesterday."

Through this kind deed, Madaki not only helped many needy families, but he also preached quite a sermon. Christians are telling and re-telling the story all over town, always adding, "That is just the way it is with Jesus." Today is the day of opportunity. The harvest of souls is waiting to be brought in. How big a basket are you taking?

Wilmer S. Beachy, Liberty, KY

The sure way to miss success is to miss opportunity.

October 3

Bible Reading: Jeremiah 17:5-8, Psalm 63

One Year Bible Reading Plan: Ephesians 4, Isaiah 24-26

Lord, how are they increased that trouble me! Many are they that rise up against me.

- PSALM 3:1

THRIVING OR DYING?

It was very warm and dry. Any moisture exposed to the elements was absorbed. Days passed. Each was the same. I kept watching the corn and wondering, *What is keeping this corn alive?* In the morning the leaves looked refreshed, but by afternoon the heat of the day and the lack of moisture caused the leaves to curl. I finally concluded that it must be the fairly regular, heavy dews of early morning that were sustaining it.

As I thought on this, my own recent spiritual life stared at me in stark parallel. When I opened God's Word, the pages seemed dry. When I knelt to pray, God seemed far away. When I was tempted, there was little strength to resist.

I knew the problem lay in me. I was not experiencing the heavy dew of morning. The busyness of summer, the long days, and the stress of everything made me push my personal devotions on the back shelf. When the sun of stress pressed, and the heat of temptation burned, there was no spiritual moisture to draw from.

So often we get our focus on the things we hope to accomplish—our work, the vacation we want to take, the reunions we would like to attend, and the list could continue. Or maybe we get sapped by the heat, the long days, or the responsibilities. Do we feel the importance of drinking from the waters of God's Word on a daily basis? Without it, we shrivel and die spiritually. May we, with God's help, be like trees planted by the waters—not only surviving, but thriving and bringing forth fruit.

Jonathan Stutzman, Albany, KY

Water early to withstand late heat

October 4

Bible Reading: Revelation 22

One Year Bible Reading Plan: Ephesians 5, Isaiah 27, 28

Thy word have I hid in mine heart, that I might not sin against thee.

- PSALM 119:11

REVERENCE FOR THE WORD OF GOD

The Bible is God's personal Word from heaven to us human beings here on earth. Can we grasp the amazing significance of this wonderful truth? The Bible is God's road map for our lives. It instructs us how to live and prepares us to die.

An acquaintance who has extensive contacts in the Middle East was a personal friend of former King Hussein of Jordan. He related how he once gave a Bible to the King during one of his visits to the palace in Amman. King Hussein, a Muslim, took the Bible with both hands and kissed it reverently. Devout Muslims express reverence for what they consider "holy" books, including the Bible. They would never place the Koran, their holy book, on the floor or lay another book on top of it.

What about us Christians who have the Bible, the true Book of books, God's message from heaven? Do we treasure the Bible? Do we spend time studying it and applying its teachings to our lives? Do we truly reverence the Bible? Or do we carelessly drop it on the floor, pitch the newspaper on top of it, and take its teachings lightly?

The real test of our reverence for the Bible, the Word of God, is our obedience to its precepts and principles.

David N. Troyer, Millersburg, OH

Can you say with the psalmist David, "O how I love thy law! It is my meditation all the day"?

October 5

Bible Reading: 2 Corinthians 9

One Year Bible Reading Plan: Ephesians 6, Isaiah 29, 30

For I know the forwardness of your mind, for which I boast of you to them of Macedonia, that Achaia was ready a year ago; and your zeal hath provoked very many.

- 2 CORINTHIANS 9:2

SOWING SEEDS OF INFLUENCE

In autumn we see a lot of seeds. Sometimes thousands of seeds drop from the many cones on one evergreen tree. Or, like a fruit tree, there may not be many visible seeds, but they are set within a well-formed fruit.

Seeds don't always stay right by the mother plant. Often the wind is the main influence on where a seed will be taken. A strong wind may blow several apples outside the orchard fence, or it may send lightweight seeds a great distance.

What about our influence? How far does it travel? Just as a seed before the wind, so our influence spreads. What influence do we leave on those who come in contact with us?

It is interesting, yet frightening, how strong influence is. For example, if one in a group seems to enjoy lifting his own ego, likely that influence will spread, and the whole group will unconsciously be attempting to put him in his place using the same technique.

On the other hand, at times we see someone who we think is "less fortunate." Perhaps they come from less-than-ideal home or church settings, but they are putting forth a strong effort to live for the Lord. They may be cheerful, willing to help, and a challenge to all. Blessed is the congregation with this type of influence!

Like seeds, our influence will grow and bear fruit. Are we influencing others into the right, or away from the right? Is our influence a weed in someone else's life that they need to struggle with? Or is our influence a fruit–good fruit that meets the Master's eye of approval? Is someone, somewhere, thanking God for our influence? Or is someone turning away from God because of it?

Tobias M. Hoover, Corinth, ON

Good influence is like sound health–the value of it is seldom known until it is lost.

October 6

Bible Reading: John 10:1-16

One Year Bible Reading Plan: Philippians 1, Isaiah 31-33

For the Lamb which is in the midst of the throne shall feed them, and shall lead them unto living fountains of waters: and God shall wipe away all tears from their eyes.

- REVELATION 7:17

LEAD ME ON

There he went again, crashing through my carefully placed gates as if they were tinker toys. That was the third time we got the bull into the barn to load him and take him to green pastures where his herd of cows waited. Each time, he decided he didn't want to be loaded and found a hole or made a hole.

What next? I decided it was time to change our tactics. I knew I could lead that bull, but I couldn't push him.

I parked the trailer out in the middle of the barn lot with no gates closed. I put a pile of enticing feed in the trailer and went into the house to watch. I didn't have long to wait before the bull had loaded himself. I quickly took him to his herd and green grass. He was a happy bull when it was all over, but he sure couldn't see it from the barn.

Aren't we a lot like this bull when we are confronted with something that needs improvement in our life? Maybe a brother has experienced something that lets him see the future more clearly. Let's take heed. Or maybe we are on the other side of the fence trying to hem someone into the fold. If it's not working, let's consider changing tactics. Let's pour our love out to them and let God lead them on board.

Wesley Yoder, Monticello, KY

When you find you can't take the bull by the horns,
turn it over to God who can.

October 7

Bible Reading: Acts 19:1-20

One Year Bible Reading Plan: Philippians 2, Isaiah 34-36

Whose adorning let it not be . . . of wearing of gold, or of putting on of apparel; but let it be the hidden man of the heart, in that which is not corruptible, even the ornament of a meek and quiet spirit, which is in the sight of God of great price.

- 1 PETER 3:3-4

PUT ON THE INCORRUPTIBLE APPAREL

Truly religious reformation took place in this Scripture reading. The Word of God took root through preaching, and the Holy Ghost did a mighty work in the listeners' hearts. Many believed and confessed their evil deeds, even bringing piles of ungodly and evil books, burning them before all. The price of the stuff destroyed was fifty thousand pieces of silver. This scene should be repeated in our day.

I would like to address a need I see in the world today. Many people live good moral lives and profess to be Christians, but on them we see earrings, finger rings, necklaces, and other jewelry. Would you be willing to consider with me how much more than fifty thousand dollars all the jewelry would amount to today?

How must God feel when He has given us His Holy Word to remind us that in the Old Testament the children of Israel had fallen into idolatry time after time. The one who truly desires growth in the way of righteousness and truth will take this matter to heart and be instructed by it. Genesis 35:2-4 indicates that to be clean included putting away strange gods and earrings. The word "earrings" is not found in the New Testament, but I do find that we are not to adorn ourselves with gold or pearls, immodest or costly array.

William Troyer, Huntland, TN

A full surrender is of great price.

October 8

Bible Reading: Matthew 25:31-46

One Year Bible Reading Plan: Philippians 3, Isaiah 37, 38

And that he died for all, that they which live should not henceforth live unto themselves, but unto him which died for them, and rose again.

- 2 CORINTHIANS 5:15

WHAT'S IN IT FOR ME?

The story is told of a grandfather who asked a self-centered and depressed young granddaughter to promise to volunteer in an old people's home one day a week for a month. The granddaughter could not fathom why he asked this of her, but she promised it and followed through. When she began to focus on the needs of others, she learned that some of the most satisfying times in life are times of living for others. Her personality and outlook on life improved dramatically.

I'm sure we have all met someone with a long face and a long sob story to go with it–the "me, mine, and I" personality. This is one of the reasons people get down and depressed. Too often life is about my needs, my problems, my agenda, my feelings, and my work. The tendency to think about myself all the time is of the nature of Adam. A self-focused life is not in God's plan if we are one of His.

You can experience a deep, rich fulfillment by sacrificing to serve those who need you. Jesus kept thinking about others all the way to the cross, and even on the cross. If He is our Lord, then that should be our focus also. When we live our lives thinking of others, we can finally escape the clutches of the "me" monster.

Lester K. Burkholder, Fredericksburg, PA

---

*Life's golden moments are when
we are focused on helping others.*

October 9

Bible Reading: Psalm 32:1-2; 51:1-14

One Year Bible Reading Plan: Philippians 4, Isaiah 39, 40

Search me, O God, and know my heart: try me, and know my thoughts: and
see if there be any wicked way in me, and lead me in the way everlasting.

- PSALM 139:23-24

GET RID OF GUILT

"Good morning. How are you?"

"I am just fine."

"No, I mean how are you?"

"Oh yes, I'm just fine."

"No, no, I mean, deep down in your heart, how are you?"

This was the conversation I had with a customer at the office where
I work. This was only part of the conversation that morning that made
him stop and look at me. With tears in his eyes he said, "Yes, I grew
up in church, but I have never received Christ as my Savior." Then he
asked the question many people ask, "How do I get right with God?"
To make a long story short, he left the office rejoicing in his new-found
faith in God through Jesus Christ and in a new peace of heart!

In Acts 2:37-38 the multitude came to Peter and asked, "What shall
we do?" The first word of Peter's answer was "Repent." Repentance
means being sorry for your sin and turning away from it. We cannot
renounce sin unless we see its sinfulness. Until we turn away from it in
heart, there will be no real change in our life. 2 Corinthians 7:10 says,
"For godly sorrow worketh repentance to salvation not to be repented
of: but the sorrow of the world worketh death."

The prayer of David illustrates the nature of true sorrow for sin. His
repentance was sincere and from the heart. David saw the awfulness
of his transgression. He saw the defilement of his soul. He abhorred
his sin. He prayed not for pardon only, but also for purity of heart.

Oh that we would experience this same healing of our soul, so we
may be able, by the grace and power of God, to help the hungry souls
around us.

Mervin Hochstetler, Auburn, KY

Thank you, Jesus, for the Calvary experience.

October 10

Bible Reading: Luke 17:26-37, 2 Peter 2:20-22

One Year Bible Reading Plan: Colossians 1, Isaiah 41, 42

Then said Jesus to those Jews which believed on him, If ye continue in my word, then are ye my disciples indeed; and ye shall know the truth, and the truth shall make you free.

- JOHN 8:31-32

REMEMBER LOT'S WIFE

Her name is not given. The Bible merely calls her "Lot's wife." She is known for her failure. In this reading Jesus was talking about how world conditions would be before He comes again.

We notice Jesus said, "Remember." The Bible gives us many examples and comparisons of warning for our spiritual and eternal benefit. The word "remember" is used 121 times in the Old Testament and 27 times in the New Testament. God knows we are forgetful. In John 15:20 Jesus said, "Remember the word that I said unto you."

2 Peter 2:5-7 mentions just and righteous Lot. But he was vexed with the filthy conversation of the wicked. It doesn't say he was in fellowship with them. His righteousness did not seem to affect his family or others. Was he a secret disciple?

In 2 Timothy 4:3-10, Hebrews 12:1-2, Titus 2:11, 12, and many other places, we see that Jesus wants us to separate ourselves from the life of the sinner and follow Him faithfully. In Philippians 3:13 Paul wrote, "This one thing I do, forgetting those things which are behind, and reaching forth unto those things which are before." Lot's wife did not press forward. She did not flee from Sodom and forget the things behind her. Instead, she stopped and looked back. There are people today who have truly repented and lived for the Lord, then later cooled in their obedience to Bible teaching and drifted back to where they came from.

Lot, who once wanted to have the best, now had lost practically everything, even his wife. We must be careful never to pitch our tents toward Sodom.

Eli A. Yoder, Stuarts Draft, VA

The Lord's sheep have no business playing around with the Devil's goats.

October 11

Bible Reading: Romans 8:1-17

One Year Bible Reading Plan: Colossians 2, Isaiah 43, 44

And lo a voice from heaven, saying, This is my beloved Son, in whom I am
well pleased.
- MATTHEW 3:17

IS GOD PLEASED WITH ME?

Suppose, for a moment, that you and I are sitting in God's office
with the freedom to leaf through His file drawer. Our attention is quickly
drawn to the status cards that tell if God is pleased with our lives. As
we look at the cards, our faults, weaknesses, and immaturity flash
vividly before our eyes. We stop. Do we dare to check our card? Is it
important to know if God is pleased with us? Should we be confident
concerning our standing with God?

If God is not pleased with our lives, we must have sin there. If God
wants us to know when He is not satisfied with our life, then we will
also be able to know when He is pleased.

Satan is ever busy. He delights in confusing the sincere follower
of Christ. He may not be able to get you entangled in obvious sin, so
he tries to make you live a guilt-ridden life even though you are not
living in sin. He longs to destroy the fruit of peace that comes from the
assurance that our salvation gives.

Praise God that we can be "accepted in the beloved" (Ephesians
1:6). We are clean as we abide in the vine (John 15:3-4), and no more
condemnation hangs over us when we are walking after the Spirit
(Romans 8:1). Let us trust our Lord to show us when we err. God
works through the avenue of a peaceful mind.

Marcus Troyer, Belle Center, OH

---

*The "Light of the World" clearly shows us
our sin and provides the remedy.*

October 12

Bible Reading: 2 Peter 2

One Year Bible Reading Plan: Colossians 3, Isaiah 45-47

Be sober, be vigilant; because your adversary the devil, as a roaring lion, walketh about, seeking whom he may devour.

- 1 PETER 5:8

SATAN'S SNARE

Years ago in the pioneer days of Georgia, there was a river that made a big horseshoe bend. A herd of wild hogs lived in this area. They were dangerous hogs that killed hunting dogs. Even hunters were fortunate to escape. Stories were told everywhere about this band of wild hogs. People stayed away.

An old man loaded his wagon with corn and set off to pen up those hogs, despite warnings from the locals. At first the older hogs would not touch the corn at all, but the little pigs started to nibble on it. When the older hogs saw that it did no harm to the young pigs, they also started eating it. Every day the old man split a few rails and put them in place. He was careful not to make a big change at once. He slowly built his corral until there was just one opening left. He kept on feeding the hogs in the corral until one day, when the hogs were used to having this old man around and were busy eating up the corn, he laid up rails in the gap and had them all penned up.

That is the way Satan works. He tries to get our young people, who cannot see the danger of the sin, to crowd the fence a little. The more they crowd it, the less harm they can see in it. The older folks also get used to it and cannot see the danger anymore. By these means, Satan is building his fence—slowly, but surely. If we do not wake up, we will find ourselves penned up in Satan's corral.

Daniel Miller, Dunnegan, MO

Usually falling into sin is not a blowout, but a slow leak.

October 13

Bible Reading: John 14

One Year Bible Reading Plan: Colossians 4, Isaiah 48, 49

Open thou mine eyes, that I may behold wondrous things out of thy law.
- PSALM 119:18

JESUS WORKS WONDERS

While Jesus was here on earth, He performed thirty-five recorded miracles. These miracles had a three-fold purpose. First, they demonstrated His relationship with God. Nicodemus acknowledged that only a God-sent man could do what Jesus was doing.

The second reason was to make it easier for people to believe in His message. In John 20:30-31, it tells us the main reason for including the miracles of Christ in his Gospel was that we might believe that Jesus is indeed the Son of God.

The final reason for His miracles was to demonstrate His care and concern for us human beings. By healing the sick and raising the dead, He showed His care for us. It showed that He was concerned about our sicknesses and sorrows. In Mark 8 He shows us His feelings for the physical needs of man.

As Jesus was about to leave His disciples, they were concerned about what they would do if Jesus would leave them. In John 14:26 Jesus promised His disciples that He would send them the Holy Spirit, which would teach them all things. In verse 17 it tells us the world cannot receive this, because it knows Him not; according to John 14:21, the promise of the Holy Spirit is only for those who have His commandments and keep them. Let us not only read the Bible, but also study it and be doers of the Word. Then His promise is for us.

Eli A. Yoder, Stuarts Draft, VA

Christ departed so that the Holy Spirit could be imparted.

October 14

Bible Reading: Matthew 17:14-27

One Year Bible Reading Plan: 1 Thessalonians 1, Isaiah 50-52

This is the victory that overcometh the world, even our faith.

- 1 JOHN 5:4

HAVE FAITH

Faith is confidence in the absolute truthfulness of every statement which comes from God.

Faith is not an emotion–a boasting confidence that God will give me what I want. It is a conviction–a persuasion that God is right. Faith is reliance on God's testimony of the redemptive work and atoning death of His Son, Jesus Christ. It is steadfast loyalty to the grace we receive in our acceptance of this redemptive work.

Jesus promised, "If ye have faith as a grain of mustard seed, ye shall say unto this mountain, Remove hence to yonder place; and it shall remove; and nothing shall be impossible unto you" (Matthew 17:20). We need to understand this verse as the disciples did, through the eyes of faith and not through carnal or immature eyes. These could be mountains of carnality, pride, and self-righteousness.

Jesus also spoke of His disciples doing greater works than He Himself did. By this He meant spreading the Gospel to the entire world and bringing people to spiritual birth. He did not have in mind that His disciples would do more healing, raising from the dead, or casting out devils than He did. The work of the Gospel in transforming people's lives is a greater work than physical miracles.

In order to have great faith, we need great humility and obedience. The three Hebrew men said, "We will not serve thy gods, nor worship the golden image which thou hast set up" (Daniel 3:18). They were fully submitted to God's will. They would accept God's deliverance whether He chose to deliver them through life or death. That is great faith.

Daniel N. Miller, Kalona, IA

Faith lets Christ do for us and with us what we could never do alone.

October 15

Bible Reading: 1 Corinthians 3

One Year Bible Reading Plan: 1 Thessalonians 2, Isaiah 53-55

Every man's work shall be made manifest: for the day shall declare it, because it shall be revealed by fire.

- 1 CORINTHIANS 3:13

TRIED BY FIRE

At my job, we sometimes work with stainless steel. To remove the residue that is left after welding stainless steel, we clean it with a very corrosive substance called pickling paste. After applying the paste, we let it dry for a little while, then it can be washed off and the entire dirty, black residue is removed, leaving a shining, clean weld. One time we applied the pickling paste and a short while later noticed that one of the pieces was turning very rusty. We had used a piece of steel that looked like stainless steel but was not. This piece went undetected through the entire fabricating process, but when the final test was done, it revealed the true substance of the material.

In the same way, people can look right on the outside, but when they are tried with fire they show what is on the inside. It is possible for someone to live a hypocritical life without revealing to others how he is living. Some people can successfully hide their sins for many years. Although they appear the same as other Christians, when trials arise, their sins are exposed. I suppose there are also people who can hide their double life from man all their lives, but it will be revealed on the Day of Judgment.

If we have Jesus Christ as our foundation, our work can be tried with fire and we can come out victorious. This should be an encouragement to anyone endeavoring to live a true Christian life.

Darrell Frey, Drayton, ON

The fire shall try every man's work of what sort it is.
- 1 Corinthians 3:13

October 16

Bible Reading: Ephesians 4:14-32

One Year Bible Reading Plan: 1 Thessalonians 3, Isaiah 56-58

A time to keep silence, and a time to speak.
- ECCLESIASTES 3:7

SPEAKING THE TRUTH IN LOVE

I have read that whenever D. L. Moody would meet someone, he would talk to him about salvation and ask him if he had perfect peace with God and was ready for heaven. Sometimes people would answer, "It's none of your business." D. L. Moody would tell them it was his business.

I read of a barber who also liked to speak to his customers about the coming of the Lord and remind them to be ready. One day a new customer came in to have a shave and a haircut. In those days they used big shaving knives. The new customer was sitting on the barber chair while the barber was sharpening his shaving knife on a razor strop. All at once the barber asked this man, "Say, are you ready to die?"

The customer did not know what the barber was referring to, but he thought he knew. He jumped off the barber chair, ran down the sidewalk, and never came back. This barber should have been more careful what he said and how he said it.

I also read of a woman who was in a shoe store to buy a pair of shoes. As she tried on a pair, the clerk said, "Your feet are too big for these shoes."

The woman left the store and never came back. She did go to another store and tried on a pair of shoes. The clerk said, "These shoes are too small for your feet. I'll get you a bigger pair." The loving attitude of the clerk convinced her to buy the shoes she wanted.

It is so important that our speech be seasoned with salt. We should always have a loving attitude so we can speak the truth in love.

Eli A. Yoder, Stuarts Draft, VA

Not only be careful what *you say, but be careful* how *you say it.*

October 17

But the fruit of the Spirit is love, joy, peace, longsuffering, gentleness, goodness, faith, meekness, temperance: against such there is no law.
- GALATIANS 5:22-23

WORKS OF THE FLESH VS. FRUIT OF THE SPIRIT

The flesh is as putrefying garbage in contrast to the fragrant, beautiful fruit of God's spirit. The works of the flesh bear the stamp of the Devil. The fruit of the Spirit bears the stamp of God. The flesh is that earthly, human nature of man apart from divine influence and therefore prone to sin and opposed to God. It is the sinful element of man's nature and that which is contrary to God's nature of holiness and love. It is all that man is without Christ.

The catalog of sins listed in today's reading relates to both outward and inward conduct and will bar a person from heaven unless there is genuine repentance.

How do the works of the flesh come about? They spring from the natural inclination of our human nature, because the flesh is that tendency within each of our lives to operate independently of God and cater to our own selfish, sinful desires.

How, then, do we obtain the fruit of the Spirit? By trying to act like a Christian? By working harder to develop this fruit in our lives? No. It is not a "reformation job" by our own effort. It begins with a transformation experience by the divine power of God whereby we become a new creation in Jesus Christ. The true, lasting, lovely fruit of the Spirit is not something we can manufacture. It is the product of God's Holy Spirit controlling and directing our lives.

True Christian character is essentially the fruit of the indwelling Spirit through our close, abiding relationship with Christ. The fruit of the Spirit will be evidenced by one who walks and lives in the Spirit, thereby radiating forth the life and virtues of Christ in our own lives.

Mark Kropf, Cataldo, ID

The fruit of the spirit comes only from a Spirit-filled, Christ-centered, God-focused life.

October 18

Bible Reading: Psalm 39

One Year Bible Reading Plan: 1 Thessalonians 5, Isaiah 62-64

So teach us to number our days, that we may apply our hearts unto wisdom.
- PSALM 90:12

NOT WITH THESE PRODUCTS

A backslidden relative of mine was a salesperson for herbal products. To be a good salesman, you need to be convinced of your product. This man was fully convinced that the product he was selling was exceptionally supportive to a person's health. At the age of 70 years, he made this statement; "With these products I am taking, I feel better than I ever have. In fact, I feel so good that I see no reason why I will not live till I am 100 years old," The person to whom he was speaking replied, "You have no promise of your life. That is up to God to decide when our time here is finished."

He replied, "Well, I'm not saying I couldn't get killed in a traffic accident or something like that, but this product will not let me die of natural causes."

Six months later, he suddenly died of a heart attack.

I was stunned to learn of his death. It reminded me that none of us have the promise of life for years and years to come. We have no claim on life.

I wondered if God let him die of a natural cause to show us that we cannot trust in herbal products, medications, doctors, and whatever else people may rely on to keep themselves from dying. Let us not challenge God by saying, or even thinking, that we know how to take care of ourselves so that we won't die.

Let us remember the shortness of time. We all will someday stand before a just and all-wise God who will determine our eternal destiny. We may not have another chance on our deathbed to make things right. Are you ready to die today? Are you ready to die right now?

Bruce Weaver, Orrville, OH

Every man at his best state is altogether vanity.

October 19

Bible Reading: Romans 12

One Year Bible Reading Plan: 2 Thessalonians 1, Isaiah 65, 66

Therefore if thine enemy hunger, feed him; if he thirst, give him drink: for in so doing thou shalt heap coals of fire on his head.
- ROMANS 12:20

HEAPING COALS OF FIRE

The story is told of a woman who had a problem getting along with her husband. She sought help from her minister. He counseled her to do things for her husband to create love. He told her that by doing these things she could heap coals of fire on his head. "Well," she concluded, "it probably wouldn't work anyway. I poured hot water on his head once and it just made him mad and things became worse!"

This may sound absurd to us, but this woman had the wrong concept of what Romans 12:20 means. If someone is unfriendly toward you but you continue to do good to that person, his motives may be thwarted, and he may be moved to a change of heart. If someone does something evil toward us, we are not to avenge ourselves. "Vengeance is mine; I will repay, saith the Lord" (Romans 12:19). If we can just leave it in God's hands and continue to do good and pray for the person, we will have our reward. We cannot overcome evil with evil. Evil will only be overcome with good. "If it be possible, as much as lieth in you, live peaceably with all men" (Romans 12:18). Let us make every effort to be at peace with all men.

Daniel Miller, Dunnegan, MO

We dishonor God when we avenge ourselves.

October 20

Thy will be done.

- MATTHEW 6:10

PEACE THROUGH FAITH IN PRAYER

I recall an incident I had while coming home from Belize. It had been a number of months since I had seen my family and friends, and I was anticipating spending a few weeks with them before returning to the mission to continue my responsibilities there. When I arrived in Houston, the line of people going through customs was so long I didn't see how I would make the connecting flight. I began to pray! Soon I began to pray without ceasing! I reassured myself that God is all-powerful and it would be no problem for Him to get me through the line in time. I ended up missing my connecting flight and didn't see my family until the next day. It seemed God didn't answer my prayer. "Ye ask, and receive not, because ye ask amiss, that ye may consume it upon your lusts." (James 4:3). My prayer should have been, "Father, Thy will be done."

Faith is revealed in our prayers when we completely yield ourselves to God's way of meeting our need or difficulty in whatever way He knows is best for us. This way may not be the way our flesh would desire. However, when we in our prayers limit God to answering in the way we think is best, we may completely miss the answer our heavenly Father is giving us.

As we pray the Lord's Prayer, we are praying that God's will be done on earth. This leaves no room for us to have our own will on earth. The more we can be committed to the will of God, the more God is able to work in us and through us. Our desires and the ways we would like to see our prayers answered need to be crucified. We need to trust the outcome into God's hands, knowing that His ways are higher than our ways.

Wendell Beachy, London, OH

Prayer is not bending God's will to ours, but our will to God's.
- Oldham

October 21

Be ye therefore perfect, even as your Father which is in heaven is perfect.
- MATTHEW 5:48

NOT AN ORDINARY MAN

Some time ago my father had heart surgery. It was a stressful and soul-searching time for our whole family. Friends and some of the hospital staff tried to assure us that this operation is usually successful and is an everyday occurrence.

I thought, *Yes, but this is not just an ordinary man. This is my father, a man I have more respect for and confidence in than any other man.*

Then I had to think of God and what He was willing to give up for our redemption. Jesus was not just some ordinary man. He was God's only begotten Son. He was someone who had done no wrong. He was completely sinless. God said, "This is my beloved Son, in whom I am well pleased" (Matthew 3:17). This was the Son of God, who "was in all points tempted like as we are, yet without sin" (Hebrews 4:15b). He is no ordinary man.

We can only imagine in a small way the pain that God must have felt to send His perfect Son to become sin for the world–to see Him be spit upon, beaten, and falsely accused.

It takes more than just an ordinary man to be able to work on a heart where even a little mistake can be the difference between life and death. Even so, doctors are limited. When a heart is damaged too much, they are unable to fix it. No heart is too black or damaged for God to fix completely. God says in Ezekiel 36:26 that He will give us a new heart and a new spirit, one that is in tune with Him as we walk in obedience. Isn't that what we want–an extraordinary heart from an extraordinary God?

Tite Miller, Afton, OK

The love of God in our lives produces "not an ordinary man."

October 22

Bible Reading: Philippians 4

One Year Bible Reading Plan: 1 Timothy 1, Jeremiah 5, 6

What shall we then say to these things? If God be for us,
who can be against us?

- ROMANS 8:31

THE SUFFICIENCY OF CHRIST

When we need to do a job, we look for the proper tools so that we can do the job properly. When we need to cut wood, we get a saw. When we need to turn a bolt, we get the wrench that fits. We should also arm ourselves with the weapons that we need in our spiritual warfare. What must we do to have Christ's all-sufficient power working for us?

Our yearnings and feelings need to be for the cause of Christ. Our interests and goals need to display the spirit of Christ in us. Christ should be evident in our behavior and in our concerns. Christ must be unspeakably dear to us, and His presence must be evident in our attitudes. Then we will live a life separate from the world, and God will be our Father and we His sons and daughters (2 Corinthians 6:18).

God has promised that He will not give us more than we are able to bear. He is faithful and gives us a way of escape so that we can bear the temptations that come our way (1 Corinthians 10:13). God has promised us that His grace will be sufficient for us in our infirmities (2 Corinthians 12:9). We can know that "Greater is he that is in you, than he that is in the world" (I John 4:4). We are on the winning side if we are on the Lord's side.

Take hold of the all-sufficiency of Christ and His power, always remaining conscious of His presence. You can go forth with His joy as your strength, for with the Lord you can and will win.

Elvin Fox, Shiloh, OH

What a friend we have in Jesus, all our sins and griefs to bear!

October 23

Bible Reading: Acts 5:1-11

One Year Bible Reading Plan: 1 Timothy 2, Jeremiah 7, 8

Neither is there any creature that is not manifest in his sight: but all things are naked and opened unto the eyes of him with whom we have to do.

- HEBREWS 4:13

NO ONE BUT YOU?

Secrets are fun. We enjoy planning a surprise for a friend. We plan birthday dinners in secret and spring them upon the victim with laughter and surprise. I think everyone enjoys a good secret. However, not all secrets are good. Some secrets do extreme harm. Take for instance Ananias and Sapphira with their secret. This secret cost them their lives. Someone has said, "You can fool all the people some of the time, and some of the people all the time, but you can't fool all the people all the time." Even if you could, you can't fool God anytime, so why try?

The scribes and Pharisees were masters at fooling the people, and Jesus said, "For I say unto you, That except your righteousness shall exceed the righteousness of the scribes and Pharisees, ye shall in no case enter into the kingdom of heaven" (Matthew 5:20). To look and sound good is not enough.

Your character is what you think and do when no one sees you. Most of us know what we are deep down inside. If you have deceived yourself, allow God to search your heart.

I like the motto on my grandmother's living room wall:

Though thy name be spread abroad
On winged seed from shore to shore,
What thou art before thy God
That thou art and nothing more.

Harold R. Troyer, Belleville, PA

No one is dressed shabbier than he who uses his religion as a cloak.
- David Young

October 24

Bible Reading: Psalm 24

One Year Bible Reading Plan: 1 Timothy 3, Jeremiah 9, 10

Moreover it is required in stewards, that a man be found faithful.

- 1 CORINTHIANS 4:2

WE ARE STEWARDS

What does stewardship mean to you–saving money, living frugally, giving a portion of your income? That certainly is part of it, but Christian stewardship involves much more and is not dictated only by economics. Following Christ may be costly and not make economic sense. For example, the Lord may call us to leave our home and our comfortable lifestyle. He might call us to serve Him in a place that will test and strengthen our faith in Him for daily needs.

Christian stewardship reaches into every facet of life, involving our whole lifestyle. The mindset of the world around us is, "This is my money, my things, and my life to use for my greatest pleasure and comfort."

Christian stewardship portrays a radically different perspective based on spiritual realities. Stewardship is the conviction that all I have and all I am is a gift from God, and we will be accountable before God as to how we use it all. It is being a manager or trustee for another, with a responsibility for that which has been entrusted to our care. It involves the receiving and giving of God's gifts to us and managing them to the promotion of His purposes and for the extension of His kingdom. It includes a total commitment of giving God first place in our lives, keeping in mind that all belongs to Him, to be used for His glory. It is the careful management of time, talents, and treasures that have been allotted to us.

Stewardship is simply making Christ Lord and Master of every area of life.

Mark Kropf, Cataldo, ID

Selfish living and Christian discipleship are incompatible.

October 25

Bible Reading: 1 Timothy 5:1-19

One Year Bible Reading Plan: 1 Timothy 4, Jeremiah 11-13

Rebuke not an elder, but entreat him as a father; and the younger men as brethren.

- 1 TIMOTHY 5:1

A SPECIAL GRANDDAUGHTER

Lisa loved to help her aging grandmother and enjoyed taking her out to eat. But now that Alzheimer's had set in, it brought with it some difficult and embarrassing moments. One day they entered a quiet little restaurant, and Lisa was glad to see that there were only a few people there. They could eat without bothering others. Grandma's endless questions and senseless remarks could be embarrassing at times. The waitress put them at a table next to a businessman who was enjoying his meal and trying to read his paper. As soon as they were seated, the endless questions began. "How did I get here?" "Who will pay for my meal?" "Why do we have to eat in a place like this?" "This is not where I live." "Can you take me home?"

Lisa tried to calm her grandmother the best she could, answering the same questions over and over. She wished the businessman would leave. She was sure that he could not enjoy his meal, and that Grandma was driving him crazy.

Lisa was relieved when he finally folded his paper and prepared to leave. To her surprise, he walked right over to their table. Lisa prepared to apologize for having disrupted his noon meal. Instead, he looked at her with a smile and said, "When I get older, I hope I have a granddaughter just like you."

Lisa had started the day with only one purpose in mind. She was going to make it a pleasant day for Grandma. She had not realized how her actions might affect others.

We may feel that what we are doing is not important, but remember the world is watching.

Melvin L. Yoder, Gambier, OH

Do all the good you can to all the people you can, in all the ways you can, as often as you can, as long as you can.

October 26

Bible Reading: Luke 10:30-37, 2 Timothy 1:1-14

One Year Bible Reading Plan: 1 Timothy 5, Jeremiah 14–16

And she shall bring forth a son, and thou shalt call his name JESUS: for he shall save his people from their sins.

- MATTHEW 1:21

SAVED BY GRACE

"Dad! The dogs are drowning in the manure pit!" My sons rushed into the house one cold morning after chores were done and we were about ready to go to church. Sure enough, our neighbor's beagle and our German Shepherd pup had walked out onto the lagoon and broken through the crust. They were paddling around in their little hole trying in vain to pull themselves up. At first, I thought it foolish to risk my own health and life over these dogs, but even in the moments spent deliberating, I could see they were losing out quickly. I gritted my teeth, gingerly walked out onto the lagoon crust, and pulled them both out.

I was reminded of the saving power of Jesus. Our key verse reads, "He shall save his people *from* their sins." Many professing Christians today live as if the angels had instead said, "He shall save His people *in* their sins." Just as it would have been impossible for me to save those dogs within their plight, so God does not save us just so we can continue living in our sin. The dogs had to be raised to a higher level in order to revive them.

God has "saved us, and called us with an holy calling" (2 Timothy 1:9). This involves departing from iniquity (2 Timothy 2:19) and not committing sin (1 John 3:9). The new birth does not remove the potential to sin but the servitude to it (Romans 6:16-18).

The Holy Spirit is the promise of present salvation, or the earnest of our inheritance (Ephesians 1:13-14). If you have a *Martyr's Mirror,* you might read on page 383, second column, second paragraph to see how our fathers further explained the Christian experience.

Kenton Martin, Carson City, MI

Without the earnest of present salvation, we cannot expect to receive the full inheritance of eternal salvation.

October 27

Bible Reading: Hebrews 3

One Year Bible Reading Plan: 1 Timothy 6, Jeremiah 17-19

Wherefore the rather, brethren, give diligence to make your calling and election sure: for if ye do these things, ye shall never fall.

- 2 PETER 1:10

TAKE HEED LEST WE LET IT SLIP

A week later the same beagle was back again, romping around with our pup. I could only visualize the same scenario we had the weekend before, so I told the boys to tie the beagle up until the neighbors could come and get him. Of course, he did not like this. He jumped and whined, chafing at the chain.

I had to think how this relates to how we act sometimes. A short while before, this dog had been rescued from certain doom, and now he seemed to say, "Everything will be alright. I just want my freedom to do what I want." Unlike God who dearly loves His people, I am not much of a dog lover and might not have been in a mood to pull him out of the pit a second time. Being tied to the chain was for his benefit, and he did not know it.

Perhaps sometimes those around me see when I am headed toward destruction and chain me up. We are to exhort each other daily. We are not told to discuss farm prices, furniture orders, or even the weather, but we are to help keep each other from becoming hardened through sin. God does not want us to doubt our salvation. Neither does He want us to become careless with it, because it can be lost. Let us hearken when the Spirit sends a brother to us with a concern for our life. Nothing is of too little significance to give attention to if it is something that would help us get on or stay on the narrow way to heaven.

For good reading on how the Anabaptists taught, I invite you to find a *Martyr's Mirror,* turn to page 404, and read the first column.

Kenton Martin, Carson City, MI

Salvation produces a change within that breaks the chains of sin.

October 28

Bible Reading: Ephesians 6

One Year Bible Reading Plan: 2 Timothy 1, Jeremiah 20-22

Children, obey your parents in the Lord: for this is right.

- EPHESIANS 6:1

ADMONITION OR ABUSE

"Do you think you will ever amount to anything?"

As a teenager living on a farm, I always had odd jobs to do. One day my father asked me to paint one of our smaller outside buildings. I complained that painting was not a favorite job of mine. That is when he asked, "Do you think you will ever amount to anything?"

Though thirty-seven years have gone by, it is easy to remember how that question felt to me at the time. Yes, there could have been a more tactful way for a father to approach a problem in a young teenager. But did he admonish (express warning or disapproval) or abuse (attack with words)?

The result depends on the receiver. It was the truth, and we know that sometimes the truth hurts. Our answer is in Hebrews 12:11, "Now no chastening for the present seemeth to be joyous, but grievous: nevertheless afterward it yieldeth the peaceable fruit of righteousness unto them which are exercised thereby."

Too often when we have problems, we tend to shift the blame elsewhere. We might blame our fathers for abusing us verbally. Let's be careful that we don't use what our father said as a crutch to lean on rather than take responsibility for our actions. Although fathers fail at times, it is wrong for us to dwell on that rather than to forgive. Let's use it as a stepping stone in our spiritual life.

Time has helped show me the answer to my question. Father was admonishing and not abusing. Let us show respect and be thankful for the father figures in our lives.

Emanuel Erb, Conneautville, PA

Godly fathers–a vital ingredient of Christian homes.

October 29

Bible Reading: Colossians 3:12-25

One Year Bible Reading Plan: 2 Timothy 2, Jeremiah 23, 24

Submitting yourselves one to another in the fear of God.
- EPHESIANS 5:21

BUILDING HOMES FOR GOD

The Bible clearly tells men to love their wives, cherish them, and treat them as their own bodies. Do we still love our wives as much as the first day or the first few months after we married? Too often we take them for granted. We go to work in the morning then come home in the evening, expecting to find our meals cooked, the house cleaned, the children all clean and in their best behavior. Did we ever stop to think about their feelings or take them away from the rigors of life and let them tell us how they feel? Do we still cherish our wives?

Wives, have you ever asked yourselves "Why doesn't my husband show me more love?" Have you considered that maybe you are not showing him respect? The Bible says that Sarah called Abraham lord. Remember that you are daughters of Sarah. Don't take your husband for granted. He is fallible and has feelings. Remember the three Cs– clean, cook, and care. Do it as unto the Lord.

Parents, are we pointing our children to the cross that leads Home? If they follow our example, will they reach that blessed shore? Let's smooth out the road for those coming behind. May God help us as we bring up our children in the fear of the Lord.

Children, you must be respectful to your parents. Be thankful for your parents and cherish them while they are here with you. Give them roses while they are alive. Useless are the flowers you give after this life is gone.

Mark G. Meighn, Hattieville, Belize

Happy the home when God is there

October 30

What is man, that thou art mindful of him? and the son of man,
that thou visitest him?

- PSALM 8:4

THE HEAVENS DECLARE

Day by day, the sun silently tells us of a matchless being. Night by night, the stars chart the course for mankind. Men measure the length of months by the stars. The power of the moon on the earth has not yet been fully determined.

We watch the sky to try to figure out weather patterns. Does it make us feel big to be able to forecast a rain shower, or does it make us feel small because we have no clue how to make it rain? Sometimes, when our ego blows too high, we should sit down and look up. What hath God wrought?

The earth orbits the sun at a speed of 18.5 miles a second. Every day we travel 1,632,000 miles around the sun.

The sun is about 1 million times bigger than the earth. It would take 109 earths to reach across the sun.

Solar flares help in the creation of northern lights, and God sometimes uses these sun storms to disrupt some of man's highest technology, such as causing radio communication to be miscarried.

There is no other place in the universe that is not too hot or too cold to sustain life. At 93,000,000 miles from the sun, the earth is just right.

When God used a number too big to write, He said, "As many as the stars." Men have yet to find an end of counting stars.

"But our God is in the heavens: he hath done whatsoever he hath pleased" (Psalm 115:3).

Raymond Fox, Shiloh, OH

God saw that it was good.

October 31

Bible Reading: Psalm 139

One Year Bible Reading Plan: 2 Timothy 4, Jeremiah 27, 28

How shall we escape, if we neglect so great salvation?
- HEBREWS 2:3

HOW SHALL WE ESCAPE?

While driving through our county seat one day, I noticed an unusual amount of law enforcement personnel in the area around the jail. Some were in their cars while others were on foot, flagging down cars as they drove through town. My curiosity was aroused. I circled the block to find a clue to the heightened security. Then I saw him, face down on the ground, handcuffed, in his orange inmate suit, and surrounded by officers with drawn weapons. It seemed his plan for early parole wasn't going well.

When I rehearse this scene in my mind, I think of the key verse. The comparison falls short, however, since this prisoner covered about two city blocks before being caught. If we neglect or reject God's free gift of salvation, there is no escaping. According to our Scripture reading, God is aware of all our thoughts, our path, and our lying down. He knows our habits and our ideas of recreation and leisure. He is aware of every word we utter and every member of our body.

I encourage you to follow the mandate the Apostle Paul gives us in 1 Corinthians 15:58. "Therefore, my beloved brethren, be ye steadfast, unmovable, always abounding in the work of the Lord, forasmuch as ye know that your labour is not in vain in the Lord."

Marcus Yoder, Grove City, MN

The world wants your best, but God wants your all.

November 1

Bible Reading: Matthew 9:9-38

One Year Bible Reading Plan: Titus 1, Jeremiah 29, 30

Go ye therefore, and teach all nations, baptizing them in the name of the Father, and of the Son, and of the Holy Ghost: teaching them to observe all things whatsoever I have commanded you.

- MATTHEW 28:19-20

FISHERS OF MEN

What is our response when we hear the word come? It all depends on where and why we are called to come. When we hear, "Come, dinner is ready," we respond to the call. When a child says, "Come quickly! Johnny fell down the hay hole!" we immediately respond.

Jesus met some young men fishing and called to them, "Come, follow Me. I will make you fishers of men." They started following Him, asking no questions. Jesus extends the same invitation to us. Are we fishing for men?

It is not always easy to allow your loved ones to go fishing for men. I well remember the day our married son and his family got a letter by mail from a mission board asking them if they would consider moving to a foreign country for several years. My heart was gripped and my mind said, "No, not you."

When our son asked us if we could give them our blessing to go, I began to think seriously. What am I doing if I throw a road block in front of their call to fish for men? But then again, my selfishness surfaced and I said to myself, "But he is a successful farmer. He has a growing family plus many responsibilities here at home." I even thought of my wife and me. What would we do when we needed help?

But then I remembered the words of Jesus, "Come, and I will make you fishers of men." How can we fish if we do not go to the waters where our Master leads us? Some are called to go and some are called to stay, but we as children of the King are called to fish for men. I can say with the authority of God's Word, "Go and fish!"

Amos B. Stoltzfus, Honey Brook, PA

Rescue the perishing.

November 2

Bible Reading: John 21

One Year Bible Reading Plan: Titus 2, Jeremiah 31, 32

By this we know that we love the children of God, when we love God, and keep his commandments.

- 1 JOHN 5:2

LOVEST THOU ME?

Three times, in the twenty-first chapter of John, this question was asked of Simon Peter. After Jesus asked Peter this question, He told him to feed his lambs. The second and the third time He said, "Feed My sheep." Perhaps Jesus asked Peter the question three times because Peter had denied Him three times. After Jesus asked the third time, Peter was grieved. I think the Lord was trying to teach Peter what real love is all about. After the third time, Peter realized the true meaning of love.

Would Jesus have to ask us three times or more, "Lovest thou Me?" Do we love Jesus enough to go out and feed His lambs and sheep? Or do we just love Him in word? When I tell people that I love the Lord Jesus, they should be able to see it in my life. The Lord wants us to love from the heart just as He wanted Peter to love. That is why He asked Peter three times, "Lovest thou Me?"

It is easy to tell someone that we love them, but only by our attitude and action toward them will they really be able to tell if our love is true. Remember, the Lord knows our every thought. He knows if our love for Him and the brotherhood is real. God's Word says we cannot love Him and hate our brother. 1 John 4:20 says "If a man say, I love God, and hateth his brother, he is a liar: for he that loveth not his brother whom he hath seen, how can he love God whom he hath not seen?"

Menno H. Eicher, Fairland, OK

But if any man love God, the same is known of him.
- 1 Corinthians 8:3

November 3

Bible Reading: Isaiah 1:10-19, Hebrews 13:10-16

One Year Bible Reading Plan: Titus 3, Jeremiah 33-35

For ye know the grace of our Lord Jesus Christ, that, though he was rich, yet for your sakes he became poor, that ye through his poverty might be rich.
- 2 CORINTHIANS 8:9

ACCEPTABLE SACRIFICES

In Leviticus 1-8 the children of Israel were instructed in offerings and sacrifices. They were to offer burnt sacrifices, the meat offering of flour and of the first fruits, the peace offering, etc.

But at times God could not stand their "vain oblations." He said, "Incense is an abomination unto me; . . . your appointed feasts my soul hateth" (Isaiah 1:13, 14). In the New Testament He says, "Sacrifice and burnt offerings and offering for sin thou wouldest not, neither hadst pleasure therein" (Hebrews 10:8).

But there are acceptable sacrifices for us. He says, "Ye also, as lively stones, are built up an spiritual house, an holy priesthood, to offer up spiritual sacrifices, acceptable to God by Jesus Christ" (1 Peter 2:5).

David gives us one of these sacrifices in the Old Testament. "The sacrifices of God are a broken spirit: a broken and a contrite heart, O God, thou wilt not despise" (Psalm 51:17).

Giving can be "an odour of a sweet smell, a sacrifice well-pleasing to God" (Philippians 4:18). We are to "offer the sacrifice of praise to God continually" from the heart. "But to do good and to communicate forget not: for with such sacrifices God is well pleased." (Hebrews 13:15-16)

Prayers can be like offering incense. The elders had "golden vials full of odours (incense), which are the prayers of saints" (Revelation 5:8).

By the mercies of God, we must present our bodies a living sacrifice, holy, acceptable unto God, which is our reasonable service (Romans 12:1).

Enos Schrock, Rochelle, VA

Thanks be unto God for His unspeakable gift. - 2 Corinthians 9:15

November 4

Bible Reading: Ephesians 6:10-20, 1 Peter 5:8-11

One Year Bible Reading Plan: Philemon, Jeremiah 36, 37

And no marvel; for Satan himself is transformed into an angel of light.

- 2 CORINTHIANS 11:14

OVERCOMING SATAN

Many teachers are clearly stating, "The best way to overcome Satan is to ignore him."

Satan thrives on this ignorance of the people concerning himself. He is the prince of darkness and must have darkness to work. The light of truth is his undoing. He tries to see to it that the Christians leave him unexposed and unchallenged. If he is challenged by the victory of the crucified Christ, he is defeated. We are not in a general fight for truth, but in a personal conflict with a roaring lion, whom we must resist, not just ignore. Nowhere throughout the New Testament can anything be found to support the teaching of ignoring Satan or his activities.

Many are blind to the Satan of the Scriptures. We must let the Word of God cleanse us from this fog, so that we can bring gain to the church of Christ and undo the adversary. We need to have our spirit stirred to wage an active opposition against the unseen powers of darkness led by Satan. We must put on the whole armor of God which has been supplied to overcome the foe.

We are called by Jesus, our Captain, to fight under His banner. No matter what conflict faces us, Jesus will be our Leader and will lead us from victory to victory. But we must have our eyes fixed on Him. He quiets the fears of His people and encourages them to rely on Him. If we fight the battle without complete dependence on our Lord and confidence that we are in His will, the battle will drain our nerves and spirit. We need to learn discipline under our Captain's generalship, keep our eyes fixed on Him, wait on His timing and orders, and simply obey Him.

Daniel Miller, Dunnegan, MO

Fear not for I am with thee, be not dismayed for I am thy God.

November 5

Bible Reading: John 4:19-24, Revelation 4

One Year Bible Reading Plan: Hebrews 1, Jeremiah 38, 39

This people draw near me with their mouth, and with their lips do honour me, but have removed their heart far from me.

- ISAIAH 29:13

WHAT IS WORSHIP?

What does worship really mean? Is it something I do at church once a week or at home during my personal quiet time with God? Or is it a way of life?

Jesus said, "God is a spirit; they that worship Him must worship in spirit and in truth." In other words, God is alive. He is real. He is not some inanimate, lifeless object upon which we heap nice words. He is the Creator and Sustainer of the universe. He is the uncaused Cause behind all the questions man has about the origin of life and man. Further, He is love personified. He is completely pure and holy—without fault. He is not just a supreme being, an eternal, supernatural God, but He is the most complete and perfect being that could possibly ever exist.

What perspective does that put on worship? Is worship something I do once in awhile because I should–because it's the right thing to do? Or does worship take on new meaning? Worship is something that takes place at a much deeper level than the surface of my smile, my words and notes in singing, my thoughts in prayer, or even my emotions during those wonderful times of praise and thanksgiving. Worship even goes farther than what I do. It extends to the farthest reaches of who I am in Christ. Jesus' words imply that worship includes the whole of our being (body, soul, spirit, and mind) and takes in our entire life. Anything less is not really worship. We may call it that, but God calls it lip service.

Worship today, and never stop worshipping. God is worthy of no less.

Michael Webb, Woodburn, IN

May my life be a living sacrifice.

November 6

Bible Reading: 1 Samuel 24

One Year Bible Reading Plan: Hebrews 2, Jeremiah 40-42

The Lord forbid that I should do this thing unto my master.

- 1 SAMUEL 24:6

GENUINE FORGIVENESS

The story is told of two Christian men who had a disagreement. Throughout their lives they carried bitterness toward each other. When the one brother was lying on his deathbed, he called for the brother he was at odds with to come visit him so they could be reconciled. When they met, he said, "Brother John, I forgive you for what you have done."

John responded with tears in his eyes, "I want to forgive you, too."

Then the brother on his deathbed said, "John, I want you to know; if I get better, this doesn't count."

We have a different example in 1 Samuel 24. David had an adversary and bitter enemy by the name of Saul. Saul was also successful in getting others involved in his attack against David. David had to spend much of his time fleeing from Saul's army. The bitter result was that David's family life was destroyed, and much of his time was spent out in the wilderness, hiding in caves.

Let us think of the emotional pain this must have caused. But David's example of love and forgiveness is beautiful. In 2 Samuel 1:12 when David received the news that Saul was killed, he wept and fasted rather than feasting and rejoicing. His love for Saul's son Jonathan remained permanent and secure. Also, in 2 Samuel 9 he wanted to bless Saul's grandson Mephibosheth and great-grandson Micha by restoring to them all the land of Saul and promising them the privilege of eating bread at his table.

This is a beautiful example of a man who could forgive past hurts, have his emotional pain healed, and find complete peace and freedom.

Joseph Kuepfer, Newton, ON

When you bury the hatchet, don't leave the handle sticking out.

November 7

Bible Reading: 2 Corinthians 11

One Year Bible Reading Plan: Hebrews 3, Jeremiah 43–45

But I fear, lest by any means, as the serpent beguiled Eve through his subtilty, so your minds should be corrupted from the simplicity that is in Christ.
- 2 CORINTHIANS 11:3

IN TUNE WITH GOD

In the year 2000, Derek Isaacs was ending a term of mission work in Cape Town, South Africa. He drove up the side of Table Mountain to get some pictures and a good view of the area he had served in the last few years. As he stopped beside a waterfall and was about to step out of his vehicle, the Spirit of God impressed on his mind the image of a viper. Just the second before he opened the door, he looked out the window. And there in the tall grass, right where his door would have swung open lay a poisonous viper, ready to strike had he stepped out.

The snake, a puff adder, is responsible for more deaths than any other snake in the area. Its nature of being lazy, quiet, and releasing large amounts of venom when it strikes makes this snake very dangerous. Being in tune with God may have saved Derek's life. He threw some stones at the snake and scared it away.

A striking parallel can be drawn with the dangers of the sinful nature of man. We as Christians need to be aware of things creeping into our lives. It often happens quietly, and subtly. Bad feelings, attitudes, or roots of bitterness can creep in behind a display of righteousness. They often don't get exposed until someone points them out.

May we as Christians resolve to maintain a vital and current relationship with God and be in tune with the Holy Spirit so we may be warned of the impending spiritual dangers. "The angel of the Lord encampeth round about them that fear him, and delivereth them" (Psalm 34:7).

Chester Mullet, Belle Center, OH

The acid of bitterness hurts nobody more than the container it is stored in.

November 8

Bible Reading: Revelation 2:1-7, John 14:15-24

One Year Bible Reading Plan: Hebrews 4, Jeremiah 46-48

Thou hast left thy first love.

- REVELATION 2:4

TRUE LOVE

"Dad," exclaimed little Thomas, "I would like to have a red wagon."

"Well, Thomas," answered Dad, "I think you are big enough to have a wagon. Don't you think so, Mom?"

"Oh, I suppose so. You can get it for him this afternoon when you go to town," answered Mom.

After Thomas had his new red wagon, he played with it constantly. He excitedly shouted to his playmates about it. He took good care of it. But eventually the newness wore off. He left it outside at night, it got rained on, and he looked for other things to do.

Isn't that the way it goes with us as individuals or as a church? At first it isn't hard to love the One who gave His only Son for us. But what happens? Through the wear and tear of life–raising our families, paying the bills, doing all the hard work, getting there on time–we lose our first love.

The Spirit told the Ephesian church, "To him that overcometh will I give to eat of the tree of life, which is in the midst of the paradise of God." Meditate on this. God said He will give. If we overcome, He gives us to eat of the tree. That tree is Jesus Christ.

It didn't help the Ephesian church to have a number of good practices. Why? Because they had lost their first love. Do we love as God loved?

True love will motivate us to keep God's commandments.

Monroe Hochstetler, Worthington, IN

How we love is a thermometer to our spiritual condition.

November 9

Bible Reading: Genesis 37:1-27

One Year Bible Reading Plan: Hebrews 5, Jeremiah 49, 50

Come, and let us sell him to the Ishmaelite, and let not our hand be upon him; for he is our brother and our flesh.

- GENESIS 37:27

CONTENTMENT WITHOUT GODLINESS

Godliness with contentment is great gain, but contentment without godliness is a vicious monster. Contentment without godliness causes people to be self-satisfied while living in sin.

In today's Scripture reading we see that the brothers decided to sell their brother Joseph. The thought of killing him and bringing his blood upon their hands was not appealing to one of them. When the opportunity arose to sell him, they agreed and were content. I believe that they well knew how wrong this was and that it would bring untold grief to their aged father. But yet they were willing and content to do so.

As I read this account, it brings to my mind the church of Laodicea. They were lukewarm and did not care. They felt secure and did not realize their needs. God said, "If you do not repent, I am finished with you," but they were content (Revelation 3:14-18).

The Pharisee was content to pray, "I am glad that I am not as other men, or even as this publican." He was proud, lofty, and lost, but he was content with his position and glad that he was not as other men. (Luke 18:11)

There are people who know they are not right with God but are content with that. There are people who know they have wronged their friend, their parents, their neighbor, or the church, but because punishment is not swift and sure, they are content to go on living in sin.

The story has been told of two mules in adjoining pastures. The pastures were identical and the grass exactly the same. The mules stood with their heads over the fence each contentedly munching the other's grass. As I consider this, I wonder if we may at times be guilty of reaching across the fence to munch on the world's dainties and attractions.

Melvin L. Yoder, Gambier, OH

The greatest loss that a man can suffer is to have contentment without godliness.

November 10

Bible Reading: 2 Samuel 12:1-14

One Year Bible Reading Plan: Hebrews 6, Jeremiah 51, 52

For with what judgment ye judge, ye shall be judged: and with what measure ye mete, it shall be measured to you again.

- MATTHEW 7:2

THE MEASURE OF JUDGING

It is possible that we sometimes, in a temper, call a judgment on others that we would consider unjust if we were judged the same. All our judgments must come under the scrutiny of the golden rule.

Nathan the prophet was an excellent story teller. He explained to David the scenario of a rich man who had a multitude of finances and animals. As the story progressed, he explained that this rich man selfishly and rudely went to a man who was poor and took the only lamb the poor man owned. David was quick to make a judgment. Part of his verdict was that the man who had committed such a crime should pay fourfold.

The irony of this judgment was that, in essence, it was measured in return to David because he was the rich man in the story. He had taken Uriah and had him destroyed. David's payment in reality was fourfold.

1. David's son born to Bathsheba did not live.
2. David's son Amnon was killed by his brother Absalom.
3. David's son Absalom died hanging by his hair from an oak tree.
4. David's son Adonijah was destroyed by his brother Solomon.

David was judged by his own judgment. He paid the fourfold payment he had decreed for the man in Nathan's story.

Joseph Kuepfer, Newton, ON

The unjust judge will be judged by his own judgment.

November 11

Bible Reading: Matthew 13:31-46

One Year Bible Reading Plan: Hebrews 7, Lamentations 1, 2

For where your treasure is, there will your heart be also.

- MATTHEW 6:21

WHERE IS MY TREASURE?

I dreamed I was out on a walk close to the mountains when I noticed a crevice in the side of a hill. I went over, moved some rocks, and peered inside. Wow! There were a large number of items, possibly from the Civil War period. In my dream I excitedly placed the rocks back carefully. I then went to investigate who owned the land and how I could purchase it.

The next morning I had forgotten the dream until I was having my devotions and read Matthew 13. The parable of the treasure in the field jolted my memory. I started meditating on what God was trying to show me. Am I really willing to sell out for God and invest everything in the treasure in heaven?

Later that morning the preacher spoke on some of the same points in a message from Hebrews 11 and 12. We need to have faith that sees beyond this life. We need to fix our eyes on the eternal promises and riches, holding them higher than the treasures of this earth.

How much do the things of this world have a hold on me? Would I be willing to sell out and move to a remote area of the world to serve God? Can I live wholly for Christ right where I am now? Am I willing to suffer persecution for the joy I can see ahead of me? Where is my treasure?

Mark Webb, Aroda, VA

How high are my sights set?

November 12

Bible Reading: Matthew 26:20-25, Mark 14:43-52

One Year Bible Reading Plan: Hebrews 8, Lamentations 3-5

This he said, not that he cared for the poor; but because he was a thief, and had the bag, and bare what was put therein.

- JOHN 12:6

WHAT GREED DID TO JUDAS

It is easy to overlook the fact that Jesus chose Judas to be His disciple. We may also forget that while Judas alone betrayed Jesus, all the disciples abandoned Him. With the other disciples, Judas shared a persistent misunderstanding of Jesus' mission. When He kept talking about dying, they all felt varying degrees of anger, fear, and disappointment. They did not understand why they had been chosen if Jesus' mission was doomed to fail.

Judas allowed his desires to place him in a position where Satan could manipulate him. He tried to undo the evil he had done by returning the money to the priests, but it was too late. How sad that Judas ended his life in despair without ever experiencing the gift of reconciliation!

Judas betrayed Jesus by his own choice (Luke 22:48). He was a thief (John 12:6). Jesus knew that Judas's life of evil would not change (John 6:70). Judas's betrayal of Jesus was part of God's sovereign plan (Psalm 41:9, Acts 1:16-20). The fact that Jesus knew Judas would betray Him, doesn't mean that Judas was a puppet of God's will. Judas made the choice. God knew what that choice would be and confirmed it.

This account should cause us to think a second time about our commitment to God and the presence of His Spirit within us. Are we true disciples or uncommitted pretenders? We can choose despair and death, or we can choose repentance, forgiveness, hope, and eternal life. Judas' betrayal sent Jesus to the cross to give us another chance. Will we accept His free gift, or will we betray Him?

Marvin C. Hochstetler, Nappanee, IN

Bring forth therefore fruits meet for repentance. - Matthew 3:8

November 13

Bible Reading: Joel 1, John 15:1-11

One Year Bible Reading Plan: Hebrews 9, Ezekiel 1-3

These things have I spoken unto you, that my joy might remain in you, and that your joy might be full.

- JOHN 15:11

WITHERED FRUIT–WITHERED JOY

Israel was in a sorry state of affairs in Joel's time. They had ceased following the Lord and had descended into the darkness of apostasy. They had forsaken the Lord, His laws, and His love. Joel 1 describes the judgment of the Lord upon the land as the crops failed, and yielded no increase. Chapter two prophesies yet further judgment in a terrible plague of locusts that would eat the little that still grew.

In the midst of this lamentation of chapter one, Joel described the withering vines and trees. Then he makes this startling statement: "Joy is withered away from the sons of men." Picture with me a withered grape vine with drooping, half-ripe grapes. Now picture God's people, weary from fruitless labor, exhausted from trying to produce food, humpbacked from labor, with no inspiration to go any further.

But that is not the whole picture. Their spirits are lifeless and not communicating with God. Their worship has ceased, obedience has failed, and righteousness cannot grow in their lives. Inspiration and blessing have ceased, and any joy of the Lord has withered away because of disobedience. Pity such a people.

God's intention for mankind is to experience true joy. But it comes at a cost–the cost of giving up self. God has so made us that deep, lasting, solid joy comes only through abiding in Christ and in obedience to His Word. When we have the joy of the Lord, each day comes with new inspiration. We can find something to rejoice about even in times of trial. See Habakkuk 3:17, 18.

Jesus expressly stated one purpose of His coming: full, abundant joy for the child of God. When we let Him have His way in our lives, that joy comes forth, springs up, and is a real motivation for Christian living.

Delmar R. Eby, London, KY

For the joy of the Lord is your strength. - Nehemiah 8:10

Bible Reading: Luke 18:1-14

One Year Bible Reading Plan: Hebrews 10:1-23, Ezekiel 46

I tell you, this man went down to his house justified rather than the other: for every one that exalteth himself shall be abased; and he that humbleth himself shall be exalted.

- LUKE 18:14

THE PHARISEE AND THE PUBLICAN

The publican was a tax collector, a trader, and a thief. He made many mistakes in his life, but he saw his sinful condition, his failures, and his mistakes. In true humility he said, "God be merciful to me a sinner" (Luke 18:13). This man received the Lord into his life.

The Pharisee was a religious person and kept the whole law. He thought he was much better than others were, and he looked down on the publican.

What is my attitude toward other people? Do I sometimes act like the Pharisee? I may think I am a good person. I fast once a week and give alms of all that I have. I go to church, abide by the standards, and regularly give testimony. I witness faithfully to those around me. I look at all the good deeds I have done and think I am a good person. I feel I should receive the praise of man for all my good works. I look down on others and make them feel I am a notch or two above them. If we would only take inventory of our attitudes, we would find out that we are filled with pride for all the good things we are doing.

Christians should do good things, but it is also important that we maintain godly attitudes for the good things we are doing. If we do things to please men, what reward do we have? When we do things as unto the Lord, He will reward us abundantly.

Samuel Beachy, Belvidere, TN

A week filled with selfishness and a Sunday filled with religious exercises will make a good Pharisee but a poor Christian.

November 15

Bible Reading: Galatians 6:1-2, Hebrews 3:1-13

One Year Bible Reading Plan: Hebrews 10:24-39, Ezekiel 7-9

Now we exhort you, brethren, warn them that are unruly, comfort the feebleminded, support the weak, be patient toward all men.

- 1 THESSALONIANS 5:14

EXHORT ONE ANOTHER

Some years ago, three boys went swimming in an abandoned stone quarry that had filled with water. The water was about two hundred feet across and thirty feet deep.

They decided to swim across, which two of them had done before. However, it was the first time for the one boy who could not swim so well. The other two, being better swimmers, soon got ahead. By the time they had gotten to the middle, the third boy panicked and called for help. The one boy went to get help, but the other boy turned back to where the third boy was and stayed close enough to talk to him.

He spoke calmly and quietly instructed him to keep paddling. He assured him that he could make it and told him to relax and swim slowly, stopping to get a breath and then keep going. He reminded the boy that they were getting closer, and so they got across safely.

When we see a brother floundering in his spiritual life, do we take time to get alongside of him to urge him on and to assure him that we're in this together? We can restore a struggling brother in the spirit of meekness. Remember, it is not required that he walk on the water but only that he keep his head above water.

Willis H. Martin, Wellsboro, PA

A friend in need is a friend indeed.

Bible Reading: John 8:1-12

One Year Bible Reading Plan: Hebrews 11:1-19, Ezekiel 10-12

And you . . . hath he quickened . . . blotting out the handwriting of ordinances that was against us.

- COLOSSIANS 2:13, 14

GOD'S COURTROOM

Come with me as we enter the courtroom of God's justice. God sits as Judge. His laws are written upon the walls. I am the defendant, seeking to justify myself.

The Judge looks upon me with the severity of justice and demands, "What is your plea?" Fearing to look up at Him, I plead, "Innocent."

The severity of His look deepens. He turns to the wall of law, takes a book in His hand, and reads my life activities aloud. As He reads, He compared each misdeed to one of the laws to see if it corresponds, and then pronounces with dreadful accents, "Guilty! Guilty! Guilty!"

He turns back to me and with yet greater severity says, "You have broken all my laws. Your innocent plea avails nothing before My divine knowledge and justice. Each broken law carries the death sentence. I sentence you to eternal death for breaking the laws of My kingdom." Turning to the guards, He orders, "Take him away, and cast him into outer darkness."

I tremble with terror, knowing the Judge is right and I am deserving of the sentence. Suddenly a door opens, and instead of the darkness I expected, a glorious figure enters surrounded in divine light. With the light of mercy in His eyes, He addresses the Judge. "Your Honor, I have fulfilled all those laws for Him. Although I was perfectly innocent, I suffered the punishment of death for Him. This man accepted my pardon and lived a life of service to You. I beg of You, on behalf of My obedience and My sacrifice, declare him forgiven and innocent."

As He spoke, I noticed His nail prints and His spear-pierced side. The Judge, with a smile of love and approval on His face, turned to me and said, "Your sins are forgiven, enter into the joy of thy Lord." I can do no more than bow down and worship at the feet of my Savior, Jesus Christ.

Delmar R. Eby, London, KY

When I've been there ten thousand years, I will be there because of love, for justice called, and mercy answered.

Bible Reading: Luke 12:22-34

One Year Bible Reading Plan: Hebrews 11:20-40, Ezekiel 13-15

But seek ye first the kingdom of God, and his righteousness; and all these things shall be added unto you.

- MATTHEW 6:33

GOD WANTS YOU IN HEAVEN

Have you ever become discouraged by the grind of life and the challenges that come with it? Sometimes we may feel forgotten and alone without a friend who cares. It is easy to forget anyone cares and to become bitter when life hands us unpleasant experiences. Sometimes we even blame others for our problems, or we may blame ourselves and live in a world of our own, brooding over our problems.

Consider what God did for us. He created the universe even though He knew man would fail, saved Noah and his family when they were the only ones worth saving, and inspired men to write the Old Testament with precise prophesies of Christ. He brought the Israelites out of Egypt and had it well documented. He recorded the bloody execution of Jesus, inspired the apostles to write the New Testament, and then kept His Word intact and available for us to read over 2,000 years later.

God did all this because He desires to have us in heaven with Him someday. He made man because He wanted worship. He inspired the Old Testament so that we could learn from history, documenting the Israelites' travels to demonstrate His love and care for us as we journey on to Canaan. He wanted us to know how and why His Son died so His death would mean something to us. He explained salvation so we could experience it. He described heaven so that we would have a longing for it.

Can you think of one reason to complain, worry, or fret? How can we complain, with a God Who loves us enough to do all this? God wants us in heaven and gives us every tool we need to get there.

Benjamin Christner, Cochranton, PA

God wants you with Him. Do you want to be with God?

November 18

Bible Reading: Luke 15:11-32

One Year Bible Reading Plan: Hebrews 12, Ezekiel 16

Come unto me, all ye that labour and are heavy laden, and I will give you rest.
- MATTHEW 11:28

THE LOST BOY WHO FOUND FORGIVENESS

I read of a little boy and his dad who went for a walk out in a big forest every day. Each time they went a little farther into the woods. One day it didn't suit the father to take their daily walk, so he told the boy they'd have to call off the walk for that day.

But the boy wanted to go very much, so the father finally said he could go, but he shouldn't go any farther than the old oak tree. "Do you understand this?" he asked the little boy.

The boy said, "Yes, Dad. Thank you very much. I think I can go by myself."

When the boy came to the oak tree, he stopped awhile. Then a temptation came. *I think I can find my way farther by myself. Dad won't know, and I won't tell him. I'll just go over the hill, that's all.* Off he went, thinking how wonderful it was to be all on his own. But before he knew it, he had gone farther than just over the hill.

That is the trouble with us today. We do not keep God's commandments, and before we realize it, we go much farther into sin than we had intended.

This boy was lost in the great woods. He tried to find his way back, but instead of getting closer home, he kept getting farther away. Then he thought of what his father had told him, "If you ever get lost, stay where you are, call for help, and pray." After the boy had called for a long time, his father finally found him. The boy said, "Daddy, I disobeyed you. Will you forgive me?"

Daddy said, "Certainly, I will forgive you. I'm just glad I found you."

Eli A. Yoder, Stuarts Draft, VA

If you would have God's guidance, you must make spiritual things your main business.

November 19

Bible Reading: Numbers 13:17-33

One Year Bible Reading Plan: Hebrews 13, Ezekiel 17-19

And there we saw the giants, the sons of Anak, which come of the giants: and we were in our own sight as grasshoppers, and so were we in their sight.
- NUMBERS 13:33

GIANTS IN THE LAND

The spies returned with a good report of the land. They said it was indeed a land of milk and honey, and they brought back fruit to show its size and quality. They had never seen such fruit before. But there was a problem—there were giants in the land.

Today we are much like those spies. We leave the world and commit ourselves to live in the peaceful kingdom God has provided for us. In this kingdom, there is no hatred, no jealousy, no pride, and no need to outdo others. Our sins are forgiven and our old nature is gone, so there is no desire for earthly pleasures. We have the promise that if we seek the kingdom first, God will supply our other needs. We could list many more good things about this peaceful kingdom. But many turn away for fear of the giants they must face.

The first and greatest giant to be conquered is self. Some feel they cannot conquer pleasure and sports. Others have no real desire to be kind, loving, gentle, and forgiving. Another giant that gets into people's way is evil imagination. Our mind thinks things that are evil, and we jump to conclusions rapidly. The Israelites need not have feared the giants. Because of the wicked giants, God intended to drive out the people of the land and give the land to His people. All they needed to do was to trust God.

Today, if there are any giants between you and God, don't despair. God wants to destroy any pride, hatred, ill will, or worldly lusts which haunt you. It is God's strength, not yours, that will win the battle.

Melvin L. Yoder, Gambier, OH

It is God's good pleasure to give you the kingdom.

November 20

Bible Reading: Isaiah 12, John 7:37-39

One Year Bible Reading Plan: James 1, Ezekiel 20, 21

For the Lord thy God bringeth thee into a good land, a land of brooks of water, of fountains and depths that spring out of valleys and hills.
- DEUTERONOMY 8:7

DRINKING FROM THE BROOKS OF WATER

Although Moses did not get to lead the children of Israel into the Promised Land, he could tell them of a land that had brooks of water and deep fountains that spring out of the valleys and hills.

We can compare the brooks and fountains of Canaan to the abundance of rich blessings we can have when we become a child of God and partake of the springs of living water. A brook is a small stream, but our key verse talks of brooks. I well remember the many mountain streams in Virginia. We would love to watch the water gush down the mountainsides after a rain. The brooks filled the rivers at the bottom. They were beautiful and reminded us of salvation, like the water Jesus offered the woman at the well. "But the water that I shall give him shall be in him a well of water springing up into everlasting life" (John 4:14). The woman left her water pot and went away with the Well. Bubbling up within her was the Well of Living Water.

Is that Well still bubbling up in my life? Does the experience that I have with God through Jesus Christ produce a depth and display of living fountains? As the songwriter says, "All my life long I had panted for a draught from some cool spring, that I hoped would quench the burning of the thirst I felt within."

Allan A. Miller, Sarcoxie, MO

One drink of Jesus satisfied my spiritual thirst,
yet made me thirsty for more of Him.

November 21

Bible Reading: Isaiah 55

One Year Bible Reading Plan: James 2, Ezekiel 22, 23

Seek ye the Lord while he may be found, call ye upon him while he is near.
- ISAIAH 55:6

MAKING GOD'S WAY MY WAY

The food that we eat every day costs us money. It only satisfies for a short time, and it only meets our physical needs.

We all like good deals and bargains. The first two verses in Isaiah 55 are offering us a good deal–food, water, wine, and milk. All this spiritual nourishment is free of charge. We are invited to come to God, to listen to what God has for us, and to seek the Lord.

Just as surely as we will starve physically if we don't eat, so we starve spiritually if we refuse to partake of God's nourishment. Isaiah exhorts us to call upon God while he is near (verse 6). God is always near. We tend to drift away from God. Let's not wait to turn back to God until we have drifted far from Him. A day will come when it will be forever too late to make a decision for Christ. God is gracious and merciful. He will abundantly pardon those who seek His face.

We see that God's ways, thoughts, and plans are far beyond what we can imagine (verses 8-9). It is not in our place to question God about the things He allows to happen in the world today such as natural disasters, famines, and wars. We are foolish to try to make God's plans conform to our plans. We should rather strive to fit into His plans.

Marlin Schrock, Whiteville, TN

Quench your thirst with the Water of Life.

November 22

Bible Reading: Matthew 23:1-21

One Year Bible Reading Plan: James 3, Ezekiel 24-26

And whosoever shall exalt himself shall be abased; and he that shall humble himself shall be exalted.

- MATTHEW 23:12

FULLY SURRENDERED

"Let your light so shine before men, that they may see your good works, and glorify your Father which is in heaven" (Matthew 5:16). Can you imagine how this verse would sound if it said, "glorify you"? How empty!

The builders of the Tower of Babel wanted to make themselves a name (Genesis 11:4). Not one of them is named in the Bible. How often are we guilty of this same thing, doing things, even good things, for the wrong reasons?

When God called Moses and David, they were tending sheep. Elisha was plowing with oxen. Peter and Andrew were fishing. James and John were mending their nets. God does choose some for a higher calling, giving them added responsibility, but even then it is important to have a spirit of humility.

What if the place God puts us seems small and unimportant? Is it perhaps pride that makes us want to be looked up to? If we go about our duties in a humble, contented way, God can bless it even if it seems no one notices.

We can try to encourage others with words of praise or with a helping hand. Everyone has the desire to feel needed. This gives us incentive to do our best for the glory of God. Only when we are fully surrendered to Him, can He work in us and through us. Let us strive to bloom where we are planted.

Henry Miller, Mio, MI

Be it big, be it small; God can bless it, give your all.

November 23

But Jonah was gone down into the sides of the ship; and he lay, and was fast asleep.

- JONAH 1:5

WAKE UP THE SLEEPING SAINTS

Jonah was running from God's call and lay fast asleep in the bottom of the ship. His disobedience brought a storm that endangered the lives of everyone on the ship. While Jonah slept, the mariners fought a losing battle against the storm. They were afraid.

Like Jonah, many Christians today are spiritually fast asleep, ignoring God's call while the world is troubled and afraid.

What puts Christians to sleep? If we hide sin and refuse to repent, we soon fall asleep and cannot see the needs around us. Materialism makes us too busy and lulls us into spiritual sleep. Christians become complacent and forget the urgency of God's work. Many church problems and troubled relationships draw our attention away from the needs of others.

Our disobedience to God's call not only puts us to sleep but also causes a storm that affects others around us. The world is afraid. Great winds of trouble are beating on their lives and their ships are about to break. Gigantic natural disasters take thousands of lives, destroy homes, and leave many grieving and discouraged. They ask why God allows such catastrophes. War and the world condition put fear in many hearts. Others are troubled by financial struggles, broken relationships, and fear of the future.

Where are the answers to the world's troubles? God has the answers. He has made His answers known through His Word, the Bible. God wants His children to show His answers to the troubled world. Repent of the sin in your life. Recognize the urgency of God's work. Don't allow materialism, church problems, and troubled relationships to put you to sleep. Sleeping saints, wake up! Show God's answers to the troubled world.

Henry Yoder, Clarkson, KY

Apathy is the enemy of evangelization.

November 24

Bible Reading: Hebrews 10:19-31, Psalm 95

One Year Bible Reading Plan: James 5, Ezekiel 29-31

Not forsaking the assembling of ourselves together, as the manner of some is; but exhorting one another: and so much the more, as ye see the day approaching.

- HE.BREWS 10:25

GOD WILL BUILD HIS CHURCH

A famous doctor once left his profession to be a minister of the Gospel. Someone asked him, "Aren't you sometimes sorry you left your practice of medicine and healing to be a despised minister?"

His answer was, "All the patients I ever treated physically either died or will die sooner or later. The people who now take the medicine that I have to give, that is the Gospel, will never die. The cure is permanent and gives eternal life."

Jesus said, "I am the good shepherd" (John 10:14a). As a shepherd cares for sheep, so the church is under the care of the Shepherd and Bishop of our souls.

The church is to be a shelter for the people of God. It is the place where we keep the commandments of God like water baptism, communion, feet washing, the holy kiss, and all other Christian ordinances. Nobody can keep all the ordinances outside of the church. The church keeps us in touch with heavenly influences. We should hear the ring of heaven in every sermon as well as the grim message of the terrible place prepared for them who do not know God and do not obey the Gospel (2 Thessalonians 1:6-10).

The church is the place where we get spiritual nourishment. Here we are warned against thieves, robbers, and wolves of this world that are liable to break in at any time and carry away or destroy members of the flock.

God warns us not to forsake the assembling of ourselves together. People who lose their fellowship with those of like faith are also liable to lose their fellowship with God.

Eli A. Yoder, Stuarts Draft, VA

The Christian who is careless in reading the Bible and attending church is also careless in Christian living.

November 25

Bible reading: Psalm 37:1-28

One Year Bible Reading Plan: 1 Peter 1, Ezekiel 32, 33

For our light affliction, which is but for a moment, worketh for us a far more exceeding and eternal weight of glory.

- 2 CORINTHIANS 4:17

OVERCOMING DISCOURAGEMENT

As a boy growing up in western Tennessee, I often saw the Kudzu vine, a prolific vine that grows up to thirty feet in a year. The vine would grow up over trees, completely covering them. It would block out sunshine, smothering and pulling down the tree until the tree gave up and died. At the edge of a cornfield, the vine would look innocent and harmless enough at planting time, but at harvest it was a tangled mess. The vines grew out into the field over the corn stalks, pulling them down and twining them together so that any attempt to harvest the crop was futile.

Discouragement is like the Kudzu vine. It grows over us, hangs onto us, pulls us down, and blocks out the sunshine. Discouragement will smother our Christian life, leaving us unfruitful.

We easily become discouraged when we try to bear the weight of sin and do not accept the forgiveness God offers. Trials can discourage us when the way seems hard and long and we don't understand why. When we feel we have no purpose in life or when we feel overloaded, we are tempted to become discouraged.

Psalm 37 offers four steps to overcoming discouragement.

Trust in the Lord (verse 3). God's purposes are eternal. Our finite minds don't see the whole picture.

Delight in the Lord (verse 4). Did you ever notice how much easier even a hard task becomes when you delight to do it?

Commit your way to the Lord (verse 5). Yesterday is past; its wrongs are forgiven. Today is a blessing and an opportunity. Tomorrow is secure in God's will for me.

Rest in the Lord and wait patiently (verse 7). Rest is a much-needed reprieve when the labor is hard and long.

Robert Nissley, Alpha, KY

To see God in everything makes life blessed.

November 26

Bible Reading: John 17

One Year Bible Reading Plan: 1 Peter 2, Ezekiel 34, 35

I pray for them: I pray not for the world, but for them which thou hast given me; for they are thine.

- JOHN 17:9

PRAYER WARRIOR

What is a prayer warrior? I have to think about this question because of the way our little four- year-old keeps telling us, "I prayed to God." He prays to God if Daddy can't find something. When Daddy finds it, he says, "I prayed that God would help you find it, Daddy." If Mommy isn't feeling well, he says, "Mom, I prayed to God that you would feel better soon." Sometimes he will disappear for awhile. When we ask where he was, he says, "I went to pray."

I am ashamed to admit, but I think my little son prays more than I do. A prayer warrior is someone who is not afraid to pray to God no matter how big or small the problem. It is a challenge for me to be more of a prayer warrior. If we parents or adults would pray like little children pray, we would all be in a better situation. I think God wants us to be more prayerful.

Prayer should always come easy. Why is it so hard to do? Jesus is our closest and dearest Friend. We should have no problem praying to Him, for He is the only One who can help us in times of need.

When someone offends you or hurts you, the way to get even is to pray for them. "But I say unto you, Love your enemies, bless them that curse you, do good to them that hate you, and pray for them which despitefully use you, and persecute you" (Matthew 5:44).

Menno H. Eicher, Miami, OK

Prayer is a direct link to God.

November 27

Bible Reading: 1 John 4

One Year Bible Reading Plan: 1 Peter 3, Ezekiel 36, 37

We love him, because he first loved us.

- 1 JOHN 4:19

CHRISTIAN LOVE

Once a man asked an aged Indian to demonstrate how he thought the love of God was. The Indian was a Christian. The Indian thought a little bit; then he took a worm and put it in a circle of leaves. He started the leaves on fire. The worm crawled around, desperately looking for a way to escape. Finally the worm gave up, curled up in the center, and prepared to die. The Indian then lifted him out and set him outside the ring of fire. He said, "That is what Christ did for me."

The best demonstration of love is the example that Jesus left us. He lived a perfect life of love. He demonstrated His love for us by dying on the cross to save us from our sins and to redeem mankind. We should love others as Christ loved us. God gave His only Son. He gave what was most dear and close to His heart. We need to take Christ's example and love our brothers.

The big day for the great race had finally arrived. John was all excited. He had been working for months, jogging and building up his strength for this race. On the day of the race, he ran as hard as he could. As he was nearing the end, his friend Bob was right beside him. All of a sudden, Bob tripped and sprained his ankle. John really wanted to win the prize, but he turned around and helped Bob up, and they finished the race together. That was a real example of love.

Jesus goes all the way to the end with us. No one loses His race except those who give in and give up.

Ronald Overholt, Whiteville, TN

The love we show for others determines our love for Christ.

Bible Reading: Job 37

One Year Bible Reading Plan: 1 Peter 4, Ezekiel 38, 39

And James the son of Zebedee, and John the brother of James; and he surnamed them Boanerges, which is, The sons of thunder.

- MARK 3:17

BOANERGES

As a teenage boy I remember a big, strong, and sometimes rough individual who was doing some concrete work in our barn. Whenever he grabbed the air hammer it would move. When he took hold of the sledge hammer the cement would break. When he would bend down to pick up a large piece of concrete it moved. I was intrigued by his strength! I remember so well the confession he made one morning after a powerful thunderstorm the night before. He said he was so scared he stood by his bed and shook. It left a tremendous impression on me to realize that this strong man could be so frightened.

It is the philosophy of the Hebrews that thunder is the voice of Jehovah and a symbol of divine power (Unger Bible dictionary). The strength of my hero is very small compared to the strength of our great God!

In our key verse, Jesus called James and John "Boanerges, the sons of thunder," recognizing that these two disciples were now considered the sons of God. God's power and actions would be transmitted through them. Now when they would speak, men who were living in sin would tremble and shake because this was God speaking. The Light they would now be radiating would convict individuals of their sin.

Will you be a son of thunder? Will you allow the power and the divine grace of God to work through you? Will you be Boanerges?

Joseph Kuepfer, Newton, ON

Live in me, Lord Jesus.

November 29

Bible Reading: 2 Chronicles 6:24-27; 7:13-16

One Year Bible Reading Plan: 1 Peter 5, Ezekiel 40

If my people, which are called by my name, shall humble themselves, and pray, and seek my face, and turn from their wicked ways; then will I hear from heaven and will forgive their sin, and will heal their land.

- 2 CHRONICLES 7:14

FORGIVENESS

What is forgiveness? Forgiveness is releasing, pardoning, or setting free. Many people, pretending to forgive, use an apology only as a means of reminding others of their wrong. This is not forgiveness. What happens when you release something or someone? You let go of that person or object. God did the same for us when we humbly confessed our sins and sought His face.

While we are proud, angry, or rebellious, turning from wickedness can be hard. We must pray to God with a humble spirit. The most important thing we can do is to prepare our hearts. God will hear our cry of repentance only as we submit to Him. Our sincere prayers will be answered. God will sanctify us.

God is watching over us. He will be there when we meet a difficulty, a struggle, or a temptation. He will help us back to our feet and give us the strength we need to face each day. We need not fear anything with God walking beside us. If we stay close to Him, He will never forsake us.

We should follow Jesus' example of forgiveness. The blessings of God far exceed any earthly good. One blessing of God is His forgiveness. Every time I fail or grieve my Lord, He picks me up with tenderness and compassion. He gives us peace as we freely forgive.

Owen Witmer, Crossville, TN

Look to Jesus for grace to freely forgive.

Bible Reading: Psalm 103

One Year Bible Reading Plan: 2 Peter 1, Ezekiel 41, 42

Who forgiveth all thine iniquities; who healeth all thy diseases; Who redeemeth thy life from destruction; who crowneth thee with lovingkindness and tender mercies.

- PSALM 103:3-4

SURRENDER ALL TO CHRIST

Full surrender to Christ requires submission and faith. We must be willing to give up all known sin and all self-will and surrender ourselves completely into God's hands. We must have faith that God is able and will do as He promises in His Word. The old saying, "Let go and let God" sums it up.

The victorious life is simply a life fully surrendered to God, a life in which our main desire is to bring glory to Jesus. It is the only way of true happiness, yet many refuse to accept it because they fear they would then be miserable. Paul had this inner happiness. Even though he was in jail, he still could say, "Rejoice evermore. In every thing give thanks" (1 Thessalonians 5:16, 18). If you love God and fully trust Him, the place where you are is the most joyful place you can be, because you know this is where God wants you to be.

A missionary who longed for victory through Christ was brokenhearted because of her past sins.

Someone said to her, "But God has forgiven you."

She answered, "You don't know what terrible sins I was involved in."

We have a wonderful promise in Hebrews 8:12: "For I will be merciful to their unrighteousness, and their sins and their iniquities will I remember no more." Also in 1 John 1:9: "If we confess our sins, he is faithful and just to forgive us our sins, and to cleanse us from all unrighteousness."

Even if we had some terrible sins in the past, if we have confessed our sins, repented, and are now living for Jesus, we can have the peace and joy of the Lord in our hearts. Thank God for His forgiveness!

Eli A. Yoder, Stuarts Draft, VA

Forgiveness is the healing which draws out the poison.

December 1

Bible Reading: Romans 6

One Year Bible Reading Plan: 2 Peter 2, Ezekiel 43, 44

For the wages of sin is death; but the gift of God is eternal life through Jesus Christ our Lord.

- ROMANS 6:23

BOUND OR FREE?

We are sinful by nature, but through the death of Christ and His resurrection we can be made free from the bondage of sin. "For he that is dead is freed from sin" (Romans 6:7). When we are dead to sin, our sinful desires cannot prevail. But Satan will come back and try us in our weak points, so we need to refresh our minds daily with the Word of God, the Truth. Meditate on the Scriptures daily. Memorize whole chapters (not just verses) to meditate on in times when the Bible is unavailable, such as when we go about our work, after the lights are out in the evening, or during times of temptation.

In the days of slavery, there was a slave who was often whipped and beaten to make him work. He had a hard life. He was unwilling to work, yet was forced to under the bondage of his cruel master.

One day his master sold him at the auction block. He had a hard look on his face as he waited for his new master to buy him. After the sale, the slave looked at his new master and with bitterness spat out, "I will not work for you."

With eyes full of love, the gentle new master told the slave his intentions, "I have bought you to set you free."

The slave's response was a melted heart. "I will work for you the rest of my life."

How is our response to God? With the precious blood of Christ, He paid the price to set us free. Are we free from sin and servants to God, or are we still bound to the cruel master of sin? We are servants whether bound or free. Let us yield ourselves to God so we won't fall when we are tempted.

Joseph Miller, Applecreek, OH

The truth shall make you free, and you shall be free indeed.

December 2

Bible Reading: Matthew 7:12-29

One Year Bible Reading Plan: 2 Peter 3, Ezekiel 45, 46

Neither is there salvation in any other: for there is none other name under heaven given among men, whereby we must be saved.
- ACTS 4:12

IT DOES MATTER WHAT YOU BELIEVE

"It doesn't matter what you believe, as long as you are sincere." This popular saying puts a premium on sincerity. We admire a person who is sincere, but a person can be sincere and still be lost. Every one respects the person who is so sincerely earnest in his convictions that he would die for them. But only being sincere is not enough. The person who crossed the railroad tracks and was killed by a train probably sincerely believed the tracks were clear, or he wouldn't have started across.

Sincerity will not save your soul if you believe the wrong thing. Being sincerely wrong is more deadly than drinking poison. The statement, "It really doesn't matter what you believe," makes it sound like any faith that is followed sincerely is alright and will get you to heaven. But that is false teaching. The heathen are sincere when they worship their idols. The Hindus are also sincere when they lie on beds of spikes for years. These and many other people caught in false religions are sincere, but they are lost. Sad to say, not all so-called Christians are saved if they place their hope on religious ceremonies or attend a plain church, although they may be very sincere. It is the Devil's lie that leads a person to believe it doesn't matter what you believe as long as you are sincere.

It does make a difference, an eternity of a difference. A person can be saved only by coming as a needy, helpless sinner to the Lord Jesus Christ and accepting His pardon. It does matter what we believe. Anchor your faith in Jesus with all the sincerity of your heart, and He will give you peace with God and everlasting life.

Daniel Miller, Dunnegan, MO

You may be ever so sincere, but you can be sincerely wrong.

December 3

Bible Reading: Isaiah 53, Revelation 5:6-14

One Year Bible Reading Plan: 1 John 1, Ezekiel 47, 48

Behold the Lamb of God, which taketh away the sin of the world.

- JOHN 1:29

BEHOLD THE LAMB OF GOD

Once there was a man traveling in another country. As he came to a certain church one Sunday, he looked up at the tower and saw a carved figure of a lamb near the top. The man asked the minister of the church why this lamb was placed in that position, near the top of the tower. The minister told him what happened one day when the church was being built.

There were some workmen working on a high scaffold at the tower. One of the workmen somehow made a misstep and fell. The men working with him saw him fall. With great fear they made their way down, expecting to see his body dashed to pieces. But, to their great surprise, the man was not hurt. A flock of sheep was being led past the church building at the moment of his fall. The man landed on one of the lambs. The lamb was crushed to death, but the man was not seriously injured.

The carved figure of the lamb on the tower of the church was placed there not only to commemorate this event, but also to remind everyone that the Son of God came into the world to die as the Lamb of God to save every sinner. "But he was wounded for our transgressions, he was bruised for our iniquities; the chastisement of our peace was upon him: and with his stripes we are healed" (Isaiah 53:5).

Eli A. Yoder, Stuarts Draft, VA

If Jesus loved me so much that He was willing to die for me,
then no sacrifice is too great for me to make for Him.

December 4

Bible Reading: 1 Corinthians 13

One Year Bible Reading Plan: 1 John 2, Daniel 1, 2

But speaking the truth in love, may grow up into him in all things, which is the head, even Christ.

- EPHESIANS 4:15

SPEAK THE TRUTH IN LOVE

In this age of overshadowing darkness and spiritual wickedness, we as Christians are finding it a greater challenge to walk in the light. Many are the offenses in this time, and many are the interpretations on how to face them.

Many times, when we see a brother overtaken in a fault, we draw up a so-called biblical judgment of the matter and prepare ourselves to face him. But wait! In reality, this is only a half truth. God has the whole truth. His Holy Spirit knows everything, even what is in the other person's heart, which for the most part we know very little about. We only see the outside of the person's heart and are unable to see to the core. The Holy Spirit knows how to apply the truth of God's Word to a person's heart because He knows everything. We don't.

In order for us to help a person see his ways, before we even draw up a biblical judgment, we need to get down on our knees with the person and lovingly try to understand where his heart stands in the matter. Only then do we stand in any place to help him.

Charity suffers long and is kind. Have we suffered long? Are we going around knocking people off the first time we see them making an error? Before we apply Matthew 18, we need to prayerfully endure another's weakness with much longsuffering. Perhaps we sometimes use Matthew 18 as a license to pacify our anger and spiritual contempt. Do we approach others in a kindly affectionate way with brotherly love? We must get down on our hands and knees and try to understand and identify with another's struggles before being so quick to tell them the truth.

Amos E. Stoltzfus, Evart, MI

Let us approach others as we also would like to be corrected.

December 5

Bible Reading: Luke 16:19-31, Revelation 20:10-14

One Year Bible Reading Plan: 1 John 3, Daniel 3, 4

In flaming fire, taking vengeance on them that know not God, and that obey not the gospel of our Lord Jesus Christ.

- 2 THESSALONIANS 1:8

ARE YOU DELIVERED FROM HELL?

Once there was a preacher who visited a glass factory. As he came to the door of the big furnace, he stood there awhile and stared at the intense heat. He said to himself, "Oh my, what must hell be like?"

The stoker who took care of the furnace happened to be close by and heard him say this. A few weeks later this man was in church. After the services he asked to talk to the minister. The minister asked him, "What can I do for you?"

So the man told him, "When you visited the glass factory and stared into the furnace awhile, you said, 'Oh my, what must hell be like?' Since then, every time I opened the furnace door I thought of your words. I came to church today to talk to you about accepting Christ as my Saviour because I never want to find out what hell is like."

The minister explained to him the plan of salvation, and they knelt together and prayed and the man received Christ as his personal Savior. He purposed to make his wrongs right and from then on live for Jesus. After that, when he opened the furnace door, he didn't have any more fear of everlasting fire, but could rejoice in the lively hope he had in Christ Jesus.

I hope everyone who reads this has this lively hope, so that you never have to find out what hell is like. If you don't have this hope, you can obtain it by accepting Christ as your personal Savior and living for Him.

Eli A. Yoder, Stuarts Draft, VA

Since it is impossible for God to lie,
it is impossible that there is no hell.

Bible Reading: Zechariah 8

One Year Bible Reading Plan: 1 John 4, Daniel 5, 6

And the streets of the city shall be full of boys and girls playing . . .
- ZECHARIAH 8:5

A REMNANT SHALL BE SAVED

Before the world began, God had a special program in mind. He would first establish the children of Israel. He faithfully rewarded them for obedience. Verse 12 indicates His intentions of blessing. In verse 14 He explains His punishments for disobedience.

Patiently God waited, exhorted, warned, blessed, destroyed, and saved. Yet He did not change His program. He followed through on His promise of a Redeemer. The birth of Jesus ushered in the fulfillment of His promise. The awaited time had come, exactly as planned.

When the creation was completed, God said, "It is very good." After Christ was baptized, a voice from above said, "This is my beloved Son in Whom I am well pleased." As Jesus died on the cross, He said, "It is finished." When God raised Jesus from the grave, His program was now completed. He followed through.

As other school teachers well know, planning a school program takes time. Songs are practiced, and then some are discarded and replaced with others. Poems need to be written, memorized, and drilled. Expression needs to be explained. This year was no exception. On the program day I glanced over the somewhat tense, nervous expressions on my pupils' faces. So many things could go wrong. Then a remark by a fifth grade girl inspired me. She asked, "If only one person came, would we present our program?"

Verse 12 of Zechariah 8 reads, "I will cause the remnant of this people to possess all these things." A remnant shall possess all things. God knew that only a remnant would "show up," but He gave them all things. The remnant was worth it all. What if God in His foreknowledge would not have presented His program for the remnant? God said, "I will."

James M. Beachy, Sugarcreek, OH

The children will possess all things. Will you?

December 7

Bible Reading: Matthew 6:19-34

One Year Bible Reading Plan: 1 John 5, Daniel 7, 8

But seek ye first the kingdom of God, and His righteousness.

- MATTHEW 6:33

LEARN FROM THE BIRDS

Birds flutter in and out of the pine tree. There must be several nests again this year based on all the traffic rushing past. My office window affords a view of our front yard and primarily of a small pine. For several years I've watched the sparrows build nests, gathering bits of this and pieces of that. I've seen the way they scavenge around the yard, seeking out a seed here and there. Occasionally they encounter a juicy worm.

Often, while paying bills and wondering where all the money is going to come from, the birds catch my eye. Many times I am reminded that God notices every one of them, and that He cares for and feeds them. Several times I have been convicted to pray and recommit myself into the Father's care, renewing my trust in our Provider.

In today's Scripture, Jesus tells us to look at the birds. He points out that they don't raise crops or store up for the winter, and yet they are fed. His question should hit home with all of us. "Are you not much better than they?" Do you worry about tomorrow–about "your" finances? Do you forget that it is He who provides? Or, maybe you don't have to worry. After all, this is America. Maybe you only worry about keeping it from the tax man or about losing it. Notice the thrust of verses 19 and 20 of our passage. The words "Lay not up for yourselves treasures upon earth" are a command, not a suggestion.

Father, help me today to lay up treasures in heaven, to trust You for today, and not to worry about tomorrow.

Michael Webb, Woodburn, IN

You can't serve God and money!

December 8

Bible Reading: Matthew 5:21-48

One Year Bible Reading Plan: 2 and 3 John, Daniel 9, 10

Brethren, if a man be overtaken in a fault, ye which are spiritual, restore such an one in the spirit of meekness; considering thyself, lest thou also be tempted.
- GALATIANS 6:1

RESIST NOT EVIL

The waiting room at the doctor's office was crowded. Most of the people waited in silence. However, near the center of the room, in the section closest to the secretary's desk, a woman was visiting on her cell phone. Without trying, most of the people could hear the woman telling someone the intricate details of her upcoming knee surgery. She finished her conversation with the gleeful statement, "If it does not work, then I'll sue and get a bunch of money!" The woman ended her conversation, rose painfully, and hobbled out the door on crutches.

It seems rather brazen to me that a doctor's patient could sit in the presence of the office staff and joke about suing the man who was trying to help her. But it made me think.

How do we feel when someone tries to help us but instead they make more problems for us? Are we nonresistant? We would not sue. But perhaps we are glad for the opportunity to defame that person. Are we glad when someone of power blunders? Are we looking for opportunities to lift ourselves up at another's expense?

When we are working on something as a group and something goes wrong, we might be quick to point fingers at another, hoping no one will think it was our mistake. Do we fault the group leader even if it likely was not him who blundered?

Non-resistance is a doctrine that should be practiced in church life. When tempted to make an issue out of something for our own benefit, remember that the Scripture's teaching on nonresistance uses phrases like "Whosoever shall smite . . ." and "If any man . . . ."

Raymond Fox, Shiloh, OH

Love is kind and suffers long.

December 9

Bible Reading: Ephesians 5:1-20

One Year Bible Reading Plan: Jude, Daniel 11, 12

Not every one that saith unto me, Lord, Lord, shall enter into the kingdom of heaven; but he that doeth the will of my Father which is in heaven.

- MATTHEW 7:21

FOLLOW GOD'S DIRECTION

One misty, cloudy forenoon I was returning from escorting a mini-barn. I was confident I knew my way back to the interstate. Heavy traffic with the mist and rain made driving more difficult than usual. After awhile it occurred to me that the landscape was unfamiliar. I was not getting to the exit where we had agreed to meet. Then I realized that I had been so over-confident when I arrived at the interstate, that I had not watched the signs and had turned west instead of east.

My first reaction was, "How could I do something like this? Why did I turn the wrong way?" Then I realized I had not been reading the highway directions in my self-confidence.

How is it in our spiritual lives? What course am I taking in my Christian life? Am I getting my directions from the Word of God and the Holy Spirit? Am I following the applications of the Church of Jesus Christ?

When I realized I was heading away from my destination, I had to change my course. But it was difficult to make a quick change. It was difficult and dangerous to make a U-turn, so I had to travel a distance to turn around at the next exit.

In the same manner, if we are taking a wrong course in our life, it will not be easy on our carnal nature to change. We need to repent, take up the cross, deny self, and follow Jesus Christ and His Word in true obedience.

Let us be "followers of God, as dear children" (Ephesians 5:1).

Enos R. Martin, Harrodsburg, KY

Watch the signs in time, or be a sign of the times.

December 10

Bible Reading: John 6:32-63

One Year Bible Reading Plan: Revelation 1, Hosea 1-4

A land of wheat, and barley, and vines, and fig trees, and pomegranates; a land of oil olive and honey.

- DEUTERONOMY 8:8

THE BREAD OF LIFE

When the spies came back from spying out the land of Canaan, they brought back a cluster of grapes that took two to carry (Numbers 13:23). Canaan was a land of milk and honey. They left little question that in Canaan you could get bread enough and then some. After traveling through the wilderness, this was a blessed prospect. However, ten of the spies saw only obstacles and wanted to turn back. They did not dispute that it was a rich land, but the giants of Anak intimidated them to the extent that they could not make a sound decision.

Today, in our experience with Jesus Christ as the Bread of Life, we are convinced that wheat, barley, and vines are in abundance, but what happens? Satan wants to scare us so that we see only the trials, temptations, the giants of self-will, and the desires of the flesh. He causes many to turn back. They forget the blessing of eternal life and the grace, peace, joy, and hope of living a pure life. Many wander in a spiritual wilderness for years as the children of Israel did, even after recognizing that there are plenty of spiritual resources. Satan plans this deception with the goal that we stumble further and die in this situation.

Let us remember, "For the bread of God is he which cometh down from heaven, and giveth life unto the world" (John 6:33).

Instead of cowering and acting like grasshoppers, we can be kings and priests at the table of God, having fellowship with Him through Jesus, the Bread of Life.

Allan A. Miller, Sarcoxie, MO

Too many Christians are trying to eat from the wrong table when God has Bread enough and to spare.

December 11

Bible Reading: Psalm 31

One Year Bible Reading Plan: Revelation 2, Hosea 5-8

The Lord bless thee, and keep thee: the Lord make his face shine upon thee, and be gracious unto thee: the Lord lift up his countenance upon thee, and give thee peace.

- NUMBERS 6:24-26

IS YOUR FACE TOWARD ME?

A young boy named Ben experienced a great loss in his life. Ben's mother had died. After coming home from the funeral with his dad, both Ben and his dad went to bed as soon as it was dark because there just didn't seem to be anything else to do. As the little boy lay in his bed in the darkness, he broke the quiet with this question for his dad, "Daddy, where is Mommy?"

The father answered the question as best as he could, but Ben kept asking more questions. After awhile the dad got up, scooped up the boy in his arms, and brought the little boy to bed with him. Ben continued to ask questions. Finally he reached out in the darkness, placed his hand on his dad's face, and asked him, "Daddy, is your face toward me?"

His dad assured him that his face was indeed toward him. Then Ben said, "If your face is toward me, I think I can go to sleep."

A short while later he was quiet and sleeping. The dad lay in the bed in the darkness and prayed to his Father in heaven. He prayed something like this, "O God, it is very dark, and right now I don't see how I can make it. But if Your face is toward me, somehow I think I can."

Ben taught his dad an important lesson. It made Ben feel at peace and able to rest to have his dad's face toward him. In the same way, we can find peace and rest when our heavenly Father's face is toward us.

Melvin Byler, Newaygo, MI

Lord, cause Your face on us to shine, give us Your peace,
and seal us Your's.

December 12

Bible Reading: Hebrews 10:1-18

One Year Bible Reading Plan: Revelation 3, Hosea 9-11

But now in Christ Jesus ye who sometimes were far off are made nigh by the blood of Christ.

- EPHESIANS 2:13

SALVATION-GOD'S PART

If you were able to provide the entire world with sufficient food, clothing, and shelter, would you not do it? There rises within us a pity, and yet a helplessness, for all the needy in the world.

Just so it is with God. He saw the sinful, helpless condition of mankind. Within Him there arose compassion to reach out and provide for people what they could not provide for themselves. Their spiritual need was so great and would doom them to eternal destruction if nothing was done.

However, unlike us, God is able to provide completely for humanity's needs. He set about a long chain of events that would draw men's attention to His provisions. To Adam and Eve, He provided coats of skin to cover their shame. For Noah, He provided complete instructions to build an ark, which enabled him to save his family. Then God put a rainbow in the sky to show His promise of faithfulness.

To Abraham, God gave rich promises of blessing for obedience and faithfulness. The promise pointed to the coming Redeemer. He further focused Israel's attention on His provision by giving the law and the sacrifices which all pointed to Jesus Christ and His work on Calvary.

It seemed God focused all His attention and resources to fill man's needs. Finally, when the right time came, He sent His only begotten Son into the world. It was through the sacrifice of Jesus that finally all the needs of mankind were met. It was at great cost, but it was worth it all for God to restore man back to a relationship with Him.

Oh, what wonderful provision! What a full salvation! God has done His part! Have I done mine?

Delmar R. Eby, London, KY

If salvation were a matter left entirely to God, every soul that ever lived would populate heaven.

December 13

Bible Reading: Hebrews 10:19-39

One Year Bible Reading Plan: Revelation 4, Hosea 12-14

That ye be not slothful, but followers of them who through faith and patience inherit the promises.

- HEBREWS 6:12

SALVATION–MY PART

Suppose you had the ability of the hypothetical giver of yesterday's meditation. How well could you meet the needs of all humanity if some did not receive your gift? What if the people refused to believe you had anything to offer?

God met with that kind of unbelief. God's part in salvation did not violate man's freedom of choice. The question facing us is, "Have I done my part to experience salvation?"

Our Bible reading contains three injunctions to move us to action to fulfill our part of salvation.

1. "Let us draw near" (verse 22). God never forces Himself on anyone. He presents Himself through the revelation of truth so we can know who He is and where He is. We draw near to Him when we confidently believe He has what we need. We draw even nearer when we allow His truth and spirit to cleanse us of all that is repulsive to Him. We cannot draw near when we have a sinful heart and life.

2. "Let us hold fast" (verse 23). When we draw near, we experience His love and fullness. It would be so easy to relax and let our flesh take over. The old life would soon overcome us. However, our part is to hold fast to what our faith has grasped. Faith must cling even if reason says, "Let go." Our faith must anchor itself in the promises of God, understanding that the promises of God never fail.

3. "Let us consider one another" (verse 24). When our hearts and experiences are firmly anchored, then the third part for us is to relate to others, helping them to a salvation experience. Our salvation will be revealed in our relationship to our brethren. As we urge them to faithfulness, we are helping ourselves as well.

May we never experience God's displeasure because we draw back from our doing our part.

Delmar R. Eby, London, KY

Man alone holds the key that allows the work of redemption to be complete in his life.

December 14

Bible Reading: Romans 8:1-29

One Year Bible Reading Plan: Revelation 5, Joel

For whosoever shall do the will of my Father which is in heaven, the same is my brother and sister, and mother.
- MATTHEW 12:50

NO GRANDCHILDREN

God has no grandchildren? Just because our parents are faithful Christians doesn't make us Christians. Many people, when asked if they are Christians, will respond with, "I come from a good Christian family," or "I go to a good Christian church." Too many people seem to think they can get through Judgment on the merits of their parents. Why do so many young people who go to Christian churches wait so long before making a commitment to serve God? Are they expecting the good works of someone else will get them into heaven?

Too often people seem to be perfectly satisfied trying to be God's grandchildren and are unwilling to do what it takes to become His children. We all need to come to a point in life when we make a personal choice to forsake sin and accept Jesus as our Savior if we want to reach heaven. Let's look at why God wants us to be children and not grandchildren.

We usually have a closer relationship with our father than we do with our grandfather because we live with our father. It is our father, not our grandfather, who provides for our earthly needs. Father knows our weaknesses best and seeks to protect us in order to spare us heartaches. Father corrects us and teaches us. Father is there when we face struggles and need answers and encouragement. Father expects us to learn obedience, patience, and other virtues.

Our grandfathers usually only come to visit us. Although we think they are great, they tend to spoil us. They don't require strict obedience as fathers and mothers usually do. They don't teach us as many things. They don't know us as well. We usually have a very nice relationship which requires very little on our part.

God wants to be our Father, not our Grandfather.

Benjamin Christner, Cochranton, PA

Quit trying to be a grandchild; become a child.

December 15

Bible Reading: 1 John 1; 1 John 2:1-11

One Year Bible Reading Plan: Revelation 6, Amos 1-3

If we confess our sins, he is faithful and just to forgive us our sins, and to cleanse us from all unrighteousness.

- 1 JOHN 1:9

CONFESSION

Do you struggle with sin in your life? Do you wonder if your sins are truly forgiven? Our selected verse for this morning gives us assurance that if we confess our sins, He is faithful and just to forgive our sins and to cleanse us from all unrighteousness.

History gives us an account of King Fredrick II, a King of Prussia in the eighteenth century. When King Fredrick II was visiting a prison, all but one of the inmates tried to prove to him how they had been unjustly imprisoned. That one sat quietly in a corner while all the rest proclaimed their innocence. Seeing him sitting there, oblivious to the commotion, the king asked him why he was there.

"Armed robbery, your honor."

The king asked, "Were you guilty?"

"Yes, sir," he answered, "I entirely deserve my punishment."

The King then gave an order to the guard. "Release this guilty man. I do not want him corrupting all these innocent men."

Our Scripture reading reminds us that if we have hatred or ill will against our brother, we are walking in darkness. "He that loveth his brother abideth in the light, and there is none occasion of stumbling in him. He that hateth his brother is in darkness, and walketh in darkness, and knoweth not whither he goeth, because that darkness hath blinded his eyes" (1 John 2:10-11).

Do you long to be free from all unrighteousness? As long as you are wrong and know it, you are in the prison-house of sin. Confession is the only way of escape.

Confess your faults and find someone who needs your help and your love.

Melvin L. Yoder, Gambier, OH

Today I will do a golden deed; I will try to help someone in need.

December 16

Bible Reading: Psalm 77:1-13; 37:1-7

One Year Bible Reading Plan: Revelation 7, Amos 4-6

Commit thy way unto the Lord; trust also in him; and he shall bring it to pass.
- PSALM 37:5

OPEN DOORS

We once had a cat that got into our shop. This cat was wild and hated to be around people. We opened the door and tried to persuade it to run outside, but it seemed the cat was blinded to the open door. Instead of running out the door, it ran and hid itself from us. The cat did not know that we were trying to help it. It simply could not see that the door we opened was for its own benefit. After three days of being in the shop, the cat finally ran out the open door.

We may think, *That blind cat! Why could it not see that big open door?* But are we not often like this cat?

We may think our ways are best for us, but God may want us to do something else in life. He continues to knock on our heart's door. The door opens for us to follow God's plan. Still in rebellion, we run away and try to hide from the open door. As God continues to call us, we finally yield our life to God. As we go through God's open doors, we can receive many blessings. We can then experience true freedom. Let us not be slow to obey God's voice, but let us be willing to follow God when He opens a door for us.

As we are fully committed to God and His ways for us, we can experience true peace, joy, and freedom.

Samuel Beachy, Belvidere, TN

When God opens a door for us, He also gives us strength enough to follow through with His plan.

December 17

But unto every one of us is given grace according to the measure
of the gift of Christ.

- EPHESIANS 4:7

WORKING TOGETHER

One beautiful winter morning as I was at home watching the snow
fall, I was thinking about the lessons God teaches us through nature.
My eyes started following individual snowflakes. Christians are much
like snowflakes. One snowflake is barely visible on the bare landscape.
But put together trillions of snowflakes, and you have a snowstorm.

Snowstorms put cars in the ditch, break roofs, keep us in the house,
give us the opportunity to go sledding, build snowmen, have snowball
fights, and many more things.

I noticed a few things about the snow. The snow knew what it was
to do. No flakes were looking at each other and saying things like, "I'm
bigger than he is" or "I'm prettier than she is." Nor did I see any flakes
riding their brakes, as it were, so as to be on the top when they came
down. On the ground I observed no individual flakes trying to stand out
from the rest, to be noticed more, or to appear bigger or better than the
rest. All worked together.

One snowflake makes almost no difference. Yet many snowflakes
together do. They can provide enjoyment or create a crisis. We can
make a difference in our community by working together. By working
together we leave a better testimony in the community. Do we provide
pleasure for people? Do we create life-changing situations? Instead of
bickering and fighting, we should work together for the common good,
just like the snow.

Owen Shrock, Shreve, Ohio

Unity is the fruit of love.

December 18

Bible Reading: John 14:1-15

One Year Bible Reading Plan: Revelation 9, Obadiah

Jesus saith unto him, I am the way, the truth, and the life:
no man cometh unto the Father, but by me.

- JOHN 14:6

ASK FOR THE OLD PATHS

A few years ago I had the privilege of meeting a retired mariner. The former Coast Guard captain was very interesting to listen to. He was not a man to laud his own experiences, yet he valued them highly. Although today much can be done with computer radar control in guidance of planes and ships, those who desire the ways of the seas must still learn to use the old pathfinder, the sextant. This is a centuries-old method of finding the position of a ship by measuring the angular distance between the horizon and a star, or the sun or moon. If everything else would shut down, the sextant could help the sailors find their way as nothing else could.

The old captain had traveled the waters from country to country, as we travel overland on the highways. The stars of the heavens were the guides along the way much as the road signs on land. He said there is hardly an unbeliever on the seas.

We also live in a day when man desires the easy way. The Lord God warns us today with the words in Jeremiah 6:16, "Thus saith the Lord, Stand ye in the ways, and see, and ask for the old paths, where is the good way, and walk therein, and ye shall find rest for your souls. But they said, We will not walk therein." How sad!

As with the sextant, the tried and proven ways are the best. Yet man is bent on having his own way. Again the Word speaks to us, "But seek ye first the kingdom of God, and his righteousness; and all these things shall be added unto you" (Matthew 6:33).

Wayne E. Miller, Rushsylvania, OH

Prayer keeps one dependent on God.

December 19

Bible Reading: Matthew 1:18-25; 2:1-10

One Year Bible Reading Plan: Revelation 10, Jonah

Proving what is acceptable unto the Lord.

- EPHESIANS 5:10

CHRISTMAS SEASON

When I think of Christmas, childhood memories flood my mind: Christmas trees and decorations, shopping for gifts, lots of food, new clothes, and most of all, Santa Claus. We lived all year in anticipation of Santa at Christmas. We sang about him and listened to many stories of him that later proved untrue. Other songs like "Jingle Bells," "Decks the Halls," and country Christmas songs brought on an emotional high that I felt was unmatched.

Later in my early teens, something happened to me. I developed a personal relationship with Jesus Christ and I discovered that He is quite different from the baby Jesus portrayed by the Christmas spirit. While it was outstanding to remember that He came, their "Merry Christmas" contradicted His very reason for coming, because Jesus does not want us to be merry in our sins. Some of my friends and family would get drunk with wine on no other day but Christmas. Merry-making was also causing the rest of us to become emotionally drunk.

As Christians, it is good for us to remember that Christ came as a babe, but it is much more important to remember that He is coming again to judge the world and receive His own. Christmastime is an excellent opportunity to show the world that, as Christians, we live in joyful obedience to God all year long.

The Bible does not tell us to worship the Babe in the manger. However, it pleads with us to believe in Jesus, our risen Lord, and to obey His commands. It also commands us to keep ourselves unspotted and separate from the world. Praise God, we can be faithful to Him and by His grace live godly lives!

Roger Rangai, Lott, TX

When we recognize Jesus' kingship, we will give Him our worship.

December 20

Bible Reading: Philippians 2:1-18

One Year Bible Reading Plan: Revelation 11, Micah 14:8

Let nothing be done through strife or vainglory;
but in lowliness of mind let each esteem other better than themselves.
- PHILIPPIANS. 2:3

THE TRAP OF ENVY

Envy is described in my dictionary as a feeling of discontent and ill will because of another's advantages or possessions. Another less familiar word, yet just as deadly, is the word "envenom," meaning to put poison into something or to fill with hate or embitter (or cause to envy).

We set a starling trap close to some trees away from our martin houses. Starlings are envious birds. When one starling goes into the trap and another is close by, both birds will probably end up in the trap. We have had as many as five in the trap at one time. The birds on the outside cannot stand the fact that the other has the advantage of a "good" situation.

Humanity seems to be no better. I have seen it happen in a neighborhood, among relatives, and in other situations. One gets a new or better vehicle and the other is not to be outdone. The same might happen with other things. The object itself may not be wrong, but the attitude often is. The bottom line is simply pride. I like what a certain German wordbook says about pride: "an over-driven opinion of oneself, a self-deception in that man is not what he thinks he is."

No one possibly can say he has never been tempted to envy, although it may have been only for a moment. Everyone needs God's spirit through Christ to check those thoughts immediately. Let us seek to put into practice the desire to see others succeed. Wishing others to succeed should be a part of our joy in Christ. When they fail, it behooves us to feel a true sorrow in our hearts because we suffer with them.

Wayne E. Miller, Rushsylvania, OH

One thing there must be, that the mind of Christ be in thee.

December 21

Bible Reading: 2 Samuel 9

One Year Bible Reading Plan: Revelation 12, Micah 4:9–7

And be ye kind one to another, tenderhearted, forgiving one another,
even as God for Christ's sake hath forgiven you.
- EPHESIANS 4:32

BE YE KIND ONE TO ANOTHER

David ordered his servants to till land that was given to Mephibosheth
that he and his son would have food to eat. This is a good picture of
God's kindness and love to us. We were completely unworthy of His
love. We couldn't do anything to make ourselves worthy of His love.
While we were yet sinners, Christ died for us.

Children usually have the features of their parents. If we are children
of God, people should see kindness in us. Bitterness, wrath, anger,
and clamor need to be put away. Kindness, tenderheartedness, and
forgiveness need to be seen.

God loved us while we were yet His enemies. God commands us
to love our enemies. Love is stronger than hate. Hate may cause us
to move people by force, but only love can make a friend out of an
enemy. It takes God's love in our hearts to do kind deeds to those who
hate us.

In *Martyr's Mirror* we read of Dirk Willems who ran across thin ice to
escape from his captor. He looked around to see his captor breaking
through the ice. He would have drowned if Dirk had not rescued him.
The thief catcher wanted to let Dirk go, but the burgomaster sternly
called on him to consider his oath. Dirk was imprisoned and later killed.

Kindness has won the hearts of many people. As children of God,
we need to show kindness regardless of the response we get.

Benuel Glick, Indiana, PA

He that is not very kind is not very holy.

December 22

He is in the way of life that keepeth instruction: but he that refuseth reproof erreth.
- PROVERBS 10:17

CHRISTIAN PRIORITIES

A small group of men was discussing spirituality and the church one Sunday evening after services. It was an intense, riveting, and open conversation. One of the wives kept reminding her husband that it was time to leave for home as she needed time to get ready for an important appointment in the wee hours of the morning. Her partner, mesmerized by the discussion's magnetic pull, paid scant attention to her wishes. After awhile the meeting broke up, and all left for home.

The next day a brother said to the one who had ignored his wife's wishes, "Your response last evening really bothered me. You missed a good opportunity to show your love and faith in action. As an older man, you could have set a wonderful example for us younger men."

"But we were having a spiritual discussion," the brother said defensively.

"God never intended us to be so spiritual that we neglect our duties," the first brother reminded him.

That is a profound and startling truth. It is the age-old struggle between the Holy Spirit and man's spirit. Are we satisfied to fulfill the smaller duties and obligations of life that are clearly ours? Living a truly surrendered yet passionate and God-centered life is not only possible, it is what God wants. There is a time for action as well as a time for words. Can we, using the tone and principle of Philippians 4:12, urge each other onward and upward? Accept your circumstances as they are. Some, of course, can and should be changed.

Roy Keim, West Union, OH

For the ways of man are before the eyes of the Lord, and he pondereth all his goings. - Proverbs 5:21

December 23

Bible Reading: Matthew 5:23-48

One Year Bible Reading Plan: Revelation 14, Habakkuk

But I say unto you, Love your enemies, bless them that curse you, do good
to them that hate you, and pray for them which despitefully use you,
and persecute you.

- MATTHEW 5:44

SHARING THE BIBLE

History books and encyclopedias yield volumes of information about
the December 7, 1941, attack on the U.S. military base at Pearl Harbor.
History records the vast destruction of property and loss of thousands of
lives.

But history books do not give us the whole story. The book, *Real
Stories for the Soul*, records the account of Mitsuo Fuchida who led the
squadron of 860 planes sent out to do the job. American bomber, Jacob
DeShazer, was eager to strike back at the hated enemy. On April 18,
DeShazer flew his B25 bomber over Nagoya in a dangerous raid. After
releasing his bombs, he became lost in dense fog, ran out of fuel, and
had to eject. DeShazer suffered hunger, cold, and torture at the hands
of his captors. He hated his captors and treated them with contempt. In
May of 1944, he was given a Bible. He clutched it to his chest and began
reading. He began to memorize verses, and when he came to Matthew
5:44, he became a changed man. He began to treat the guards kindly and
respectfully. Soon the attitude of the guards changed and they started
helping him.

After the war, DeShazer returned to Japan as a missionary. One day
a man came to DeShazer's door. It was Mitsuo Fuchida, who had led the
Pearl Harbor attack. He had been led to Christ by a man who had given
him a pocket Testament. The two became dear friends and considered
each other brothers in Christ. They learned forgiveness and exchanged
hatred for love. Mitsuo Fuchida spent the rest of his life as a missionary.

Never tire of giving away Bibles. We may never know the effects of
giving away one Bible. God can use our feeble efforts as seeds to grow
into a great spiritual harvest.

Melvin L. Yoder, Gambier, OH

*One soul saved is worth more than the whole world and
everything in it.*

December 24

Bible Reading Matthew 1:18-25 Matthew 2:1-11

One Year Bible Reading Plan: Revelation 14, Habakkuk

Behold a virgin shall be with child and shall bring forth a son, and they shall call his name Emmanuel, which being interpreted is, God with us.
- MATTHEW 1:23

THE VIRGIN BIRTH

Someone told me we make too much of Christ's birth–the way He came is not important. The man suggested that Jesus could have been an illegitimate child. Was Christ conceived of the Holy Ghost or was there a man involved?

If Christ would have been illegitimate, He could not have been the true Light (John 1:9), and He could not have given anyone the power to become a son of God (John 1:12). He could not have been the Bread of Life and could not have satisfied anyone's hunger nor quenched anyone's thirst (John 6:35).

Our reading in Matthew 1 tells us what was going to take place. If Jesus would have been an illegitimate child, Mary would not have been considered a virgin, she would not have found favor with God, and the angels would not have had good tidings of great joy to all people (Luke 2:10). The Holy Ghost would not have come upon Mary; neither would she have been overshadowed by the power of the Highest; and Jesus would not have been the Son of God. That would have nullified Isaiah's prophecy about Jesus (Isaiah 7:14). The angel Gabriel would have lied to Mary; Christ would not have been the Son of the Highest; and His kingdom would have ended like all others.

If Jesus would have been illegitimate, all prophecy concerning Him would still not be fulfilled, and we would still be without a Savior. Do you believe in the virgin birth?

Nelson Yoder, Hartville, OH

Unto you was born that day a Savior.

December 25

Bible Reading: Luke 1:67-80

One Year Bible Reading Plan: Revelation 16, Haggai

For mine eyes have seen thy salvation, which thou hast prepared before the face of all people.

- LUKE 2:30, 31

CHRIST–CHILD OR KING?

What should be the focal point of joy on this Christmas Day? Judging by the religious world around us, it would be Baby Jesus. It is proper that we rejoice in Christ's coming as a baby. Christ's advent was a marvel of grace that only God could perform. But the emphasis on Christ as a baby is off the mark. The infancy of Jesus was but a means to an end. It provided proof of the complete humanity of Christ. The babyhood of Christ, however, provided nothing for our salvation.

It may seem nice to think about a cute baby. Babies are the epitome of innocence. They endear themselves to us by their helplessness. However, we need to avoid reducing the exalted Christ of heaven to a perpetual baby in our lives. Yes, a baby can claim our affections easily. But did a baby bring salvation? Is a baby Lord of our lives? Does a baby have a spiritual claim on us?

The world's effort to keep Christ in the manger is not much different than promoting Santa Claus. Both take people's minds off their accountability to Christ. Both serve as idols to turn our affections away from God. In the name of religion, Christ Jesus, the Lord of glory, is pushed aside and forgotten.

We are glad God sent Jesus into the world as a babe. We are happier yet that He grew up into perfect manhood, providing an example of life for us. But our joy is complete when we remember the great salvation He wrought for us, and that He continues His work in heaven at God's throne. Worship Christ for Who He is, not only for Who He was two thousand years ago. May the joy of Christmas find its true expression as we serve the King of glory.

Delmar R. Eby, London, KY

Christ is born, the great Anointed; Heaven and earth His praises sing!
Oh receive whom God appointed, For your Prophet, Priest, and King.

December 26

Bible Reading: Romans 12; 13:10-14

One Year Bible Reading Plan: Revelation 17, Zechariah 1–3

This is the day which the Lord hath made; we will rejoice and be glad in it.
- PSALM 118:24

TODAY'S TIME

One account says the average person at seventy-five years of age has spent nine years playing, seven and a half years dressing, six years traveling, six years eating, four years sick, and one year in the house of God. I was once seventy-five years old, but I hope I spent more than one year in the house of God.

Today is a day that has never been here before and will never come again. We need to be careful what we do today. It will affect our eternal destiny.

It is good for us to get up early enough every morning to spend time reading God's Word and praying. It is very important to have family devotions every day with the family, but it is also important to have personal devotions alone with God. As the Bible says, "Go into your closet and shut the door."

It may be good to make some resolutions about how we are going to spend the day. Today I will start the day with a smile. I will rejoice in the Lord. I will not criticize anybody. Today I will not spend time worrying about things that might happen. Today I will study to improve myself. Today I am determined to do the things I ought to do and stop doing things I should not do. Today I will not imagine what I would do if things were different. They are not different. I will work with what material I have. Today I will act toward other people as though this might be my last day. Tomorrow may never come.

Eli A. Yoder, Stuarts Draft, VA

Tomorrow never comes, and yesterday never returns.
Today is all we have. Use it wisely.

December 27

Bible Reading: Jude

One Year Bible Reading Plan: Revelation 18, Zechariah 4–6

He that dwelleth in the secret place of the most High shall
abide under the shadow of the Almighty.

- PSALM 91:1

KEEP YOURSELF IN THE LOVE OF GOD

Many modern conveniences using micro-chips have replaced mental
attention, decisions, and effort. We have automatic transmissions,
dishwashers, washing machines, and cruise control. The danger we
face is that we would like to apply this automatic convenience to our
spiritual lives as well.

After our conversion and baptism, we assume that the initial fire,
enthusiasm, and joy we have will continue automatically. However, we
tend to cool off over time and then we wonder why. Jude admonishes
us to, "Keep yourselves in the love of God" (Jude 21). It is our
responsibility to be where God can bless us. We will grow if we are
by the River of Living Water. To keep ourselves in His love we must
maintain daily communion with the Son and obey and absorb His
Word.

We might also think that if we could just find the perfect church or
own an expensive study Bible we would automatically become more
spiritual. As good as those things might be, they do us no good until
we put those truths into practice. Spirituality is seldom spawned under
ideal circumstances but rather in adversity. "Knowing this, that the
trying of your faith worketh patience. But let patience have her perfect
work, that ye may be perfect and entire, wanting nothing" (James 1:3,
4). Our faith needs to be applied and tried to prove its quality.

The Devil cannot hinder God from blessing us, but he uses every
means at his disposal to keep us away from God. He will keep us so
preoccupied with entertainment, work, hobbies, sports, and just plain
busyness that we will have little or no time to receive God's blessings.
Let us set aside the cares of life and give God the time He deserves.
Time spent with God will keep us in His love and we will grow.

Steven Taylor, Stoystown, PA

The Word is delicious to him who despises the world.

December 28

Bible Reading: Genesis 6:11-22; 7:1-12, 22-24

One Year Bible Reading Plan: Revelation 19, Zechariah 7–9

Thus did Noah; according to all that God commanded him, so did he.

- GENESIS 6:22

GODLY OBEDIENCE

God told Noah to build the ark. Noah obeyed. It took effort for Noah to obey. It was a large project. The ark was approximately four hundred fifty feet long, seventy-five feet wide, and forty-five feet high. Building the ark took nearly one hundred years. Noah probably didn't have a large crew. It wasn't what the ungodly people around him were doing. But Noah obeyed.

God will also call us to things that look hard to the flesh. In the Bible He commands us to live holy lives and to gain victory over sin. He calls us to love our enemies and forgive those who hurt us.

He speaks through men also. He has created a network of people in authority above us. He calls all of us to obey in the home, the church, and the civil government. He can also speak through the admonition of our peers.

Sometimes God calls through circumstances. He may present an opportunity for greater service when we think we are too busy to fulfill the task. Perhaps we fear what others would think if we obeyed such a call.

Noah obeyed God, and God rewarded him for it. During the flood, the ark he had made saved his life. Noah's family was also saved because they obeyed God with Noah. Even many animals were kept safe from the flood because of Noah's obedience.

Works can't save us from sin, but God does call us to a life of obedience. He has promised, if we obey Him through His grace and power that our reward will be in heaven with Him. There we will be safe from the destruction of the world in a calamity worse than the flood.

Jonathan E. Mast, Crossville, TN

Trust and obey. Today.

December 29

Bible Reading: Matthew 24:1-13, Revelation 16:17-21

One Year Bible Reading Plan: Revelation 20, Zechariah 10–12

But he that shall endure unto the end, the same shall be saved.

- MATTHEW 24:13

PREPARE TO MEET GOD

On December 26, 2004, there was a 9.0 magnitude earthquake in the Indian Ocean. It was the most powerful earthquake in forty or more years. A section of the ocean floor nine miles wide and 745 miles long rose straight up one hundred feet and dropped again. The earthquake unleashed a destructive wave that traveled four thousand miles across the Indian Ocean at 500 miles per hour. When it hit land, it became one of the worst natural disasters in history.

What is God trying to tell us? Are we listening? We weak humans cannot fathom the great power of God. A man said, "This is one time God made a mistake!" We serve a God who makes no mistakes. We are not able to understand God's ways, but we can accept them as God's will. Many people feel the earthquake is one of God's ways of showing us that the end is near. Others blaspheme God. In Revelation 16 we read of two different plagues God sent. The people blasphemed Him and didn't repent.

Although I cannot verify the following account, I heard it from several sources. It is reported that someone picked up a hitchhiker. The hitchhiker told the driver, "Jesus is coming very soon." All of a sudden he was gone. The driver reported it to the police, and they told him he was the fifth person to report the same thing that day.

Even if Jesus does not return in our lifetime, our days are short. Are we ready, or are we just going on, more concerned about making money and living a life of ease? Prepare to meet thy God!

Daniel Miller, Dunnegan, MO

The greatest business of life is to prepare for the next life.

December 30

Bible Reading: Psalm 139

One Year Bible Reading Plan: Revelation 21, Zechariah 13, 14

And unto the angel of the church in Thyatira write; These things saith the Son of God, who hath his eyes like unto a flame of fire, and his feet are like fine brass.

- REVELATION 2:18

THE EYES OF GOD

Our key verse says that God's eyes are like a flame of fire. Fire speaks of piercing and penetrating. God's eyes are not limited like ours. He sees into our heart as easily as we can see through clear glass. He knows the thoughts and intents of our hearts. We might be able to deceive people around us, but we cannot deceive God. His eyes are everywhere, beholding the evil and the good (Proverbs 15:3).

It makes ungodly people uncomfortable to think about having God's eyes looking into their lives. At the Judgment Day they will call on the rocks and mountains to fall on them and cover them from the face of God (Revelation 6:15).

It is a great blessing for God's people to know that God is watching over us. He knows when we face trials and temptations, and He cares about us. He gives us the grace we need to live in victory. No matter where He sends us, He promises to be with us and protect us. He will never leave us nor forsake us. As we look to Him, He will give us strength and courage to be faithful.

It should help us to be reverent toward God and not harbor evil in our hearts when we think of God's eyes upon us.

Dan Troyer, Deer Lodge, TN

You can't do wrong and get by.

December 31

Bible Reading: Proverbs 4, James 1:5

One Year Bible Reading Plan: Revelation 22, Malachi

Wisdom is the principal thing; therefore get wisdom:
and with all thy getting get understanding.

- PROVERBS 4:7

GODLY WISDOM

The Bible says that the fear of the Lord is (see Job 28:28) wisdom. Everyone wants wisdom and understanding. Eve committed the first sin in hope of gaining knowledge and understanding. Today much time and money is spent to gain worldly knowledge and understanding in many different areas. But God's Word says that the wisdom of this world is foolishness to God (1 Corinthians 3:19). The wisdom that is from above is pure, peaceable, gentle, easy to be entreated, full of mercy and good fruits, without partiality, and without hypocrisy (James 3:17).

If we are Christians, God will give us wisdom from above. It is God's good pleasure to give us wisdom and understanding through His Word and through the Holy Spirit. If anyone lacks wisdom, let him ask of God who gives liberally to all men (James 1:5). We all need to ask God to give us wisdom with humility.

Solomon confessed his weakness and ignorance by asking God, "Give therefore thy servant an understanding heart" (1 Kings 3:9). Because of this, God made him the wisest of men. Yet Solomon's wisdom did not teach him self control. He taught well but failed to practice what he taught. He describes the fool in Proverbs and it draws a vivid picture of his own failings. We can have a lot of head knowledge, but unless we put to practice what we know and use the wisdom that God gives us, God will not bless us with more wisdom.

Ben Gingerich, Burkesville, KY

It is a wise man who knows that he isn't.

CONTRIBUTORS INDEX

SCRIPTURE INDEX

Dates in bold identify the daily key verses

SUBJECT INDEX

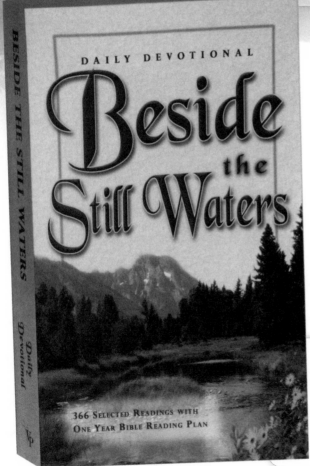

DAILY DEVOTIONAL

Now with Index

Beside the Still Waters

Volume One

366 SELECTED READINGS WITH ONE YEAR BIBLE READING PLAN

BESIDE THE STILL WATERS

Daily Devotional

Beside the Still Waters

Volume One • Indexed

400 pages \\ Paperback \\ $12.99

Item #STI76051

Junto a aguas De Reposo

Beside the Still Waters - Spanish Edition
Volume Two
370 pages \\ Paperback \\ $8.99
Item #JUN76136

To Purchase
Print Books
or
Ebooks
go to
vision-publishers.com

ORDER FORM

To order, send this completed order form to:

Vision Publishers
P.O. Box 190 · Harrisonburg, VA 22803
Phone: 877.488.0901 · Fax: 540-437-1969
E-mail: orders@vision-publishers.com
www.vision-publishers.com

_____ _____
Name   Date

_____ _____
Mailing Address   Phone

_____
City   State   Zip

***Beside the Still Waters** Vol. 1 Non-indexed* Qty. _____ x \$9.99 ea. = _____

***Beside the Still Waters** Vol. 1 Indexed* Qty. _____ x \$12.99 ea. = _____

***Beside the Still Waters** Vol. 2* Qty. _____ x \$12.99 ea. = _____

***Beside the Still Waters** Vol. 3* Qty. _____ x \$12.99 ea. = _____

***Junto a aguas De Reposo - Spanish** Vol. 2* Qty. _____ x \$8.99 ea. = _____

(Please call for quantity discounts - 877-488-0901)

Price _____

Virginia residents add 5% sales tax _____

Ohio residents add applicable sales tax _____

Shipping & handling - Add 10% of your total order plus \$3.00

❏ Money Order   ❏ Visa   Grand Total _____

❏ MasterCard   ❏ Discover   **All Payments in US Dollars**

Name on Card _____

Card # _|_|_|_|_| _|_|_|_|_| _|_|_|_|_| _|_|_|_|_|

3-digit code from signature panel _|_|_| Exp. Date _|_|_|_|

Thank you for your order!
For a complete listing of our books request our catalog.
Bookstore inquiries welcome

ORDER FORM

To order, send this completed order form to:

Vision Publishers

P.O. Box 190 · Harrisonburg, VA 22803

Phone: 877.488.0901 · Fax: 540-437-1969

E-mail: orders@vision-publishers.com

www.vision-publishers.com

_____ _____
Name   Date

_____ _____
Mailing Address   Phone

_____
City   State   Zip

Beside the Still Waters Vol. 1 Non-indexed Qty. _____ x $9.99 ea. = _____

Beside the Still Waters Vol. 1 Indexed Qty. _____ x $12.99 ea. = _____

Beside the Still Waters Vol. 2 Qty. _____ x $12.99 ea. = _____

Beside the Still Waters Vol. 3 Qty. _____ x $12.99 ea. = _____

Junto a aguas De Reposo - Spanish Vol. 2 Qty. _____ x $8.99 ea. = _____

(Please call for quantity discounts - 877-488-0901)

Price _____

Virginia residents add 5% sales tax _____

Ohio residents add applicable sales tax _____

Shipping & handling - Add 10% of your total order plus $3.00

❏ Money Order   ❏ Visa   Grand Total _____

❏ MasterCard   ❏ Discover

All Payments in US Dollars

Name on Card _____

Card #__|__|__|__| __|__|__|__| __|__|__|__| __|__|__|__|

3-digit code from signature panel __|__|__| Exp. Date __|__|__|__|

Thank you for your order!

For a complete listing of our books request our catalog.

Bookstore inquiries welcome